Tales of an Internet Dater

Tales of an Internet Dater

Rob Morgan

To Dave,

Best wishes,

Rob Morgan

To my family, thanks for all your love and support.

PROLOGUE

Down on my luck, beginning to feel lonely and a little depressed, I was searching for happiness in my life. I'd had one stable and mostly happy relationship for fifteen years and was a father to three adorable children. But now, after separating, I was single again and wanting to meet someone new. If possible, I wanted to fall in love again. As meeting women in bars, pubs and clubs had failed miserably, it was now time to try the wonderful world of internet dating. What followed was a rollercoaster ride of emotions and experiences that culminated in this book.

Tales of an Internet Dater is the true reflection of the hilarious and sometimes ludicrous adventures of my pursuit of happiness and love. Could I really find love by tapping on a keyboard? Did my perfect match really exist? Or was it really all just about a quick bonk? Dating sites certainly covered every possibility, whatever anybody was craving. I was ready to enter this world and try to have fun, whilst trying to find my soul mate.

As these tales are all true, I've changed the names of all the ladies in the book to protect their identities and avoid any embarrassment. Most of the women I met were genuine in their pursuit of love and affection. But, often, the pure physical urge to copulate was evident for women too. In fact, I found that most ladies enjoyed sex just as much as men and craved physical satisfaction in the bedroom too. And there's absolutely nothing wrong with that.

Sometimes, people find it difficult to discuss sex and relationships in detail. This book tries to eradicate such nonsense by sharing with you some of my sexual encounters in graphic detail, albeit with a comical element. After all, sex isn't perfect at all. It's far from perfect and my recollections reflect that too. My stories also give an honest male viewpoint about dating, relationships, women, love and ~~shagging~~ romance. I hope that you find it funny too, after all, it's my intention to make you laugh, smile and occasionally cringe.

Rob Morgan

CHAPTER 1: WHO THE HELL IS WAYNE?

I'm just an ordinary guy really. Not particularly good-looking, but not ugly either. My grandma always told me that I was handsome, but she had funny eyes and was slightly biased. I was once told that I had one of those faces that looked as though I was gazing into the back of a spoon. At this point in my life, I'd been single for a couple of years, after my only long-term relationship of fifteen years had come to an end.

If truth be told, I was rather depressed, quite lonely at times and wanted to meet someone who I could call my girlfriend. In reality, I was struggling to meet anyone really. I wasn't bothered about modern technology and had only recently bought a decent mobile phone. I guess you could've called me a technophobe. That's why I had to invite a couple of my friends around to set up my new shiny laptop.

My friends told me that it would be ideal for communicating with others online and even joining a dating site or two. It hadn't crossed my mind that people actually met online and could develop long-lasting relationships. I assumed it was more about having fun and maybe finding friends with benefits. Yet, at the time I was ready to give anything a go. I'd been informed that it was the new way to meet people and, well, you could say I was looking for love again. I had a new world to explore online and it was a world I was willing and ready to enter.

As time went by, I really wanted to meet someone special. I was fed up with chatting to drunken women in bars and dodgy nightclubs looking for some intimacy. I guess you could say I was looking for a bit of sex to keep me happy and empty my bulging sack. My friend, Big Col, and I frequented a particular club which catered for an older clientele. People in their 30s, like us, and even 40s and 50s were not out of place. There were also a couple of guys in their 60s trying it on with any lady who had a pulse. It certainly wouldn't matter to them if she had a bit of sick down her top.

You know the kind of venue I mean, full of uninhibited middle-aged people desperate for some physical contact, whether it be a snog, a fondle down some back alley or a kneetrembler if lucky enough, or possibly unlucky if you caught crabs as a result. As the alcohol kicked in, even the old, wrinkled, caked in make-up types seemed decent, if you ignored the belly overhanging those trousers that were two sizes too small. I was beginning to be part of this world, as I was now in my mid-thirties and very much single. Unfortunately, the beer goggles certainly kicked in at the end of many of these nights.

My friend was single too, so we often had the intention of trying to meet someone on a night out. Failing that, it was usually a kebab with chilli sauce instead. The amount of times I woke up with hot chilli sauce down my jeans compared to waking up with a hot woman told a story. However, on one particular occasion I actually pulled a lady within about 10 minutes. I walked around the club and surveyed the possible options like a lion stalking a gazelle. Only I was not king of the plains and the women were nothing like a majestic gazelle type creature. It was more like a hyena chasing a hippopotamus to be honest.

Anyway, the chat up lines I used were nothing too inventive. They didn't have to be in a place like that. A simple, 'Can I buy you a drink?' usually worked when they'd had 13 vodkas already. A few compliments didn't go amiss either - 'Nice jugs love!' or 'You've got a great ass,' for example. In reality, I was far too polite to say things like that, but I'd heard others use such wonderful terms of endearment. My favourite line at the time was along the lines of 'I've got a frozen pizza at home; would you like to share it?' which sometimes worked believe it or not. Often the ladies would ask what type of pizza it was, and my response was simple – 'Meat feast!'

At the time I thought I could also strut my stuff on the dancefloor, but subsequent videos have made me realise what a complete knob I was. My dancing was described as a monkey on stilts - just going everywhere with no rhythm. After a few drinks I was doing spins, then more spins, and gyrating like a mad man. Most of my moves involved me pulling funny faces and sticking my tongue out without realising. I tried to be like Michael Jackson but ended up looking more like Ann Widdecombe on *Strictly Come Dancing*. I could empty a dancefloor faster than a snowman would melt in the middle of the Sahara Desert.

Although I tried to pick up women on the dancefloor, I usually had a little more success talking to them on the sticky carpet. Alcohol allowed everyone to remove their inhibitions and most people in that club would have a chat. One time I asked a lady, 'What do you do for a living?' and she replied, 'Oh, I'm an opera singer,' smiling. I was obviously very sceptical to say the least. 'I really believe you, of course,' I said laughing, but she was insistent. It transpired that she was classically trained and taught youngsters how to sing properly. I went out with her a few times, but we just didn't hit the high notes. In all honesty, it just all fell flat.

My friend, Big Col, also had some success and we had a few mutual friends who often appeared on nights out. Don't ask me why they called him Big Col. He wasn't that big; he wasn't that small either. I was under the impression that the ladies knew him as 'Tiny Col' for some reason. Anyway, Tiny Col, I mean Big Col, was a fantastic friend during this period in my life. Without him I'd be single, desperate and lonely. At times, I was still desperate and lonely though and usually single too. However, I certainly would've felt worse without Big Col as my mate. He was single and still lived at home with his parents, for fuck's sake. At least I had my own place.

Having said that, once I'd separated from my long-term partner, I lived temporarily with my parents too. I did meet one nice young lady, who was quite a bit younger than myself. I'd gone to a cricket dinner with Big Col and was wearing a suit for once. I reckoned there was something special about wearing a suit on a night out, as opposed to the typical jeans and shirt. Or in some places I frequented, a tracksuit or a soiled T-shirt – and that was just the women. The suit made me feel smart and attractive, which in turn gave me extra confidence. In fact, that night I was simply oozing sex appeal and couldn't fail.

On the night in question, I walked past a group of ladies in a nightclub and one of them squeezed my bum. Some people may have been outraged or offended in today's modern society full of equality and feminism, but I took it as a huge compliment and started talking to her, with a huge semi developing. You know, my trusted chat up line of, 'I've got a frozen pizza at home if you'd like to share it?'

As I didn't have my own place at the time, I had to refrain from offering her a meat feast. Well, the one from my freezer anyway. We had a lengthy chat and swapped numbers which felt like a success. She was called Debra and was about 10 years younger than me. She was fairly pretty in the faint light of the club and sure had a cheeky sense of humour. A few hours later I was walking home at about 3 a.m. when I got a text message on my shitty cheap mobile phone saying, 'I WANT YOU! I WANT YOU NOW! XXX' so I thought carefully about my response. I thought I'd play it really cool so I responded in a sexy, teasing and tantalising way that would really turn her on - 'I'll try and get a taxi. Where do you live?'

She lived about 6 miles away, but I was merry and determined to see her. I got back to my parent's house and started looking through the phone book to find a taxi number. I don't know why I just didn't use the number in my bloody phone. I tried to be quiet but alas woke my mum. 'What are you doing at this time?' she said half asleep. 'Oh, sorry mum. Didn't mean to wake you up. I'm getting a taxi to someone's house,' I responded. There was a pause and then my dad spoke up, 'I'll give you a lift son. If you've met someone go and have a good time.'

I was surprised by my parents' reaction to say the least. Instead of being annoyed for waking them up, my dad offered me a lift at 4 a.m. to a place about 6 miles away. We had an idea where the address was because my mum knew and started giving my dad thorough directions. My dad drove the six miles and then around the area my mum had described before we eventually found Debra's address.

I knocked on the door and hoped it was the correct house just in case she was teasing me for some sick, disgusting, twisted, unfathomable reason. My mind was playing tricks. What if it was a drugged up, shaven headed thug with a snake tattoo on his neck and he was pissed off that I'd just woken his family up in the middle of the fucking night. I waited, but there was no answer so knocked again with trepidation. This time, she answered thank goodness, but I think she was shocked when my dad introduced himself. In hindsight, maybe he should've stayed in the car.

Actually, my dad dropped me off and tried to get a sneaky glance as she answered the door before driving off. I felt like I was about 16 again instead of in my mid-thirties, waving to my dad as he gave me the thumbs up. Having separated from my only long-term partner it was now time to play the field and have some fun. But, of course, I did want to fall in love with someone eventually, if I ever met the right person. Would this young desperate lady be the special one?

Inside the house it became apparent that she was really keen and couldn't get my suit off quick enough. I didn't want to crumple it on the floor though, as my only suit was precious to me, so I hung it carefully over a chair. We did the deed all night long until the birds started tweeting and I remember sweating like I'd just run the fastest 800 metres in history. My performance must've been extraordinary because the mattress was soaking wet, unless she just enjoyed pissing in bed. What had become apparent to me was that she had a tattoo just above her arse which said the word 'WAYNE' in big letters. It did make me wonder though, who the hell was Wayne? What if it was her boyfriend and she wasn't single after all? Every possible scenario was playing around in my mind, as I continued to pump away.

I must admit that the tattoo was a bit of a passion killer for me. I wasn't keen on tattoos anyway, but who the fuck was this Wayne dude? We changed positions and as I gave her one from behind, all I could see was the word 'WAYNE' in front of me. The letters seemed to get bigger and bigger the harder I pumped. There was only one Wayne I'd ever heard of. Images of Wayne Rooney appeared in my mind. No wonder I could keep going longer than my standard average time – I was thinking about bloody Wayne Rooney. I thought that this could be a good tactic in future liaisons with attractive ladies, if I ever had to control my elite performance in the bedroom. Better still, thinking about the bloody BREXIT negotiations would probably allow me to go even longer. Although, it may lead to a soft exit, I guess.

I did see Debra again a few times, despite that hideous tattoo. The next morning, she told me all about her young son Wayne. Everything made sense now, although I still didn't fancy getting tattoos of my kids' names on my arse. Or anywhere else for that matter – it doesn't mean I don't love them of course. I can usually remember their names anyway. I just don't love them enough to have a permanent reminder of them every time I look in the mirror. I'm sure little Wayne was a lovely boy, but I never got to know him. I did see him in his cot once and he reminded me of a baby Wayne Rooney, or maybe it was just the light. Debra told me that her ex, Wayne's dad, was a bit of a nutjob who had a propensity for violence. He was currently stalking her and would not let go of the relationship. This was all I needed in my life right now.

One night, I was at Debra's house when her mobile kept ringing and ringing all bloody night. It started around midnight and didn't stop for the next few hours, as well as a number of text messages saying she was being watched. The next text she got then stated, by the way, that she was still greatly loved by him. It was then that Debra told me that he'd attacked her previous boyfriend with a bottle and had smashed it over his head, in a fit of jealousy. She said he sometimes sat outside in his car for hours staring at her window. In fact, she said, 'He's probably outside now and will kill you if he sees you so please sneak out the back when you leave,' in a deadpan manner. I thought for a minute then responded, 'Is he called Wayne too?'

I thought I could take anybody on at the time, though I guess some of it was bravado and trying to impress Debra. I said, 'I'm not sneaking out the back, I'll go out the front door like a man. If he attacks me, I'll sort him out don't worry,' as a gentle fart made its way into the room. She pleaded with me again and said any trouble should be avoided. As I pumped myself up for a vicious encounter and a potential bottle on the head, she opened the back door and tried to push me out. 'I'm really tough me,' I bellowed as I ran out the back gate at the speed of light trying to find my car. I'd have probably given Usain Bolt a good race, to be honest.

My heart pounding, I got in the car and sped off thinking her crazy ex would chase me in a stolen supercar. In fact, I looked in my mirror and saw nobody at all. Maybe she was genuinely worried for my safety, or maybe she wanted me out the house so she could have a big dump in peace. I never found out because I didn't want to find out. I thought about the situations I may encounter again if I saw her and decided to send a massively long text, about 7 pages long, explaining why I didn't want to end up drinking through a straw.

I felt bad about dumping her, but it seemed the only sensible option at the time. Why would I want to subject myself to the wrath of her ex-boyfriend? He was the kind of person to avoid at this stage in my life and it just wasn't worth the hassle, although I did fancy her. It always amazed me about how many ladies loved the so called 'bad boys' who were tough, uncompromising and often treated their partners like something they'd stood in. Personally, I couldn't understand it at all as I thought most women would want a reliable, trustworthy and respectable partner. In fact, I found reliability to be an admirable quality because the kind of lady I wanted to meet would be the type who never let me down. The type of lady who would always be there in times of need, when I was feeling low. The type of lady who never messed me about or played games. Maybe Debra was actually that type of person, but I never gave her a real chance in the end, which was a little sad, I guess.

CHAPTER 2: UNIVERSITY BLUES

I'd not long had my new laptop when a few more of my friends started suggesting I could meet people online and communicate with people using social media or online dating sites. 'What's this Facebook thing?' I asked them, as everyone was talking about it. At the time, I simply didn't understand or realise that millions of people used it every day. You could say I'd had my head buried in the sand when it came to digital relations.

However, I managed to join up and some women I hardly knew requested me as friends. I thought it was fantastic that someone I'd only met once would want to be my friend. They must fancy me, I thought, so they want to message me and seduce me using a recognised social media platform. It turned out that these women were usually married and really did just want to be friends. Well, not real friends obviously, but friends who you never saw again, but just spy on from afar.

They wanted to add me to their 3571 other friends who they also never saw, so they could be more popular than everyone else, whereas I knew I'd be happy if I could make it to 100 friends. If I liked a lady, was it worth looking at her profile and her millions of pictures to find a revealing picture in a bikini on some foreign beach? Not really my kind of thing to be honest, although some people were posting pictures that didn't leave a lot to the imagination. I'd dabbled and flirted online to a degree, but I found it more useful for keeping in touch with mates from university, who lived all over the world. Joining a dating site, however, would be a totally new and different proposition for me. I would have to think long and hard before I did this, but what would I have to lose?

Many of my initial experiences with the opposite sex occurred when I lived in Manchester whilst at university. I lived with two great friends,

Nick and Gary, in a flat whilst studying and we had some fantastic times in Manchester. My friend, Nick, was very posh compared to me and his accent very different from mine. He lived in Nicosia in Cyprus and his mum was German and his dad was Lebanese. He'd once lived in London and had been christened in Jerusalem, so had an interesting and eventful life. I'd grown up in a northern town in England and my life had been relatively uneventful. You could say we had rather disparate backgrounds. However, we bonded well, and Nick invited me to Cyprus during the summer at the end of our first year of university and showed me around the beautiful island on his motorbike.

The first time I met Nick was whilst we were lodging in a house, with our landlord near Manchester. On the very first night in our new digs, I was asleep in my room when I heard a massive scream coming from his room. I jumped out of bed and sat on the edge, wondering what the commotion was. Again, he screamed as though he was startled or fighting an intruder. I wondered if a burglar had broken into the house and he needed some help. Either that, or our new landlord was some crazy axe killer.

I grabbed my cricket bat from the room just in case and leapt up ready to defend my new housemate. I stormed into his room and asked what was going on. 'They never told me they had a bloody cat,' he yelped. 'I was asleep, and it crawled under my covers.' I was in stitches laughing, but he was quite flustered with it all. In the three months we lodged in that house, I never had a pussy in my bed.

Gary was a big-muscled, well-toned black guy who introduced me to weight training and weightlifting. He was a bodybuilder and, though fairly short in terms of height, could lift huge weights. We became training partners for a while, and he persuaded me to take some supplements to help improve my muscle mass. I remember popping these pills that made my piss turn luminous yellow. I'd never seen anything like it. When I urinated, it looked like something from a science-fiction movie. After a while of training, my body became more toned, but I gave up on the pills.

I remember one occasion when we were training, and I was trying to perform a weightlifting exercise called the clean and jerk. Gary commented, 'Normally, you do it the other way around mate – the jerk then clean!' I had to drop the bloody bar as I was laughing that much.

Gary certainly had a good sense of humour and we had many nights out on the pop. On one particular night, he dropped a battered sausage in a dirty gutter. It was covered in muck and all sorts of shit, but he was so drunk he still ate it. The morning after, his head and bed were covered in pools of vomit and me and Nick had to keep him alive by placing him in the recovery position and clean up the mess. Those were such happy times.

When I went to visit Nick in Cyprus, I was introduced to two of his friends who were sisters. They both drove their own £50,000 Mercedes cars as their father was super rich and some sort of top politician on the island. I'm convinced one of them liked me, but I didn't really have the hots for her acne covered face. However, she was a lovely friendly person and invited us all to play cards in her father's private suite. We went up to the suite in a private lift and onto a balcony overlooking fruit trees in a splendid garden. We drank beer and played cards most of the night, but obviously at some point I needed to urinate. I asked which part of the palace the toilet was situated in and she pointed me in the right direction, along the East wing.

Having had a few drinks, I was fairly tipsy by this point and stumbled down a corridor towards the luxury bathroom. On my way, I nudged what looked like an incredibly expensive ornament with my foot. It was Chinese, probably from the Ming dynasty, and probably worth over a million. It was like slow motion as it spun round and wobbled more and more. I reacted as quick as I could, but this valuable piece of history was on its way down. Then it finally happened – it actually fell over and the beautiful figurine on top lost its fucking head. I was distraught, and my heart was pounding like a bongo. I barely knew this girl and had decapitated her favourite piece. What would her father do to me? He might throw me in prison for 10 years for criminal damage to an ancient antique.

I looked around in horror but all I could hear was laughter coming from the balcony outside. They hadn't heard it smash or seen a thing. I stood motionless for a few seconds and then grabbed its head from the floor. I'm an honest person I thought – I'll show her the decapitated head and hope she doesn't take too much offence. Suddenly, I heard someone get up and panicked. I simply balanced the head on top of the ornament.

I'd even put it the right way around, although the smirk on its face made it look like the decapitation had caused considerable pain. It had one of those faces that you can imagine someone has during a bout of extreme constipation. It was passable – not perfect by any means, but passable.

Did I leave it as it was or tell her the truth? I considered the options as I pissed in her luxury bathroom, which was fitted with gold taps and marble sinks. It was so posh, I considered having a dump even though I really didn't want to squeeze one out. It made Harrods look like a public toilet in a northern seaside town. Then, I realised that if I played ignorant nobody would know a thing. And even if it was discovered, nobody could prove it was me. It could have been her fucking cat. Nobody knows till now. Jeez, I hope they had insurance cover.

Nick also took me to Aya-Napa and in those days, it was just developing as a modern resort, with a fantastic nightlife. We went to Nissi Beach a few times and I'd never seen such beautiful women before. I'd only been abroad once before – on a school football holiday to Germany as a spotty 14-year-old. The only women we saw there were big busty German women who looked like they could beat our 15 stone PE teacher in an arm wrestle.

Having said that, when we bought some pottery from a place called Rüdesheim the woman behind the counter wrapped our presents up in pornographic magazines. I'm sure it was a marketing tactic to sell more items. Our football team queued round the block. One lad gave his mum and dad 13 different pieces of pottery as a present. Even I bought my mum a genuine German tankard, which stated in big letters on the base, 'made in Stoke-On-Trent'.

Many of the women who frequented Nissi Beach at the time were Scandinavian and had beautiful bronze bodies. Most only wore a tiny thong too, so I had to lie on my front. Whilst Nick had a nice tanned olive skin, I was the whitest person in Cyprus at the time – until I saw a couple of ginger ladies who made my white body look positively tanned. Luckily, my face tanned very nicely so at night-time I could hide my body and have a decent chance of pulling. I did meet a lovely Finnish girl, but my success was measured in a slow dance lasting 3 minutes.

In Manchester, we lived in a student area called Rusholme. It was known as the 'Curry Mile' and presented an array of brilliant restaurants which I tried to sample as often as I could. I guess this very fact didn't help on the ladies' front, however, as my breath probably stunk, and my trumps smelt worse. The curries were bloody fantastic though, as were the numerous kebabs I demolished. Looking back, my dress sense hindered my chances of meeting the opposite sex. My mum had bought me some brown cords, which I wore quite often on nights out. I also had a diamond jumper and a green donkey jacket. I looked like I'd entered a 70's fancy dress competition and the impression I must have given to the ladies makes me shiver. What the fuck was I thinking? When I discovered jeans, I felt like a new man.

Nick was a great friend during these days and my parents invited him to stay at their house a few times, as his family lived so far away. He had a fantastic sense of humour and we bonded very well right from our first meeting. At the time, Nick had a lovely Thai girlfriend who I got to know well, and he tried to give me plenty of advice about women. I was looking to meet someone or at least play the field a bit but was having little success if truth be told.

I tended to get smashed on most nights out so having a proper conversation with anyone was rather difficult in my inebriated state. Some nights I was that bad I could hardly fucking speak. Whilst sober, I met a few gorgeous girls on my course at university, but I was far too nervous to ask anyone out in that environment. I couldn't imagine myself discussing some complex concept with them in the library and then saying, 'By the way, please, please, please will you go to the pictures with me tonight, please?'

The university disco was obviously a place I fancied my chances – especially when prices were around £1 a pint. I had a mate everyone called Chuey, who was a big black guy, about 6 feet 7 tall. His hands were as big as my head and his cock was halfway down his leg. His nickname should've been 'Rhino' – because he was hung like a donkey. We played badminton a few times and whilst we had a shower after, he always made a point of his huge manhood - which was nearly touching his knees. He made me feel inadequate, but I was sure glad he was my friend during those times.

When he walked up to the bar, people moved out the way for him. At one point, I started wearing a bandana like Chuey did. I thought I looked cool, but in hindsight I probably looked like a real knob. One night, he took me to a club in Manchester city centre and I was the only white guy in there. I didn't feel out of place, though, as I was wearing my precious bandana. I did a few moves on the dancefloor, until Chuey told me to calm down a bit.

One time we were dancing on a night out at the university disco and I fancied an attractive girl. I told Chuey that I liked her, and he said that he knew her from previous nights out. He said, 'I'll put a word in for you,' giving me a wink. 'Ok, make sure it's a good word. I wanna play it cool as I really fancy her,' I said. He told me not to worry – he walked over and without further ado simply pointed at me and said to her, 'My mate over there, do you wanna fuck him?' Needless to say, I spent the night alone once more.

Another night at our university disco was memorable because the fire alarm went off and the whole place was evacuated. There were hundreds of half-pissed students waiting outside in the cold, hoping to get back in as soon as possible. I was dying to empty my bulging bladder in any decent place where I wouldn't be seen. I didn't whip my knob out in front of the kebab shop like some lads did, as I had a touch more class.

I found a few bushes nearby and felt elated as the urine exited my trembling body. Suddenly, I heard a voice right beside me in the dark – 'Lovely evening, are you having a good time?' she said. I looked down and literally right beside me was a girl crouching down, knickers round her ankles, having a piss too. We had a proper conversation whilst having a wee next to each other – it was all rather strange. To this day, I don't know why but I ended the chat by saying, 'Lovely bush!' and sniggered. Surprisingly, she laughed – I should have got her number really.

I did meet a few girls at university, but they rarely saw me more than once. Not having a mobile in those days meant that arranging to meet was a matter of trust. I obviously trusted them to turn up and they either didn't trust me or wanted to stand me up. I had a meeting point in Piccadilly Gardens in Manchester, fairly near the bus station. I vividly remember waiting and hoping that the evening's date would turn up. She never did of course, and I began to feel somewhat deflated. The third time this happened I returned to our flat feeling sorry for myself. I was dejected and in need of some cheering up by my housemates, Nick and

Gary. I knew they'd be supportive and make me feel better as I got back to our flat.

It was silent as I entered the kitchen with tears in my eyes. Suddenly, Nick and Gary burst out laughing hysterically. They laughed and laughed as I stood there feeling like shit. Then I realised I just had to join in and began to laugh too. They'd had a bet that I'd return on my own just like the other times. Gary said, 'Why don't you change your meeting point next time mate?' and I realised that that was the problem. Of course, the problem wasn't me as I was such a good catch. It was the bloody meeting point – in the dark near a sex shop was far from ideal. I'd been such a fool but could laugh about it now. I realised too that I'd have to ditch those fucking brown cords.

Another time I met a lovely Dutch girl called Sabrina. She was leggy and blonde and spoke with that really funny English accent that Dutch people do. I must admit, her strange accent really turned me on. I'd never had the pleasure of meeting a Dutch person before and I found her to be a sweet, exotic lady. Her smile was beautiful, and her demeanour was something to behold. At the time I liked bands such as the Stone Roses, U2, A-ha and was a massive fan of guitar music by Dire Straits and Chris Rea. The latter had had a big hit with *The Road to Hell,* which was a moody, depressing song with superb guitar solos. It was a real man's song that I would sometimes play air guitar to, or even grab my cricket bat and pretend to be Rea whilst dancing around the room strumming tunes on my bat between my legs.

I'd seen Sabrina at the university bar a few times and somehow managed to invite her to the flat. Surprisingly, she willingly came up to my room and I began to feel all tingly inside. I fancied her big time and wanted to make a good impression. I didn't want to rush things too much and go for a sloppy kiss too quickly, so I decided to put some music on first. Instead of putting on some mellow romantic music to set the right mood, maybe some Gloria Estefan or Whitney Houston, I decided to put on the full 12-inch version of *The Road to Hell.* To make matters worse, I turned off all the lights, so we were sat in near darkness, just to add to the atmosphere. Then, I blasted the song out loud with Rea's gruff voice bounding round the room trying to impress her.

When I turned the lights back on, I knew I'd made a big mistake. She seemed in a state of shock and a tear rolled down her cheek. She probably thought I was some sort of nutter who was trying to frighten her. Maybe she thought I would tie her up and kidnap her too. What the fuck had I done? She may have expected me to make a move in the dark in a romantic sort of way, but I was listening intently and nearly got my bat out for a bit of air guitar. I'd misread the mood and really didn't know how to treat a lady back then. I'd blown it big time, that's for sure. I'd been a complete knob and had an awful lot to learn. Even my cut-price shitty frozen pizza from the cheap supermarket that I'd made her for tea didn't do the trick. Unfortunately, I never saw her again. I really did have a lot to learn when it came to the opposite sex. I'm still a fan of Chris Rea, however, and when I play that song I sometimes think of that moment. I wonder what became of Sabrina.

CHAPTER 3: TORQUAY TALES

As I contemplated if I should join a dating site, I also began to reminisce about the first time I fell in love. I say fell in love, but really it was unadulterated infatuation. How had I changed since then? I was 17 years old and on my first holiday away from my parents. Five of us lads from the Sixth Form had booked a hotel in the lovely seaside resort of Torquay. It was the English Riviera, a hotbed of fun in the sun. I'd never seen a palm tree until I arrived in Torquay and I discovered it to be an amazing place. People had told me it was full of old codgers, but I didn't care – being away for a week was just magic.

On the very first night we got ready to go out, feeling excited about the evening ahead. We went to a local pub and had a quick pint before walking down into the town centre. As we walked down the street a group of girls were walking towards us. I saw a lovely looking blonde, with long flowing locks and a gorgeous smile. As she looked like a younger version of the attractive one from ABBA, for a joke I just said, 'Hello, are you from Sweden?' and laughed. Unbelievably, she smiled at me and said 'Yeah, I'm from Sweden,' in a rather Swedish accent.

This was like something from a sit-com. I was a little shocked by her response so simply said, 'Do you like ABBA?' as it was the only thing I could think of at the time. I then proceeded to ask her if she shopped at IKEA, whether her father drove a Volvo, if she lived in Stockholm and whether she had regular saunas. For some reason, she didn't walk off or ignore me at all, but her group of friends chatted to us for quite a while. They were on a group exchange and this meant that there were lots of Scandinavians in town.

Her name was Ami and apparently, she lived on an island east of Stockholm called Lidingö. We had a brief kiss, though nothing too passionate. The chemistry was amazing, and I was elated with having met the most beautiful girl on the planet. It was the first night and within a couple of hours I'd met the girl of my dreams. She told me that she was staying at the opposite side of town and actually gave me her address. However, we made plans to meet each other the following night in the town centre. It was all surreal for a 17-year-old.

That night we got drunk on cheap beer and I remember some superb pubs around the harbour area. It felt like we were abroad, with expensive yachts bobbing up and down in the picturesque harbour, surrounded by lovely palms. The Swedish girls we'd met thus far had been slim, beautiful and exotic. As we sat in a bar, another group walked in. They looked more like the type of girls from back home – podgy, spotty and fat-arsed, with a bit of crack poking out the top of their pants. My mate Jonny started a conversation with one of this group of Swedes – big, fat and slightly hairy with a touch of bulldog features. He must have been wearing his beer goggles by this point and thinking with his knob.

They got along very well and ended up back at our hotel. Jonny managed to pop his cherry but was rather under-whelmed with the whole experience. He seemed a bit deflated the next day when we all took the piss and said he may have a disease or may become a father. What was he thinking? She was a hound to say the least, but to be fair he'd scored and admitted that he didn't wear a condom so went bare-back riding.

Fast forward twelve months later. We'd had such a good time in Torquay that we decided to do the same the following year, albeit in a different hotel. We went about the same time of year and retraced our steps, going to many of the same bars and clubs. We made a visit to the very same bar, by the harbour, as Jonny had met his conquest from the previous year.

We began to tease him about her turning up again and having a general laugh about the previous trip. It was all light-hearted and Jonny took it in good spirits as we had a drink or two and said he may have a child in Sweden somewhere. Then, unbelievably, incredibly, like something out of a movie, the very same girl walked into the bar with her friends! I looked once, twice, and several more times to make sure it was her. We almost fell onto the floor in complete fits of laughter, except Jonny of course.

Jonny slivered down in his seat and tried to hide behind a table. But we couldn't let this go, not after a full year. Another of our group, Graham, went over to them and pointed over to Jonny. By this point he was almost on the floor struggling to breathe. However, she came over and said hello. Jonny ignored her so Graham tried to chat her up, but eventually thought better of it. It was an unbelievable coincidence and something that still makes me chuckle to this day. By the way, she didn't have a child, so Jonny sighed with relief, but his sheer embarrassment took a while to vanish.

During our first holiday to Torquay twelve months earlier, I was determined to see Ami again after our meeting on the very first night. I had the address she'd given me and plenty of energy after our night on the pop. My friend, Mad Mick, came with me on the adventure to discover where she was. It seemed bloody miles, but we asked a fair few people and managed to locate the street towards the end of the night. Outside and still fairly drunk, I began shouting her name in a romantic fashion I thought. After a few minutes of waking everybody up, she opened the curtains and window. She stuck her head out of the window and asked what I was doing. I shouted, 'What do you mean, I've come all this way just to see you!' rather excitedly. We exchanged a few words, but she told me she wasn't allowed out after a certain time.

The positive was that she seemed pleased to see me, although she said I was being far too loud and waking people up. Then, suddenly, a big bloke opened the door and started shouting at us - 'You're waking everyone up. If you don't go now, I'll call the police!' He had an angry look on his face, and I could tell his blood was boiling. I tried to reason that I'd met a wonderful girl, but unsurprisingly it fell on deaf ears. We had to leave quickly and with a wave to Ami I ran down the street in haste.

Soon after, without any warning, the rain started. This was not rain like I was used to at all, but more like a tropical storm. It belted down and soaked us through within a matter of seconds. We only had shirts on, but I felt rather liberated being in love and piss wet through. Then, after about ten minutes of being drenched, Mad Mick picked up a big advertising board from outside a shop to carry above our heads. It certainly did the job as we seemed to walk for miles back to the town centre. Then, as we walked down the main street carrying the sign above us, a police car pulled up next to us. Mick saw them and absolutely legged it, leaving me with this fucking big sign. They asked where the sign came from and I was clueless, although I said it was not far from the street I'd been to. They told me it could be theft if I didn't return it there and then. I knew it would be difficult to carry on my own due to the size and weight, but I turned around and began to walk back on my own.

After a minute or two the car pulled up beside me again. A butch female copper said, 'Get in the car. You can't carry that on your own. We'll give you a lift.' She gave me a dirty look as I got in and then asked my name. Rather stupidly, I said 'John Smith' as it was the first name that came into my head. I'd never been asked by the police before and it was just a reaction without thinking. I could've been called John Smith, some people must be, but I reckon they knew I was telling porkies. In fact, when the female officer said, 'You're lying, tell us the truth,' I knew the game was up. She then went further, 'What have you been up to tonight? Smashed a few windows, smashed a car up, come on tell us.'

By this stage I was feeling very sober and slightly fearful. It seemed that this female officer, a very butch and joyless soul, had it in for me. The male driver appeared to be far more sensible, until he asked if I'd been drinking. What could I say? I'd already lied about my fucking name so was honest when I said it was my first holiday away from my parents and I'd had a few beers. They drove around for ages trying to find the shop and then I recognised which lamppost it had been leaning on. They put it back and then Butch asked me where I was staying. The man grunted, 'We'll take you back and find out your I.D. so come clean now.'

Outside my hotel, I confessed my real name and said I would show them the tag on my suitcase. It was the very first night of my holiday and I was followed into the hotel by two bloody police officers. We walked past the bar and my mates were playing pool and supping pints. There were a few guests in the bar and the hotelier behind the bar. Everyone just stared at me as we walked past, with my mates gobsmacked. I showed the bloke my tag and he said 'I'm gonna find out if any charges are to be pressed so I'll make a phone call.'

My whole world was crumbling at this point in my life, as I waited for the call to finish. In hindsight, I think he was just shitting me up a bit. The sign had been returned so it couldn't be theft, but I guess there was always underage drinking. To be fair to him, he gave me a lecture and told me not to drink again on the rest of my holiday and they left. However, I went straight into the bar to see everyone and the hotelier offered me a drink. I was that relieved by the whole episode, I had a pint and regaled the entire story in detail to everyone in the room, including lots of people I'd never met before. Everyone laughed and then Mad Mick walked in. 'You bastard!' I shouted.

The hotelier wasn't impressed a couple of nights later, however, when Mad Mick set off the fire alarm at about 2 o'clock in the morning. Everyone had to evacuate the hotel in their bloody pyjamas. He'd been fooling around and claimed it was accident, but it had caused a lot of people to become very pissed off. Whilst we were all stood outside waiting, I used this opportunity to get talking to a young girl with long brown hair, who looked rather nice in her nightgown. It transpired that she lived only about ten miles from me and was a year younger than me. We exchanged numbers and vowed to meet up at some point, when we got back up north.

Of course, I didn't think things would materialise in a romantic way. But, having met outside in the cold on that night in Torquay, she became my girlfriend for a while and even bought me a Chris Rea album for my eighteenth birthday. Though I liked her a lot, it was stupid of me to keep comparing her to Ami. I couldn't stop thinking about Ami and she just wasn't her. The Swedish princess was the girl I dreamed about and the girl who'd really stolen my heart on that trip. I'd put her on a pedestal, and nobody would come close to her. You could say I was fucking besotted and crazy too.

I saw Ami a couple more times on our holiday, but it was just an hour or two having a milkshake with her friends. Unfortunately, I never got chance to slip her the finger. She was only 16 but had made a very big impression on me. We swapped addresses and I promised with all my heart to write to her on a regular basis and try to visit her in Stockholm. She seemed genuinely sad when we hugged goodbye and I was smitten. A week or two later, I received a letter with a Swedish flag on it and she sent me a photograph which I treasured for years.

Of course, I replicated her gesture and spent ages trying to find the best possible photo to send her. I had my mates taking photos from every conceivable angle to get the right one. We wrote to each other for years and I called her several times, usually whilst drunk, telling her that I loved her and missed her terribly. I was determined to see her again as I had dreams that maybe we'd get married and I'd move to Sweden to start a new life. Then, one of my friends from university suggested we did Euro-rail and fit in a visit to see her in Sweden. I called her up to tell her the good news – 'I'm coming to see you!' I proclaimed.

CHAPTER 4: SWEDISH DELIGHT

Now, as I considered whether to create a dating profile, I wondered what would be appealing to the ladies out there. I thought it would be wrong to lie on any profile that I created, but that I should be totally honest and be myself. Afterwards, I thought that everyone else must be economical with the truth and probably told a few white lies. And probably many people blatantly lied, in order to sell themselves and ensure a better impression to others. In fact, it felt like I was marketing myself to others and it would be a bloody marketing exercise. How would women perceive me? Would I appeal to them? Lots of questions whirled around my mind as I pondered whether I should delve into this world. You could say I was slightly confused by it all.

By this point in my life, my athletic body was turning a bit podgy. I mean, I wasn't fat or that much overweight, but my body shape had changed from my prime and I'd started developing moobs for the first time. I'd heard about these bastards, but I thought my pecs were solid and would stay that way. One day, I looked in the mirror and saw some small tits. To compound matters, my hair was turning grey in some places. My eldest daughter made me feel much better by buying me some *Just for Men* hair dye and telling me to use it, as I was beginning to embarrass her. She was probably just trying to help, but I wanted to grow old gracefully. I had to consider whether I should reflect these changes in any profile I created, but I guess everyone had to go through this. Everyone was in the same boat. People grew older but tried to cling on to their prime. Nevertheless, I knew I was getting older and the doubts began to creep into my mind. Would anyone really want to date a greying man with moobs? You could say my former confidence was dwindling by the month and my head was spinning with negative thoughts.

Back when I was 17 when I'd first met Ami in Torquay, I was clueless as to how life would pan out in the future. At that age I almost felt invincible. I'd written to her for a few years and thought about her for hours and hours. It must have been infatuation. At 20 years old, I was going to visit her with another friend from university and make all my dreams come true. I'd bought my Inter-rail pass which allowed unlimited travel around Europe for one month. I'd got myself a massive backpack and stove and we had a two-man tent to sleep in.

Being students, we didn't have much money at all but reckoned we could plan everything on the cheap. For example, a hearty meal to us was a packet of flavoured rice with a tin of tuna plonked on top. The plan was to go to Denmark first and then on to Sweden to see Ami. She'd asked her parents and it was agreed that she would put us up for three nights. She told me her parents were going away for a couple of these, so I thought I was on a promise.

Copenhagen was a very clean and lovely place, with some splendid architecture, even if I didn't really appreciate all that kind of thing at that age. What I did notice in Copenhagen, however, was the sheer beauty of the ladies who lived there. I called it the 'land of the beautiful.' Walking through my local town you may have seen one beauty every now and then, about once every three weeks. Walking in the 'land of the beautiful' it was the complete opposite – every now and then, you saw an ugly one. Nearly every woman was stunning to me – I was simply amazed.

As I walked around the pristine streets, I seemed to get a few glances too, but that was probably because my tongue was hanging out and I had a semi on which made a slight bulge in my pants. The one thing I didn't like too much in Copenhagen was the price of everything. I remember the only food we could afford there was bread and cheese. Luckily, I liked both as we ate them in abundance. We were students so bread and cheese turned out to be a decent meal for us at the time, I guess.

Later, we made our way to Stockholm and I remember the excitement building up inside me. But also, I began to feel a tad nervous because I'd built everything up in my mind over the last few years. What would I do when I saw her? Should I try to be intimate, if the moment was right?

Lots of stuff whirled through my mind, it was just weird. Once in the city I remember using a phone box to call her so she could meet us and pick us up. I didn't know how to operate the damn thing and money kept dropping out. There were no instructions in English, and it all felt very foreign to me. My hand was shaking with nerves too, which didn't help matters. Eventually I got through and thankfully she picked up the phone. She told us a place to meet and we went there to wait for the girl I'd dreamt about for three whole years. Some of them had been wet ones too.

As I waited and waited, my heart was racing and there was sweat on my brow. Suddenly, I saw a blonde figure walking towards me – it was her! It was Ami looking radiant, with that gorgeous smile I'd remembered. The way she walked was like poetry in motion, with her hair blowing gently in the cool breeze. But then I saw a big guy next to her as they walked towards us. My immediate thought was, who the fuck is that? Was this really happening? She embraced me with a big hug and then said, 'Lovely to see you, this is my boyfriend Goran,' smiling. After all that, she had a fucking boyfriend!

Jeez, I was crestfallen beyond belief. All these years I thought she'd been dreaming about me too and devoting her entire life to me. But she'd probably been shagging this ugly buffoon behind my back. My whole world was caving in right here, right now. The girl of my dreams was at it with this big lump, bloody Goran. To be fair, he was very polite and made me feel welcome to his country. But it took quite a while for my head to adjust to this situation. I thought I was on a promise with Ami, but the best I could hope for now was a friendly chat, although a threesome wouldn't go amiss.

Once I'd regained my composure and wiped away all my tears, we could head back to her house in Lidingö. We had to cross a long road bridge, which seemed to go on for miles and miles from the city. It transpired that Lidingö was a small island attached to the mainland, on the east side of Stockholm. We got to her house eventually and I was surprised to see it made out of wood and standing on what appeared to be huge wooden stilts. It was a bizarre piece of architecture in all honesty, but it was how you imagine an IKEA house would look, with different shades of wood everywhere. Inside, it was all wood, more wood –

everything was fucking wood. It was all very ironic, because I'd wanted to give her my wood too.

Ami made us fresh pizza, using her wood burning stove of course. We sat on her wooden balcony, overlooking a small wood, and sat in some lovely wooden chairs. Goran gave me a beer and we had a good chat about what it was like to live in Stockholm. I told them I loved how they made such natural use of the wood that was all around them. They told me how expensive it was to buy alcohol in Sweden compared to England - they nearly fell off their wooden chair when I told them it was only £1 per pint at university.

The next day, Ami introduced us to a friend of hers called Pia. She was pretty fit too, but I didn't want to appear desperate when they were simply showing us around the city. We went to some museum with a massive wooden ship inside and had a look at the Royal Palace, which wasn't made of wood. They told us that Stockholm was so clean that salmon could swim in the city centre. It made where I lived look like a bloody rubbish dump. It was just normal to see rubbish strewn around everywhere, whereas here the streets were spotless, and everything seemed immaculate. I wondered why people just didn't respect where they lived and looked after the local environment.

After exploring the elegant city all day, we went to McDonalds for a meal - which was very similar to back home. However, after eating my usual 12 cheeseburgers, I was dying for a dump. I hadn't emptied my load at Ami's house because I didn't want to stain the natural wooden toilet seat or leave a nasty surprise for her. I wandered over to the men's toilets, but unfortunately, they were closed due to being out of order. This was like being in England again I thought. So, reluctantly but desperately, I had to go to the ladies around the other side of the restaurant.

I waited for a while behind another lady, but then the cubicle was vacant. I expected rows of cubicles - but there appeared to be a single toilet ready for my immediate use. I must admit it was a bad one - a real stinker. I'd not been for a while, so managed to shit half my body weight. It was like a fucking python writhing around the bowl. I was also sweating like an Olympic weightlifter trying to squeeze the bastard out in a very confined space. There was no window and the toilet extractor fan was sadly broken, so I began to panic a bit.

I tried to be as quick as I could, but this python was a slow mover, as well as a rather sticky creature. Having managed to lose about half a stone in the process, I opened the toilet door to make my escape – although half the python was still planted in the bowl despite a couple of flushes. When I opened the door, the hideous smell wafted to the other side of McDonalds. I positively put half the restaurant off their big macs and fries. To make matters worse, there was a sizeable queue that had developed outside the door. Their faces told a story when I opened that door. Each and every one coiled away in a look of sheer disgust, faces screwed up as though they had just seen a dead dog lying on the pavement. And as I looked up, who was next in the queue waiting? Ami of course.

We had a pleasant few days in Sweden, but it hadn't transpired how I'd hoped. I was only alone with Ami a brief time in her kitchen and I'd decided that it would be wrong to make a romantic move, when Goran had been so good to us and I got on well with him. It was clear that Ami saw me as a penfriend from England and I continued to write to her for another couple of years, although I didn't perceive her in the same way.

I'd been bloody naïve and stupid in any case. She moved to the USA to be an au pair I believe, in Long Island, I think. Anyway, after about 5 years of letters it all ended as my new girlfriend at the time, understandably I guess, wasn't too keen for me to maintain the friendship in case I fled to the USA if we had a bad argument. It was probably a poor idea to show her all the letters and photos Ami had sent me though and tell her that I dreamt about Ami every night.

On our European tour we also went to Holland, Germany, Italy and France. In Amsterdam, I was taken aback by the sheer weirdness of the city. I'd anticipated a big sign introducing the red-light zone so that children wouldn't venture there. In fact, we walked around a corner and a very large lady who looked about mid-forties, wearing skimpy knickers and bra, started waving at me and gestured that she wanted me to enter her booth. At that age I was slightly shocked and put my head down to avoid eye contact. There was no way I would go into one of those places, although it became more tempting when the ladies began to look more attractive. There was anything you wanted or craved – oriental, black, white, blonde, brunette, old, young, lady-boys, fat, thin, ugly, normal, attractive – it didn't matter. To a twenty-year old, it was a real eye opener.

After walking around for a while, I became more confident to have a proper gawp and look at the offerings on display. It's fair to say that some of the women were really rather stunning, but you still wondered just how many pricks had entered them in the past. It did put me off just a tad. In the red-light area I also saw groups of Japanese people, with children as well, carrying massive cameras and having a good look at the scenery. Blokes trying to sell tickets for sex shows also shouted to us, 'Come on lads, wanky, wanky,' as we wandered down the street. In one red-light window I saw a couple of gurning grannies with saggy tits wearing their skimpy panties. It was such an attractive sight for a young man to witness. They looked about 70 years old and must have known how to handle a cock or two. I guess everyone had different tastes and the grannies appealed to some punters. Not just the grandads either.

I'd never had a proper look at a sex shop before so spent some time in one, seeing if there was anything on offer. However, I didn't fancy a gimp mask or leather body suit and all the sadomasochistic stuff was just plain weird to me. I didn't understand why people wanted to be hurt for sexual pleasure like masochists did. I'd never really thought that sticking hooks in my testicles or using a scrubbing brush on my cock would turn me on, although I could understand handcuffs and whipping to a certain degree. There was also a massive selection of vibrators, which incorporated every size and colour you can imagine in readiness for satisfying pussies from all over the world.

Inside the sex shop, there were also secret booths and I could hear the sound of porno movies and some bloke bashing one off. It was all rather bizarre. I looked in another corner and saw false vaginas and dolls, some of which looked very life-like indeed. Some of the dolls were very tempting in fact, as they permanently had their mouths gaping open. My mate told me that you knew a doll was ready for throwing away when its nose started running. In all honesty, I found Amsterdam a peculiar place all round, but certainly a different cultural experience.

In Germany, we visited places such as Hamburg and Cologne, as well as a few small towns on the beautiful River Rhine. Near the Rhine we found a picturesque campsite overlooking the majestic river. We got told to pitch our tent in a certain spot and went to see what food was available on the site. I remember the only food in stock was a tube of *Pringles*, so we got one each for our evening meal. I mean, I liked *Pringles* for sure, but it was a bizarre end to the day.

In the morning, we were abruptly and rudely woken by an old German man spraying our tent with a hose pipe and ranting at us. We couldn't understand what he was screaming, but it was clear he was apoplectic with pure rage. He was basically shouting at us to move our tent away from his precious caravan. Well, I tried to reason with this buffoon that we'd been told to pitch our tent in that very position.

Unfortunately, this fell on deaf ears as he continued to rant at us. His fucking ugly wife then popped her melon shaped head out of the caravan window screaming yet more abuse. They were acting as though we'd robbed them or pissed through their windows, but we'd done no such thing. Eventually, I lost my composure at this point and shouted the only swear word I knew in German which basically translated as 'Shithead,' as he began to back off.

I could see that he didn't like this so said it several more times, trying to use the best German accent I could muster from my school days. My German teacher would've been so proud of me. However, this ploy seemed to be working. He threw the hose down and ran back into his shitty caravan probably fearing some sort of retaliation. In fact, I picked up the hose and began squirting his caravan in revenge. Then my mate piped up, 'You're doing him a fucking favour now. You're washing his caravan for him!'

After our experiences in Germany, we then ventured to Italy and visited such cities as Verona, Florence and Venice. On a memorable train journey between two of the cities in Italy the train was packed with people and it was standing room only. Luckily, I had a seat in a carriage when a trim Italian woman stood in front of me. It was a very hot summer day and she had a white blouse on with rather large gaps under the arms. As the train pulled away from the station, she reached up to the handgrips above her and exposed her beautiful breasts. She must have known that I'd see from the angle I was sat at and clearly didn't wear a bra for a reason. She knew exactly what she exposing to us.

Her breasts were just the right size as far as I was concerned, not too big but firm and pert. Her lovely nipples seemed to jiggle about as the train gathered speed and I began to get flustered. This bizarre situation which I'd not anticipated began to turn me on and I had to place my cap over my groin area so as not to be too embarrassed. She glanced down at me, but I turned my head so as not to make it too obvious. My mate had also noticed by now and we began to smirk like naughty schoolboys. The faster the train went the more her boobs jiggled about and the more my semi developed. Suddenly, I realised it was our intended stop next and I'd have to get up.

However, there was no way I could stand up in such a state as my semi had now developed into a full-blown stinking hard-on. I was transfixed and so was my friend. I half-heartedly stood up but realised this was a situation I couldn't avert so quickly. She looked at me again and my red face, with perspiration rolling down it. I started thinking about other things, such as what type of pasta we may have for lunch, but nothing seemed to work. I'd never wanted a stiffy to diminish so quickly. We had long missed our intended stop and all our plans went out the window. Where would we end up? Did it really matter? The answer was we nearly ended up in bloody Switzerland!

Eventually, we had to make a move. By now I'd started thinking about all sorts of shit so I could stand up properly. A voice in my head kept saying, 'Don't look you dirty bastard,' but then I looked again. Having purposely thought about my university exams in great depth I was thankful that something like that allowed me to stand up and make way to the exit. It was over, I'd overcome a tricky situation albeit about 150 miles later. On reflection, it was terribly wrong of me and out of order. I should have given my seat up for a pensioner like that.

CHAPTER 5: SNIP AWAY

Of course, the Italian girl on the train wasn't really a pensioner. She was a similar age to us, had a lovely olive skin, tidy body, long dark hair and a pretty smile. A year later, whilst in my third year at university, I saw someone similar dancing in a nightclub when out one night with friends. I really fancied her and thought I'd show her how to move on the dancefloor and did my usual spins and twirls, probably making a tit of myself again. However, she appeared to like my enthusiasm and sort of danced with me, looking slightly embarrassed by my moves.

At the end of the night, despite my moves we ended up talking, then kissing and exchanged numbers, which was promising. However, as my previous experiences at university had all been failures after the first night, I wasn't brimming with confidence. Nevertheless, we arranged to meet and this time she amazingly turned up as planned, possibly because my meeting place was now totally different. The first proper date went really well, and we continued to see each other regularly from then on. From this initial meeting at the nightclub, it then developed into a long-term relationship, the first in my life.

As our relationship prospered, we had three fantastic children who we both love dearly, of course. For a large part of our time together, we had fun, both as a couple and as a family unit too. I tried my best to be a good dad and worked hard to support my family. Though at times we didn't have much money and lived month to month, we were happy. It seemed, however, that as the children grew older, we somewhat drifted apart as a couple. Unfortunately, as our relationship faltered, we'd had less and less time for each other. Everything was about the children and providing the best life for them. In hindsight, we were probably too young when we started a family and ended up becoming only parents, rather than having time for each other. Despite this, we remained together for a considerable number of years.

When we separated, it was a really difficult time for both us and the children, as you can imagine. Neither of us entered the relationship thinking it would end, but the statistics proved that it was a real possibility. Having children made it so much harder though and I had to adjust to being with the kids much less, instead of being there all the time. The early days of the separation were the worse by far, but gradually I learned to cope without the children around all the time. Yet, I always tried to spend quality time with them, mainly at weekends, and still do. It was something that many absent fathers have to adjust to after a separation and I was no different. My parents and friends were very supportive around this time.

One thing was for sure, there was no way I wanted to rush into another relationship. I was mentally shot, somewhat depressed and needed to adjust to life as a single man. I needed to get my head right and only then could I move on. After a couple of years, I thought I was ready to meet someone special again. I looked in the mirror and tried to envisage what women would make of me. I was now past my mid-thirties and beginning to feel older and looked older too. Surely, I thought, the best years of my life were behind me. I was beginning to doubt myself and wondered if I could connect with someone who was maybe in a similar situation. But a voice in my head kept telling me that if I didn't try to meet someone, then I was sure to remain single. Probably forever and ever.

Was I ready to begin my journey looking for a new partner? Maybe not at first, but you never knew what was around the corner. As I had children myself, I knew that I'd have to be honest if I met someone, as they would have to accept my kids. However, I also realised that I didn't want to introduce lots of different women to my children. I envisaged only doing this if I met someone special, after a lengthy time dating. I certainly didn't want any more kids of my own though and vowed to be honest with any ladies that I met, just in case they wanted to start a family.

After my third child was born, my second beautiful daughter, I decided to have the snip. We'd only planned one of the three after all and I could've ended up with about 16 kids at that rate. Don't worry, my kids know this fact as I've told them in detail – they are the best mistakes ever as far as I'm concerned. In spite of that, I realised that unless I took some action there could be several more mistakes and it would become almost impossible to stay sane. Nobody could deny that kids were fucking hard work at times – mainly mornings, during the day and evenings.

Three children were enough for anyone I thought, especially since my oldest two hated each other. When my son was born, my eldest daughter bit him on a regular basis. Of course, she was only a toddler herself but her dislike of him began young and seemed to last. The biting stopped, but that was replaced by her simply pretending he didn't exist. Of course, they love each other really, but just pretend they don't sometimes!

My two daughters were both beautiful babies when they were born, but my son was one ugly baby if truth be told. Nobody would have the guts to say anything though, apart from me, but I had eyes so knew what they were thinking. Thankfully, he actually grew some hair as he got older and became a good-looking lad, just like his father. Though he now swears vehemently that he doesn't look anything like me. I don't know why, in all honesty.

So, after three kids, I volunteered for a vasectomy even though the thought of it sounded rather squeamish. Before the operation occurred, I was given a magic pill to relax me, but it didn't have any effect at all. I should have had a few vodkas instead. I arrived nervously at the clinic and was met by the doctor dubbed as the 'Butcher of Baghdad' by those in the region who'd already had it done. His reputation was legendary.

I had to lie down on a sort of operating table ready to have my testicles sliced open by the Butcher. I looked at him again and then realised why his nickname existed. He was a dead ringer for the for the former brutal Iraqi dictator Saddam Hussein. So, here I was, laid down with my tackle exposed with a Saddam lookalike stood over me and holding a rather large scalpel. My balls retracted even more, and my cock nearly disappeared, like a snail hiding its head in the shell.

Before he got to work a nurse joined him and introduced herself as the staff nurse on duty for my operation. She looked at me carefully and I looked twice at her. It was only my mate's fucking mum! She was a nice friendly woman, but I really didn't want her staring at my shrivelled cock and retracting balls. I was already fearful and now my mate's mum was fondling my genitals in order to assist the Butcher. She told me not to worry and that she wasn't allowed to tell her son she'd seen me, as it was all confidential. Yeah, yeah – I bet she told him that night whilst having her sausage and mash for tea. Maybe she had chipolatas and thought about me.

Anyway, I managed to cope with the slicing and tying and was even presented with some evidence in a jar. It seemed strange but I took it home and put it on my mantelpiece as though I'd won a trophy. Once every visitor to my home had seen its lurid contents, I decided to throw it away.

The next part of the challenge was far more enjoyable. I was told by the doctor that I had to empty my sack of as much semen as I could, before taking a sample to the hospital for testing. This was to rid myself of any existing sperm that was still inside my testes. This obviously involved lots of masturbation whenever I could. I told my partner that, of course, I wasn't enjoying it at all, but it was an essential medical process that needed my due care and attention. I basically had a valid excuse to bash the bishop as often as possible. When she asked where I was going, my usual response was, 'Oh, just going to bash another one out that's all.'

After a couple of weeks, I reckoned I'd emptied my balls good and proper, so it was time to take in a sample to the hospital. The sample had to be a very recent one and stay fresh, so I had to ejaculate just before we went. I remember vividly my partner was waiting in the car with the kids and the engine running, whilst I had a tiny pot to aim for. Talk about pressure. Of course, it wasn't easy in that situation. I could hear the kids outside asking what dad was doing and why he was taking so long. Sweat was pouring from my brow as I had to release my load imminently, in this tiny pot. I was worried that I'd over-shoot the target and it would end up all over the toothbrushes. It wasn't as easy as I'd imagined, especially when she was honking the bloody horn telling me we'd be late. Eventually, I managed to release my sample in the pot, mission accomplished, and felt rather excited as we set off.

When we arrived at the hospital, I tried to find the right place to submit my sample. It was like a bloody maze in there and the signs were misleading. I was basically walking around everywhere with a pot of hot seed in my hand. Finally, I had to ask an attractive nurse where the appropriate place was located, and she asked what sample I had with me. Instinctively, I held up my transparent tub of semen and showed her my handy work. She stuttered slightly and explained where to submit it. The sample failed miserably, which meant my special tadpoles were still firing on all cylinders.

Basically, despite all my hard work, there was still lots of sperm in my semen which meant I was able to impregnate again. Disappointing, of course, but it meant I had to repeat the wanking process with far more intensity thereafter. Thankfully, after another few of weeks of frequent masturbation my sample passed. I felt proud after all the hard work I'd put in and had lost a bit of weight with all the exercise. It meant I could also have sex without the fear of having any more children, which was a huge relief to me. Having three kids was bloody draining at times. Although, not nearly as draining as all the masturbation I had to put up with.

Of course, I love my kids, but having the snip was just taking a sensible approach. I couldn't understand those people who had massive families, with 7 or 8 kids or more. It must be fucking unbearable living in a household like that. Let's be honest, children could be rather difficult at times with all the attention they craved. Babies just shat all the time and cried for no reason. Well, I thought they cried for no reason but obviously they probably had trapped wind. Or needed yet another smelly shit. The amount of times they puked over my shoulder as I gently winded them was immeasurable. As toddlers they had tantrums and started screaming for no good reason. Then they got to the age when they started fighting with each other and being cheeky brats. It was all good fun, I guess, if you were a fan of sleepless nights and enjoyed cleaning up sick and poo on a regular basis.

So, as I contemplated meeting someone else, I pondered whether I'd really want to take on another woman who had lots of kids. That was a definite 'no' then. Would I mind if she had just one or maybe two children? That felt different to me, and something I considered doing.

I certainly wouldn't reject a lady purely because she had children. But could I really cope taking on lots of kids? I could only just cope with my own and they actually loved me. Well, they always told me they did! What would it be like trying to become a new father-figure in another child's life? All these questions were swirling around in my overactive mind.

Then, I realised I had three children of my own and that whoever I met would have to take them on so to speak – which made me think that this could be a very difficult process. I was already jumping ahead in my mind, thinking all these silly thoughts. First, though, I actually had to sign up to the dating sites and complete all the required information. Compiling a suitable profile may have been much more difficult than I anticipated.

CHAPTER 6: PROFILE PORKIES

After thinking about my options carefully, I called my friend Tiny Col – I mean Big Col and asked him if he could help complete my dating profile one Friday night. He came around to my house with a few beers and a few ideas to put on my first ever attempt to meet someone online. In hindsight, bearing in mind he was in his mid-thirties and still living with his parents, I'm not sure he was the best person to ask for help. I'd not even seen the type of stuff that these sites asked you to complete, but I could guess some of the details required and was faced with something of a dilemma when the questions appeared online. My state of mind at the time was demonstrated by my response to these details:

NAME – This sounds an easy question to be honest, but do I make up a false name like some people do? Maybe just 'Dave' or go for some extended artistic licence, like 'Monster Cock' for example? Or maybe just tell the truth, like all decent people out there. I don't mean 'Normal Cock' but write my actual name. Obviously, not my full name like when doing an exam at school.

AGE – Oh shit! Do I lie again? Surely, people tell white lies here I thought. But if I did tell porkies then how many years shall I actually knock off? Maybe just one or two I reckon, don't push it. I bet some people knock at least 5 years off. That's ridiculous though, I want to be genuine and honest and be well respected. Just be bloody honest, I thought. I'll knock one year off. This was really difficult; I needed more beer.

HAIR – Oh no! I'm fucking turning grey in some places and I don't want to dye it. Surely, I can't lie about this shit, as I'm posting a photo or two as well so people can actually see me. I'll have to tell the truth. Hang on, what's this box – salt and pepper? Is that a polite way of saying grey? I'll go for that as it's partly brown too, with grey flecks. Yes, that's right – I'm fucking salt and pepper. How exotic!

HEIGHT – This is easy, just think of my real height and then add an inch or two on. A bit like estimating cock size really. Small men must add on a good few inches then wear massive Cuban heels on dates. I mean on their feet, not cock. I'm about average height, say 5 feet 10. So, I'll put down 5 feet 11 inches then. That extra inch may swing it my way.

BUILD – Again, this is tough, but make a bloody decision man. I used to be athletic, very athletic. But that was ten years ago, shit. What am I now? I've put weight on recently and my fucking moobs are developing. At least it doesn't ask for weight – nobody would be honest then, would they? The options in front of me include athletic build and average, but not fat, very fat or morbidly obese – this must be for marketing purposes. I'm not fat anyway, honest. I'm now carrying a slight belly that's all. Why is there no option for Dad Bod? So, I'm undoubtedly average build and weight here.

ETHNICITY – That's an easy one, I'm white. I can't lie on this point. My photos would give it away.

SMOKER OR NON-SMOKER – Again, easy decision. I can't stand fags and hate the smell of smokers, but I won't say that here yet. It may reduce my chances of getting my end away.

INTERESTS – What would the women out there like me to be interested in? I can't mention stuff like masturbation and sex as that would surely put them off. But is mentioning cricket worse? I bloody love cricket. I've played it for 20 years, been to watch county games and even been to watch England play. I've been first team captain, coached youngsters and managed junior teams. If I put all that shit in, I've no chance as most women I know hate cricket. In fact, I bet if a survey was carried out, more women would prefer a bit of anal sex than cricket. What's interesting to women? No, no, I can't put shopping down as I hate that myself. I hate being dragged around shops all day while she tries to find the perfect dress, visiting every shop in the universe before deciding the first one was right after all. It's my idea of hell to spend all day at the Trafford Centre. I'd probably prefer to stay in all day with the trots. I know, I'll put badminton down. Most women I know don't mind a game of badminton every now and then – it's a better bet than cricket. Women like hitting a dead budgie over a net for some reason.

So, it was plain to see my mind was clearly all over the place when wrapping up these details for my profile. I'd anticipated it being a quick and easy process – but the reality was very different. I wanted to get it just right and make an impression from the outset. However, I was really confused about whether to include cricket as an interest. Remember, this was a long time before a big resurgence in the game following England's amazing World Cup win in 2019 against New Zealand when the match was tied, and England won after an unbelievable super-over. New heroes like Ben Stokes have now sold the game to a new generation of fans and shown how great the game can be.

Bizarrely, for some reason I'd always enjoyed standing in a field for hours on end, waiting for a catch to come my way. My own personal hero was the mighty Ian Botham, who I'd seen destroy the Aussies on television as a kid and it made me take up the game. I was lucky enough to see him play for Worcestershire once and my great uncle got his autograph for me, as he was a member of Somerset Cricket Club. More recently, I admired Freddie Flintoff as a local Lancashire icon who was a fantastic player and a likeable character. I was a decent club player in the local leagues and enjoyed the social side of the game as well. Many a night we had a few beers and ended up on the razzle after matches.

One Saturday evening when we had another game the next day, we ended up on the pop again and went in town for a curry. A few of us ordered different curries, but they all came to the table looking identical. I reckon they just had one big pot of curry for all the pissheads at 1 o'clock in the morning. It tasted good at the time, but the following morning I paid the price with a vengeance. I was basically on the bog all morning before the game and suffering from an acute bout of the dreaded 'ring-sting'. I had to put the toilet roll in the fridge just to cool my stinging anus. I made it to the ground but had to fight another couple of players to get to the shitter first. I was still suffering badly, as were a few others, and I promised I'd never to go back there again.

I struggled to make it out on the field and was constantly checking for any brown marks on my lovely white flannels. Unfortunately, one of the other players was not so lucky and had already shit himself before the game. He had a massive brown stain on his arse and was understandably rather sheepish. It was hilarious for those who hadn't been out with us and, of course, they took the piss big time.

I had to inform the umpire that I may have to run off at any time, including in the middle of an over. I was bowling first, and the slips were shouting plenty of encouragement, as you can imagine – 'Come on mate, let it rip!' or 'Make sure you follow through properly!' were just a couple I can remember. Fortunately, I managed to clench my butt cheeks for the whole game, as I didn't enjoy the prospect of defecating in public.

On another occasion, I was about to bat but had forgotten to pack my jockstrap to hold my protective box in place. Their quick bowler was storming down a hill at one end and making our batsmen flinch. I was only wearing a pair of boxer shorts underneath my flannels and was next man in. I reckoned I couldn't risk my precious crown jewels without a box, so had to try and hold it in place by applying pressure with my left wrist as the bowler ran in. It wasn't ideal to say the least. Several times my box slid down my leg as the bowler charged in. I was lucky to escape with my gonads intact.

Only once did I forget my box altogether and had to use the only manky box in the club kit bag, out of pure desperation. Unfortunately, another batsman had forgotten his and had already used it just before me. I picked it up from the dirty old kitbag and it was still rather sweaty, stinking a little. Then, I noticed a couple of pubes stuck to it. I tried to blow them off, but they were stuck good and proper. I pondered how many cocks had been in this box over the years – probably a lot more than in Joan Collins' box.

To relate to women properly, I also assumed that I'd have to get in touch with my feminine side just a little. I'd been in a couple of local musicals, playing comedy roles and enjoyed trying to hold a note with the chorus. I wasn't good enough to sing a solo, but my dancing could make anyone laugh. So, I reckoned, if I posted that I enjoyed stand-up comedy shows and the theatre, that would be a big tick for loads of women. Well, those that enjoyed comedy and musicals maybe. I wasn't the hunky type I guess, the rugby playing type with a 20-inch neck. I didn't have a six pack either, although in my peak I had a two-pack this had now turned into a more of a keg, but I thought it was still on the firm side, just about.

I'd had a go at stand-up comedy a few times and realised how tough it could be. My first gig lasted about 45 minutes and went down a storm, as I used fairly smutty material that appealed to the audience at my local cricket club. I also did a funny dance at the end which brought quite a few laughs, just like my club days when I didn't realise, I looked like a complete knob. The next time I thought I'd try to appeal to a wider audience so changed the material to a few more subtle jokes and some political satire, but this was a big mistake, as some of the material bombed. I didn't consider the make-up of the audience and it felt bad to bomb in front of some friends.

I was deflated and it certainly set my confidence back. It made me respect comedians so much, knowing how nervous they must feel and how much resilience they must possess. Nobody fully appreciates how difficult stand-up comedy can be until they give it a go themselves. Having bad gigs and dying on their arse is all part of the experience for comedians, but I didn't know whether I had the sheer perseverance to do more gigs after that.

My favourite show I was involved in was called *Trafford Tanzi,* when I played a 1960's sexist comedian – a bit like playing myself really. Actually, I wasn't alive in the 60's and am certainly not sexist – I like women honestly. Anyway, I had to wear a big wig, false moustache and plenty of bling, including a big medallion. I thoroughly enjoyed dressing up for the role and being part of a cast created some camaraderie between us. I got to perform some near the knuckle stand-up comedy and sing ABBA songs with the chorus. It was great fun, especially dancing with a pink feather boa to *Super Trouper* and getting in touch with my feminine side.

I certainly enjoyed performing arts and thought I'd put that in my interests. Surely, I thought, some women must appreciate comedy, musicals and visits to the theatre.

I also liked rambling in the countryside and trying to spot birds and other wildlife. However, I thought this made me sound like an old fart and a bit lonely too. I wanted to come across as an exciting human being, a risk taker and an adrenaline junkie. I wanted to get their pulses racing by reading about my hobbies. I considered whether I should admit to liking snooker, golf and hiking. No, no – I mean sky diving, rock climbing and white-water rafting.

Truly, I didn't want to lie here though as the women out there would have to accept me for who I was. I shouldn't have to change as a person for anyone, I thought. I'll put down walking in the countryside and travelling. I'd been to a few places in the past, but I wanted to travel more extensively. My trip around Europe by train had given me a flavour of different cultures and people and I wanted to see more of the world, like many others did. I thought that may be appealing to some ladies too. I also enjoyed visiting places of interest such as historical buildings, museums and art galleries. What could be more exciting than a day out at a military museum? Jeez, I DID sound fucking boring. How would anyone want to go out on a date with ME?

CHAPTER 7: TICKING ALL THE BOXES

ABOUT ME AND MY IDEAL MATCHES - This was the part I could go to town on, I thought. I'm intelligent, I'm funny with a great sense of humour, and I'm just so interesting. But how did I start this? Who was I looking for? I said I was a professional male, hoping to impress, although I didn't want to let people know my real job. I was hoping this may attract some professional ladies with good jobs, who I may relate to and get on well with. I wouldn't be bothered, however, if they simply worked in a shop or had a menial job at all, as long as they gave me a fantastic blowie on a regular basis. When you're looking for an overall 'package' the occupation of a potential partner doesn't really mean that much - unless, of course, you're purposely seeking to be a footballer's wife or live that kind of lifestyle. That's pretty shallow I guess, but there again, many of those people are really shallow - they simply want attractive partners and plenty of cash to hand.

I'd seen the film *Shallow Hal* starring Jack Black and found it both funny and fascinating. It was so true how people judged others simply by their appearance. I'd been guilty of that myself when it came to the opposite sex. If there was an attractive lady, with a great body and a beautiful smile I wouldn't care if she had a stinking personality, no brains and treated people like dirt - I'd probably want to go out with her. Conversely, the grossly overweight type with a face like a slapped arse didn't really appeal to me - but they may have been a lovely genuine person, with a heart of gold and a wicked sense of humour. Maybe, I thought, I should go out with all sorts of people and not be so stereotypical in my approach. Personality was something that needed to be considered for a long-term partner. Then, it occurred to me that you actually had to fancy someone too for it to work properly. This was going to be difficult to 'tick all the boxes' as they say.

It then crossed my mind, what does it mean to 'tick all the boxes'? Nobody, I mean nobody, is perfect. We all have our faults, our idiosyncrasies, our moments of sheer bloody-mindedness or petulance. We're all human beings after all. What I wanted primarily was to try to tick as many boxes as possible, in terms of a potential partner. Personality was obviously important as it drives the relationship and people have to be compatible. I wanted someone with drive and an enthusiasm for life. At times, I'd been rather depressed about my situation and felt I'd be alone for a long time. I was beginning to feel loneliness in my daily life and wanted someone to share life with again and bring me some happiness. If that person had spark and zest, it could rub off on me and make me smile. I was becoming a miserable bastard and needed to do something about it.

The physical side also had to be right for both partners, I reckoned, to maintain a long-term partnership. I knew that falling in love encompassed more than lust or sex, but the overall package had to include that surely. Fancying your partner would be high on the agenda too. In fact, this whole process was very business-like in places and felt like a true marketing exercise. I was trying to sell myself to others out there, whilst trying to think about who my perfect match would be. Then, I realised I was being far too serious and sensible about this and just had be instinctive and see what happened.

I didn't want to sound desperate in my profile, but there again, I didn't want to sound as though I just wanted lots of one-night stands either. Getting the balance right would be the key I assumed. So, the line, 'I'm looking for lots of casual fun' wouldn't suffice but neither would, 'I'm hoping to meet the woman of my dreams and my future wife,' of course. They were both true statements, but I had to hit the right tone to succeed. By this point, my friend Big Col was losing the will to live as I laboured over this part of my profile. He probably thought it would be a quick job and bam, sent off to see what would happen. He certainly didn't envisage that I'd be writing a bloody essay to say how fantastic I was and what a brilliant catch I would be.

Despite knocking back a few cans of beer, I was really getting into this now. By this point, I was basically wondering how I could entice the ladies and get inside their knickers. It was all rather surreal and at times I giggled like a naughty schoolboy. The whole concept of setting up a profile and talking online was completely alien to me. I'd only recently bought a laptop and now I was using it in a way that I'd not anticipated at all. I was moving with the times and finally seeing sense.

I considered trying to crack a few jokes and demonstrate my silly sense of humour. For example, I nearly wrote that, 'It would be rather novel if our first date was in a library.' Then, I was tempted by, 'If our first date was in a museum, we could look at some old relics. But that's enough about the people who work there – it would still be a top day exploring,' before deciding that was fucking terrible. I even thought about including a quote or two, such as, 'Life is like a box of chocolates – you never know what you're gonna get. Well ladies, with me you'll know for sure. For a start, I look great, I'm rather sweet, smell nice and I'm not sickly at all. I also last a long time and can be easily swallowed. There's no bitter after-taste. In fact, you'll simply want more and more...'

The more I thought about it, though, the more ridiculous some of the quotes and phrases appeared to be. They were like corny answers to questions on the TV show *Blind Date,* which I used to watch when the fabulous Cilla Black presented it. They may have been funny or amusing in the context of a show – but on my profile they just seemed childish and daft. I was struggling to think of adequate material and didn't want to come across as big-headed, too confident or a nutter. Even less, I didn't want to seem like a real knobhead intent on one objective. It was bloody difficult to get it right, that's for sure.

Eventually, I settled for something a little safe, not too different from what I imagined many people posted. I was looking to meet someone to share dates in restaurants, outings to the theatre and walks in the countryside, as well as cosy nights in watching films and cooking meals. Obviously, I was hoping the 'cosy nights in,' part would lead to rampant sex, but I left that bit out. Sounds a bit sickly doesn't it? Let's be honest, it wouldn't get their pulses racing. I wasn't into clubbing all night, as those days had gone. I wasn't into kite surfing, hand-gliding or water sports. I wasn't into dangerous liaisons, drugs or heavy metal. Then, I realised the beauty and wonder of all this. Everyone was totally different, and everyone was looking for different things and different people. Surely, there was bound to be someone who liked my rather safe profile – someone similar to me maybe.

By this point Big Col was nearly asleep, but he still had to help me upload some photographs to make everything complete. I thought this would be easy but trying to find a couple of decent ones that I was happy with proved more elusive. For a start, I didn't have that many on my laptop and many of them wouldn't do my cause any good. On every picture there was one bloody thing I wasn't happy with. From some angles I maybe looked a little podgy, from others you could see a wrinkle. In others, I looked plain miserable and in some I simply looked like a complete dick. However, after a while searching and laughing at some old photos, I found a couple that would definitely find me the woman of dreams – or so I thought.

In one photograph, I was wearing a neat shirt and looked prim and proper – very smart, if a little uptight. Most ladies would probably assume I was a boring banker or something similar, if you know what I mean. I thought I'd have to portray a clean-cut image though, as I didn't have long hair or tattoos or any jewellery. I didn't own any outrageous clothes or have any piercings. The other photograph uploaded was more casual, in which I was wearing a pair of jeans and not brown cords I hasten to add. The green donkey jacket was also long gone. I tried to look cool, with a slight smile but not too happy. It probably looked as though I was trying to break wind in public, without being spotted. I assumed these two pictures would change my whole life. Come to think of it, I was a bit of a boring bastard. I was Mr Average in nearly every way.

It made me consider whether I should shatter my boring image by being blatantly graphic in what I was searching for. Maybe I could say, 'When I'm riding your arse, I'd like to pull your hair too.' Maybe that'd get their pulses racing. Maybe my inbox would be flooded with offers from sexy ladies after that statement. Believe it or not, I'd actually seen that quote once on a car window – driven by a female. It was along the lines of 'If you're going to ride my ass, you may as well pull my hair.' So, at least one lady out there would like it. Mind you, I'd only seen the back of her head. She may have been a real minger.

I was now ready for lift off. My whole world was about to change for the better. I was going to be a new man and begin a new exciting chapter in my life. And then I did it; I deleted everything by accident. No, not quite, but nearly. Clearly my IT skills needed to improve fast. I woke Big Col up from his slumber and managed, with his considerable help, to submit everything. Then it finally dawned on me. What the fuck have I done?

CHAPTER 8: A TINY TALE

I waited with bated breath. Well, I'd had about 6 cans by this point so was rather relaxed about the whole thing. Or so I thought. Big Col said it shouldn't take too long as there were always people on these sites. After submitting my profile, it then stated that it was searching for my ideal match. My heart was racing now, Jeez. What will she look like? I liked tall women, with long legs. I didn't mind hair colour as such - blonde, brunette, ginger, purple or red. I didn't mind race or body type. In fact, I liked most women in all honesty. But who would be my ideal match? This was a very intriguing prospect. All the magical algorithms went to work to find my match. Suddenly, the screen changed and my ideal woman, the woman who was surely about to change my whole world was in front of me. She was a fucking dwarf!

Big Col was hysterical with laughter and we both fell on the floor and rolled around hollering. This was unbelievable and not what I had in mind. I'd nothing against dwarfs at all and wasn't against dwarfism, but this couldn't be right surely? I was looking for a leggy blonde and was given a small person. A very small person, in fact. Not a good start I thought. Then, it dawned on me that I was open to new experiences and had never dated a dwarf before. Maybe this was a good start after all. Maybe I would end up with a dwarf fetish and be happy with my little date. In fact, I'd never considered dwarfs in an erotic way before – but now I was getting excited by the prospect. Lots of dirty little thoughts went through my head.

I pondered whether I should speak to her and try to go on a date. It may turn out rather fun, going out with a dwarf. Then I thought about my mum. She was only 4 feet 9 and once I'd googled whether she was actually a dwarf herself. In fact, google notified me that she was a midget – a small person. I loved my mum dearly, but I didn't want to go out with someone similar – a midget or a dwarf. I reckoned that I must have recorded my height down in error; either that or someone had a good sense of humour. Or the mathematical algorithms were just plain wrong. Something was wrong, surely.

The dwarf sent me a tiny message, but it was just small talk. Soon after, however, I had a message from a woman who looked a fair bit older than me, even after a few beers. She had dirty blonde hair and looked like a German shot-putter. Then again, I bet she was bloody dirty in bed and could go like the clappers. I sent a few messages in return, just to play along and found myself getting mildly aroused by the whole episode – talking to another lady online. It was strange – and fascinating too. Nothing materialised that night, other than a few messages sent and a brand-new profile set up and ready to go but I was excited at the prospect of more evenings talking online.

When I explored the site the next day, all these faces just popped up at me. It was like being a kid in a sweet shop again, figuring out what I wanted. For example, would it be cola bottles, sarsaparilla tablets, sherbet lemons, fruit salad or midget gems? (I've already said no midgets though!). You must understand the analogy; it was all exciting stuff for someone new to this experience. The vast majority of the women looked tempting to me. It was probably more like liquorice all sorts to be honest. There were just so many ladies to choose from – well at least send a message to.

I had to realise that just because they were on the site it didn't mean they would reply to any message I sent, never mind arrange to go out on a date. I thought it would be best to look at their profiles in more depth, to get an understanding of the type of person they portrayed themselves to be. But, of course, having clicked on their profile it was more about their photographs. Who gave a shit if they liked knitting, if they looked like a film star or supermodel? Who cared if they loved cricket if they looked like a bulldog chewing a wasp? The very thing that I wanted to avoid, being shallow, was happening again. Why go just for the person who looks stunning on their photographs? I realised I should read the bloody profile and see who had something in common with me. But human nature was all about being attracted to a potential mate.

I sent one lady an opening message. I didn't want it to be too forward, but I had to inform her that I found her very attractive. I also wanted to pick something from her profile to indicate that I'd read it carefully too. So, my opening gambit may have been along the lines of 'Lovely profile and great smile on your photographs. Would like to get to know you better, if you like.' If I could, I'd mention a specific piece of information from their profile too such as, 'You say you have a horse, that's nice. I rode one once on holiday in Wales...' I cringe now about some of the shit I used to write. If they liked animals, which many of them did, I used to offer a possible date at a zoo. Most people loved a day at the zoo after all. But from what I remember, I've only ever had one such date, at Chester Zoo. More about that later.

I never had any animals whilst living on my own, although my children badgered me to get a cat. The reason? I had a cat flap in my new bachelor pad. They reasoned that as the cat flap existed, I simply had to get one. As a family together, we'd had a hamster called Daisy which Santa brought one year, complete with cage and wheel. We bought a hamster bowl and she used to roll around the kitchen in it. I used to let her run around occasionally and she often escaped under the cooker. The only way to bring her out was to entice her with coco-pops, which always worked a treat.

Thinking about it, I wished I could've enticed some women with a bowl of coco-pops. But now, on my own, I didn't want a bloody cat – even though as a child I adored our family cat, Matilda. I reckoned that I could only just look after myself – never mind have to feed and look after a cat. The kids were very disappointed, but I tried to cheer them up by turning the heating on. They'd complained they were cold, but I let them in eventually. They were forever testing the cat flap and seeing if it was possible for a young child to squeeze through the gap. I was apologetic but made several excuses why their loving dad would not be getting a fucking cat.

When online, I reasoned that if I put all my hopes and dreams into just one message, I'd be very disappointed. Therefore, I selected a few women who I thought looked nice on their profile and fired out similar messages. I guess you could call it the scattergun approach. I didn't want it to be appear like a message from a robot, so tried to make it as personal as I could. By this stage, I'd also received a few messages myself in my inbox, which was quite exciting. Until I opened them, that is. Instead of the type of women I'd selected myself, they were mainly from real mingers. I don't mean to sound cruel, but some of them looked like Ken Dodd on a bad hair day. And they all seemed much older than me too. I'd done searches in an age range that would suit me, not too young, but just a little younger than me up to my age or a few years on. Most of those contacting me were probably ten years older at least. I reckoned I should message an older lady for a chat at least, just to see how it went.

The initial messages I sent didn't all get a response, which was hard to swallow at first, but I knew it was the dating game. Obviously, some women didn't fancy my pictures or just thought I was boring or not their type, and that was despite not mentioning cricket. I got a couple of messages back from very polite ladies too. They said they always replied to messages out of courtesy but were declining to take anything further. I felt like I'd been rejected after a bloody interview.

My heart sank a few times after these rejections, in all honesty. At first, I was hopeful but some of my replies knocked me down a peg or two and it didn't feel great. I just wanted to go out on a few dates and being rejected was hard to take. Being alone and being ignored by those I liked felt cruel and exacerbated my loneliness further. However, I vowed that this was all part of the process and I had to accept plenty of knockbacks along the way.

However, I did manage to strike up conversations with some ladies online and this gave me some confidence. I then discovered that some of them were just timewasters who simply liked to chat online, without moving on to the next stage. When I asked for mobile numbers to text, they gave up chatting. What was the point in that then? I assumed people signed up to go out on dates and meet up.

In reality, there were plenty of weirdos on the site who just liked to talk to fill a hole in their loneliness. I just wanted to fill a hole – but I had to get myself a date first. In fact, in reality I was somewhat lonely too. Living on my own and using dating sites at night to talk to others and meet someone could be a soul-destroying existence. I tried to stay positive, but the reality was that I came home to an empty house without my kids being there, made a shitty meal for one and had the radio or television for company. I just wanted to connect with someone else who was feeling the same.

After a while of chatting online and not really finding my ideal date to go out with, I figured I may have to stop going for the model types basing it on looks only. That was simply shallow anyway and I was no match for the hunky types who were probably younger, fitter and better looking than me. I'd started talking to an older lady who seemed very keen on me and she seemed a lovely person too. We swapped mobile numbers and spoke on the phone a couple of times before agreeing to meet up. She was local to me, so we knew the same pubs and restaurants and agreed to meet up in a pub. In all honesty, I would say she was attractive for an older lady but was probably around 10 years older. I'd never been out with anyone older before, so thought I'd give it a go and agreed to meet her.

CHAPTER 9: A SICK STORY

I was nervous, really nervous actually. I'd never been on a blind date before. Well, I guess it wasn't a blind date as I'd seen photographs, but you never truly knew what people were like until you met up. Photographs could be misleading and could be altered by lighting or angle. Meeting in the flesh was different for sure. On the profile Alexandra had long blonde hair and an attractive face but wore quite a bit of make-up too which concerned me slightly. I wasn't into orange faces and people with different colours on their hands, neck and face. I preferred natural looks more, not women who applied their make-up with a trowel. In short, I hated the TOWIE look with ladies all dolled up like a waxwork with Botox lips, false tits and an even falser sense of beauty.

I'd had a couple of drinks before we met, just to relax me. I was also aware that the more I drank, the nicer she would look. Firstly, I was just glad that she'd turned up for a start. She was attractive, without being a stunner. She was certainly older than me, but that was part of the attraction too initially. I'd heard that some older women could be really dirty in bed and she might open my eyes to a few things. I noticed that she had sizeable breasts too and she was wearing really tight black leather pants that looked too small, in all honesty. Not that I'd tell her. In fact, we hit it off really well and the conversation flowed really easily. She certainly liked a drink and I wasn't complaining, as I did too. We knocked back a considerable amount of booze in several pubs and had a real laugh. This was just what I needed, a woman with a good sense of humour who liked to let herself go.

Towards the end of the night I considered playing it cool and then I started to get horny, having drank about 8 pints at least. I knew she liked me by her body language and, well, her actual language. She turned to me at one point and said, 'I really like you,' which made me think she liked me. Of course, by now I was thinking with my knob and said, 'I've got a frozen pizza back at mine if you'd like some,' with a big smile. 'That'd be nice. I really like you,' she replied with a prodigious grin. We were both drunk by now but made our way back to mine.

We got back and started kissing passionately, in that drunken sort of way. I didn't ask again whether she wanted pizza as it seemed the right moment to take things further. We didn't even make it up to the bedroom – in my lounge I started to take her top off exposing a big white bra. It wasn't the sexiest I'd ever seen, but it had to be sizeable as she was carrying a large pair of jugs that needed playing with. I took off her bra at the sixteenth attempt and her boobs fell in front of me. I took one in each hand and gave them a good jiggle, like playing with a fucking toy. She knew I was drunk, however, and was giggling a lot like a teenager.

Then, the hard part was getting those extremely tight leather pants off. Not mine, but hers. I was pulling and pulling and pulling and they moved about an inch. Jeez, they were tight. I thought I might have to get some olive oil from the kitchen to help but she was determined to get them off. Eventually, she got them down a little more and exposed a bulging belly that had been squeezed into those tight pants, leaving a large red mark across her stomach. Not the most attractive I'd seen, but I could understand that she wanted to look good and tried to hide that marauding piece of flab. I struggled more and got them further down to expose her matching panties. Not too sexy, but she was surely in her mid-forties by now.

Then, I slowly and sexily removed her panties in order to go down on her and give her heavenly pleasure, despite feeling a bit queasy after all the beer I'd consumed. As I pulled them off however, the smell was immense. I'd never had to deal with this problem before. It was fucking rancid, like some out of date chicken that'd been in the bin a week. The smell wafted around the room and up my bloody nose. It must have been those tight leather pants, and an extremely sweaty fanny I reckoned. Surely, she'd had a shower before meeting me – but whatever – it was simply gross. No matter how drunk I was I couldn't go down there now. If she'd been menstruating and there was a bit of gore, I'd probably have had a go, but not this time. Not with this putrid scent lingering in the air. I was nearly sick and began to honk. Oh fuck, I felt like I was going to be sick all over her jiggling breasts.

She stopped giggling and began to realise I was in some sort of trouble. If she'd a nose that worked, she'd surely have smelt the odour rising into the atmosphere. I ran to the kitchen in some dismay and feeling a little embarrassed. I told her I just needed a drink of water, as I honked a little more. Being sick on my first internet date would not be a good start. I composed myself and asked if she wanted that frozen pizza I'd promised. I conjectured that a spicy pizza may take away some of the smell. Yet, she didn't want pizza, but she certainly couldn't have any sausage either for a while, as my cock had withered by now. I'd wanted sex for ages and now I had a chance, I was wasting it. I thought I had to do the deed as she was naked and waiting for me.

I had a drink of water and pulled myself together. I felt like a soldier having to overcome the final challenge of an assault course with everyone watching. I walked back into the lounge and she was on the sofa waiting, though not in a sexy way. She asked if I was okay and tried to help me become aroused again. The smell was still lingering somewhat, but now the worse was over. I was going to have another bash down there, but I really didn't want to vomit. So, I scrambled to put a condom on my member and rammed it inside whilst trying to close my nostrils, and indeed my eyes. She moaned a bit, like it was really good, but I knew it wasn't. Not for me anyway, as it was a struggle to perform in that situation. Nevertheless, she was a lovely person and we got on very well – apart from in the bedroom.

I did see her again a few times, hoping the issue with the smell was a one-off. Thankfully, it was a unique occurrence and I noted that she never wore those ridiculously tight pants again. I had visions of rampant sex with an older lady, but alas, it wasn't to be with Alexandra. We fumbled about a few times after the first encounter, but I just didn't fancy her in a sexual way. She was more like a friend for a while, who I could talk to about things in my life. She gave me advice about life as she was older and wiser in some ways, but the physical side was disappointing for me. I didn't feel the attraction to her that I'd craved, although I did appreciate her as a genuine person. I wanted to find someone nice like her, but I needed that physical desire and attraction as well. Everyone does. I needed more and I needed to move on.

Another older lady called Brenda contacted me quite soon after I'd posted my profile. She had long dark hair and a lived-in face with a few wrinkles, but nice olive skin. She described herself as average build and looked like an attractive older lady on the photographs. I was growing in confidence and was up for meeting people, so decided to give it a go. When we met, she wasn't what I'd envisaged at all. She was certainly older than me but seemed much bigger than in the photographs and a lot uglier I'm afraid, to be blunt. I wouldn't say I was totally surprised as I knew these things could happen. However, I endeavoured to have a good night and the drinks flowed. When I first met Brenda, she appeared a little unsightly, but now towards the end of the night I had my beer goggles on again.

She must have fancied me, as she asked me back to her place. Maybe that was the advantage of dating older women, I thought. We stumbled back to her dingy flat and I felt a bit uneasy about the situation as I didn't fancy her too much. I should've learned from my previous experience with Alexandra, but I'd been boozing, and it'd clouded my judgment yet again. This time, however, it wasn't me who felt sick. Brenda had taken off her top to expose a huge pair of breasts that sagged a little and I was about to lick her dark nipples when she ran into the bathroom, feeling sick.

A minute or two later she came back saying that she felt a bit better but hadn't been sick after all. It didn't bother me too much though. I was ready for action and took off my shirt and exposed my toned body. Well, partly toned, I guess. She mustn't have been impressed though because she ran straight back to the bathroom! This was really fucking sexy I thought.

After another few minutes she came back, and this time took off her jeans and knickers. Unfortunately, she exposed a giant hairy fanny that matched the décor of her flat – from the outdated 1980's. However, growing up I'd seen plenty of porn magazines and some videos of 80's porn stars with their hairy pussies on display. It wasn't particularly attractive, but it didn't faze me outright either. I guess everyone liked a hairy bush every now and then. I was about to get stuck in and lost in that bush, when Brenda ran to the bathroom yet again. This was fucking annoying now. I followed her in to check that she was okay. Unfortunately, she had her head over the toilet and was vomiting wildly, which this time resembled the disgusting yellow lino floor. Hairy bush and vomit, what a bloody great combination.

She seemed in quite a bad way, so I tried to make her feel better by talking to her. It wasn't a great conversation to be honest. 'Do you want me to leave?' was about the gist of my question. I pulled away a bit and then it dawned on me she was bent over the bowl with her arse sticking out, exposing her giant hairy pussy and a sizeable chocolate hole. Despite her puking her guts up, I began to get aroused.

This shouldn't be happening, I thought, but her pussy was staring right at me and it looked rather wide and tempting. Her arse was big but shapely and waiting right there for me. I was now stiff and was about to act out a scene I'd seen in a porn film whilst at university. Give her one hard from behind whilst she was vomiting! Jeez, I was a sick fucker myself for wanting this now. She was turning me on, but probably knew it. Maybe she got a kick out of this sick fantasy.

Then, as I got closer, she retched, and I saw a tiny bit of poo poke out of her arsehole. That really turned me on. Not. My stonking erection went down in about 0.1 seconds and I was flaccid again, listening to her honks. Then, she said, 'You're a nice kind man. Some blokes I know would've fucked me from behind whilst I was being sick,' retching once more. 'Oh, I'm not like that. I couldn't do that,' I stated with authority. I went in the other room and began to get dressed, ready to leave. I brought her some water and checked she was fine before making my way to the door.

By this point, she'd slipped on a robe and was asking me to stay, when she had a call on her mobile phone. It was bloody late by now, probably 3 in the morning, but Brenda took the call then said it was a bloke she knew. She said he was coming around soon. I asked who it was, and she admitted he was her fuck buddy – they were mainly friends who shagged at weekends. Then she said, 'Please stay, he won't mind at all,' in a serious tone. I was aghast at the thought of another man coming to the house. He may have been a decent guy, but then again, he could have been a serial killer who was into kinky three-way sex.

In spite of this, it dawned on me I could even watch or join in. This was an unexpected opportunity that had now arisen. She piped up, 'It's always been my fantasy to have two men,' almost pleading with me to stay. This statement was made despite the fact she'd just violently puked up and had a bit of shit on her bum hole. I stood motionless, with everything jogging through my mind. It looked good fun in the porn films, I thought, having a threesome. Though, undoubtedly, I'd prefer it with two women instead like every other man whose ever walked the earth.

I thought carefully for a minute and then realised I didn't know who this bloke was, or even who this woman really was. For all I knew, they may plan this manoeuvre every bloody weekend. My head was spinning. What if she pinned me down by sitting on my face with her big shitty bum while he sexually assaulted me? What if he tried to bum me if I was in a delicate position? I was half tempted to try it for the experience, but politely declined. I really didn't fancy poo on my face or a cock up my arse. Not this particular night anyway. I was tired and just wanted to go home by this point and get back to my own bed. I've regretted it ever since. Not.

CHAPTER 10: WOLF WOES

After talking a while with several women and having dates with a couple of older women, I managed to find someone a few years younger than myself. She was actually very good looking – blonde hair and blue eyes and what appeared to be a shapely body. By this point, I'd been rejected by a few ladies at the last minute for some reason. I was beginning to discover that some people just played games and would talk online, but not want to meet or even exchange phone numbers. Plain and simple, they were bloody timewasters and it annoyed me. I was genuinely trying to find a partner, or at least a decent fuck buddy for a while.

I met Katarina in a local drinking establishment, and we ended up getting blotted in town. She was generally good company and dragged me to a club, where we danced a while. I made sure that none of my silly moves came out and tried to play it cool, as far as I could. So far, the women I'd been out with had wanted to take things further on the first date. This was a good sign in a way, because I could empty my sack, and be physically fulfilled. However, it was also a bad sign, as they may have tended to fuck anyone and everyone. The chances of a long-term liaison with someone like this was probably remote. However, the chances of a sexually transmitted infection were a lot more likely. Nevertheless, I was along for the ride and would see what happened.

Katarina suggested getting a taxi to her place, at her side of town. I'd heard it was a rough area but was gobsmacked when the taxi driver asked for the fare upfront. I'd never ever seen that before. Jeez, I thought, this must be a fucking rough area. Either people do runners on a regular basis, or they simply refuse to pay or rob the driver. We went down some back streets and I was now unaware of our location. For all I knew, she could be taking me to be fucking robbed. We could be going to a drug den, full of users and thugs who'd inject me with heroin for a joke if I had no money. Mind you, I only had about £8 left now as I was a tight git and had no card. I began to consider how I would get home and wish I'd gone for a kebab. I'd have got a decent mixed kebab, with salad and chilli sauce for £8.

We got to her abode, which was a run-down house from the 1940's, or so it seemed. Having entered the foul-smelling front room, I noticed holes in the doors where someone had clearly punched them. The lousy smell was partly tobacco and partly dog. I say dog, but when this massive creature entered the room it was unlike any fucking dog I'd seen before. It was a white wolf. I was shitting myself. I was on the sofa but stood up when I saw this wolf staring at me with its big blue eyes. It stared and stared and began to growl. She said, 'Oh don't be scared, he's not going to bite you,' laughing at my fear. I responded, 'Everyone says that about their wolf, I mean dog,' and let out a small gentle fart.

The beast began barking loudly and I just wanted to get out of there fast. It must have been a Husky or something similar – but it was a wolf in my eyes. Luckily, at least there was only one wolf and not a pack ready to devour me for their supper. Then, I heard another dog barking. This sounded even bigger, like a Doberman or Alsatian. By this point, my heart was pounding, and my hands were sweating. The Alsatian type dog walked in and stared at me too. I now had a wolf and gigantic dog staring at me and growling in discontent. I got ready to leave, but she lit a fag and asked me if I wanted a drink. Katarina seemed relaxed and calmed me down somewhat, by stroking my leg.

Next, she asked if I wanted a cigarette. I was going to tell her that I hated smoking and hated kissing anyone with a nicotine breath. But I was truly worried that she'd set her dogs on me. I envisaged that they would kill and eat me, and she would put me out in the bins for collection. I needed to pull myself together. She had some whisky and poured me a drop, even though I didn't like it. I just needed to relax and was even half-tempted with a fag. I'd not smoked since I was 17 and tried six one night. I'd also eaten a garlic bread that same night and the foul taste in my mouth lasted about three days. That was also the very same night I'd got drunk and vomited all over a girl's shoes when she stood next me. A girl I fancied for two years that is. I vowed never to smoke again, as I found it disgusting.

She lit me a fag and I had a couple of drags. Jeez, I was living life on the fucking edge right now. Smoking and drinking whisky with a stranger, pretending to like her monster dogs. I coughed and spluttered a little, trying not to inhale all those dreadful toxins. The last time I smoked was when I'd been offered a Cuban cigar at Nick's wedding, my friend from university. He'd got married at 'The Waldorf' in London – an amazingly posh place full of posh people.

It was like an alien world to me, but when offered a £30 Cuban cigar, you didn't turn it down. It was fucking horrible, but I thought I looked so cool puffing away trying to impress all the other posh rich people. The Cuban was so large it was like holding a huge courgette between my fingers. I was also pissed on all the free wine, downing it like lemonade whilst the others sipped it pretentiously. I also pretended I was stockbroker to impress all the affluent businessmen, bankers and lawyers. The problem was, everyone had their own business card apart from me and these were being passed around like milk vouchers at clinics for pregnant women. So, I just offered people a chewing gum instead. That's all I possessed in my pocket, along with a few snotty tissues.

At least now I also had a nicotine breath, I could kiss Katarina without feeling too bad. We had a snog on the sofa, and I began to feel more comfortable. I even saw the wolf give me a quick wink as I fondled her. After a while, she led me to the bedroom. We walked past her son's room and he gave me a wink as well. Only joking, he wasn't there at the time thank goodness. Her bedroom was cluttered with lots of perfume and sprays, so I was hoping for a pleasant-smelling minge after the episode with rancid Alexandra. Then, when in the bedroom, she removed her top. To say I was dumbfounded would be an understatement.

Fully clothed, I thought her boobs were big, but I'd never seen anything like this. When her special bra was removed, and it had to be very special believe me, her humongous breasts looped downwards towards the floor. Gravity could not be avoided with these monster melons. Her boobs simply didn't match the rest of her body, which was shapely and trim. I was speechless in that moment, because I was simply shocked and astounded. She'd obviously concealed them very well, but it just wasn't for me. Some men would have loved them, no doubt. I reckon lots of men would have loved them actually. To me, they were just too big. Far too big. I reckon it was probably uncomfortable for her, in all honesty, and it must have been very difficult to walk with them banging into her knees.

Despite the shock of the pumpkin breasts and the wolf trying to push its way into the room, I was determined to perform. I felt much better when she turned over and displayed her lovely arse, covering up those giant melons. In fact, she used them like cushions to balance on. I had a right good go from behind and she was howling all along. Well, I couldn't tell if it was her or the fucking wolf who wouldn't leave us alone. It was scratching at the door and doing its best to gain entry so it could bite my balls clean off. Having eventually climaxed, I was ready to leave. I felt a little heartless, as she wanted me to stay. However, I told her I had to be up early in the morning for something and she seemed okay with that.

In hindsight, maybe I should have stayed until the morning, but I still felt slightly uneasy about the wolf. Maybe I'd used her just for sex, but then again, she'd wanted the same thing and it was a mutual understanding on the night. It was one of those things that happened. I knew she wouldn't be the one for me long term, but I'd had an enjoyable evening on the whole – if I could get home alive. All I had to do now was dodge every dodgy geezer on the dodgy estate and I'd be fine. As I left, I ran like fuck but still had a horrible taste in my mouth, and it lasted a few days. I vowed never ever to try a fag again.

CHAPTER 11: CHICKEN LEGS

One day, sometime after my night of passion with Katarina, I went shopping at my local supermarket and saw a ginger-haired girl wearing an extremely short skirt. She was fairly attractive but had lots of make-up on and looked like she was trying to make an impression. It seemed strange to be dressed like that whilst shopping, as it was late, and the shop was nearly deserted. I was mildly surprised when she gave me the eye a few times and I even began to feel slightly uncomfortable. However, I'd heard people could meet in shops and supermarkets. For example, I knew someone who once met a girlfriend whilst buying a stereo. Maybe they simply liked the same music or were simply in tune with each other.

Anyway, her glances at me were turning into stares after a while. I didn't normally go for gingers, but I was beginning to get mildly aroused by her. Her tartan skirt was so tiny, and she was flirting with me big time. I was almost following her route around the store, so she probably assumed I was following her, which I was. I considered simply going to the other side of the store, where the bread was located, but then decided to continue on my route behind her. It wasn't my fault that I was focussing on the frozen pizza aisle – after all they were my babe magnets. She kept turning around and probably thought I was some weirdo checking out her arse, but her signals and smiles were intense.

After a while she made her way past the frozen veg, where I always picked up peas and corn, and towards the frozen chicken. Apart from burgers I didn't buy that much frozen meat, unless it was on offer. By this stage my heart was racing, and I was wondering whether to chat her up in the frozen food section. I was still behind her and that miniscule skirt, when it happened. She rummaged around in the giant freezer for something she couldn't reach and bent right over in front of me; I mean right over. And then I saw it appear in front of my disbelieving eyes – 'Buy one get one free on packets of frozen chicken legs!'

After almost 45 minutes of this flirtatious game of cat and mouse, I plucked up the courage to say something. It was a great chat up line. I said, 'There's some fantastic bargains today – especially on chicken legs,' with a smile. She also made small talk and we seemed to have a mutual attraction. However, I didn't have the guts to simply ask her out or even ask for her number. When I unpacked my frozen chicken legs at home, I kept thinking about her sexy legs though and a missed opportunity. I was sure she liked me, and I'd blown it.

A couple of months later, I was perusing the options online again and saw a ginger haired lady. It was definitely the same girl and I was excited. In her profile, she said her name was Jenni and that she liked shopping and dining out on chicken legs. Not quite, but her profile was encouraging, and I felt like I was in with a great chance. I messaged her, making it clear that I was the man from the supermarket. I was the man who'd followed her around the store for 45 minutes. I was the man who told her about the deal on chicken legs. Jeez, this sounded like I was fucking stalking her. I hope I didn't come across as a nutter who wouldn't leave her alone. All I wanted was to meet up and see how it went.

I waited for a reply, but it wasn't forthcoming. I was terribly disappointed as I felt there was some connection between us – it may only have been chicken legs, but it was still a connection. Despite my knockback, I continued to talk to ladies online and developed another connection with a local lady. She appeared genuine and honest and we spent a considerable time chatting before we agreed to meet up. But the very day we were due to meet, she texted me and said something had cropped up and she couldn't make it. I was obviously disappointed once more, but it could've been a genuine reason, so I gave her another chance. Our chats had been fun and amusing at times and I thought she was a nice person.

We continued to chat and arranged once more to meet up. Almost inevitably, on the very day we were due to meet up she made another excuse again. Once was understandable, but to let me down twice was just ridiculous. I'd put a fair bit of effort into chatting with her and getting to know her, but I guess I knew nothing at all. Everything she said could've been a pack of lies. Her pictures may have been fakes too. Something just didn't add up and I felt terribly let down and rather low at the whole experience. It seemed that she was just playing games or wanted to chat to someone that she simply had no intention of meeting. It was certainly a learning curve for me, and I realised that I couldn't accept everyone at face value. There were some strange characters out there.

Around this time, I was also messaging a Thai lady and agreed to meet her for a drink. She looked rather stunning in her photographs and I'd never dated a Thai before. In fact, I'd never even eaten Thai food at the time, but enjoyed a Chinese for sure. That had simply nothing to do with wanting to meet her at all, but I did wonder if my frozen pizza would be good enough for her taste buds. That's if I could ever get this beauty back to my bachelor pad. I must admit, having looked at her pictures online I was surprised that she'd agreed to meet me at all. She appeared to be a classy lady, with a penchant for the high life.

I met April in a posh country pub, in May. I knew April was not her real name, but some Thai ladies had an English name as it was easier to pronounce. Maybe her real name was June. Anyway, her name was simply irrelevant when I saw her in real life. She was absolutely stunning – one of the most beautiful women I'd ever seen. Her dark silky hair was so long she could sit on it. Her legs were so long and sexy she could wrap them around me all day long. Her face was a picture of beauty, with a gorgeous smile. However, when she spoke to me her accent was a little strange and her voice a bit deep. I'd heard about lady-boys in Thailand and tried to look at her hands and Adam's apple. Surely not? This simply couldn't be a man, could it? Stranger things had happened.

I didn't want to ask if she was a man, just in case it'd upset her. But, having studied her properly for a while I concluded that she was all woman. She was definitely a lady alright. I was thrilled to be with her and wanted to take it further there and then. I tried to compose myself and stop dribbling as I spoke to her. Then, she began to ask questions about my job and where I lived. She asked about what car I drove, what my pension was like and all about the equity in my property. She then started asking about my financial means and savings and if I had any stocks and shares in any of the FTSE 100 index. Next, she wanted to know my fucking pin number - well not quite, but it felt like it. I was basically going to be used as a bank to fund her lavish lifestyle.

I was in a dilemma as I found her very attractive and so agreed to meet her again - this time for lunch. We met in town and she probably expected some posh restaurant, including a bottle of champagne to wash her exquisite meal down. My friends had advised me to be careful, in respect of the previous questioning and her motives. I could've tried to impress her and paid for a lovely steak somewhere or a Thai banquet. Instead, I settled on a café that sold bacon baps, hot beef butties and cheese and onion pie.

I was being myself and was hoping she'd respect that. I could tell by the look on her face, that she was disappointed to say the least. She was sulking, like a sulky brooding woman with a sulk on. The bacon baps went down like a pork roast at a vegan's wedding. She told me that her last boyfriend had taken her to lots of posh restaurants, Paris for the weekend and then up the Eiffel Tower. Funnily enough, my ideal date would've been taking her to Blackpool and then up the arse. I never saw her again.

That episode was a strange disappointment, but I was happier one day when Jenni replied to my initial message. She said she'd been busy and hadn't seen my message for a while, which was understandable, I guess. Whatever, I was willing to give it a go because of the initial time we'd crossed paths. I was fairly nervous when I met her, because I liked her look and hoped we'd get on. It had been a chance meeting initially and the fact that she was also on the same dating site was a good omen, I reckoned.

When I saw her again, my initial impression was one of slight disappointment. She didn't look as nice as the original meeting and was wearing these huge dangly earrings, which I wasn't keen on. I had this weird phobia that she'd catch her gigantic earring on something and rip her lobe clean off. It just went through me to be honest. I was rather fond of nice ears for some sad reason and didn't want to end up searching for her ear lobe on the floor. Nevertheless, we had a laugh on our date, and I thought there may be something to work with. I was hoping things may progress but was relieved that she didn't just jump into bed. Not with me anyway. This seemed more like the type of person I could have a relationship with. I saw her a couple more times – it wasn't electric between us in all honesty, but there was some attraction. Either that or I'd just been without sex for a while. In fact, I was probably getting a bit desperate by this point.

On the third date we got rather drunk and I was hoping that it was the right time to take things further. Fortunately, she invited me back to her house and I was keen to get on with it. After all, I'd never seen ginger pubes before and wondered if it was true what they said about gingers. However, as she was clean shaven or totally waxed, I couldn't tell at all. She certainly made sure she had no ginger bush, that's for sure. She made me look quite hairy, which was unusual, as I wasn't renowned for my body hair. I did notice, though, that she had massive lips dangling down – and that was before we got started. I'd never seen a vagina quite like it. Was it deformed in some way? Did it matter that her labia were nearly touching the floor? No, it didn't to me. It was unusual, sure, but she was obviously quite excited too. In fact, her dangly fanny lips rather matched those massive dangly earrings.

She was also very keen to pleasure me and did the business with aplomb. She was definitely an expert at fellatio and had probably practised on lots of men in the past. I reckon she could've got a bloody cucumber down her throat, no problem. She kept on giving and giving and giving – I felt like she was trying to suck my precious organ clean off. In fact, there was more suction than a powerful Dyson vacuum trying to remove a giant cobweb from a skirting board. I wanted to return the pleasure and put my head in that general direction. However, by now her pussy looked like a fresh roadkill and was splattered really wide. It was as attractive as a squashed squirrel on a country road. Her labia were dangling like two gigantic, dangly things and she was so wet that it was like licking a small waterfall.

When my shaft entered her squirrel cave, it was the equivalent of a cheese string entering the mouth of a hippopotamus. I doubt she felt anything – and I didn't feel much either as nothing touched the sides. Needless to say, this was not what I'd anticipated. It was all rather strange, and it taught me a lesson – until you've experienced the physical side of the relationship, you can't make a true judgment about the future. The difference between the initial meeting and this moment was vast, and another learning curve for me. I'd fancied her but this was a major turn off. Then again, she may have thought the same about me and my performance.

Many surveys suggested, in fact, that women often faked orgasms and I wondered whether Jenni was the same. Would she really tell me if she didn't enjoy it? I doubt most women would tell someone if they were dissatisfied. Would they really say, 'Small cock, I'll give you 5 out of 10 for effort and 4 out of 10 for performance!' To compound matters, I had to sleep in the wet patch. Well, I say wet patch. Trying to find a bloody dry patch was difficult. It was like sleeping in a shallow paddling pool. I'd had some wet dreams before, but this was just ridiculous. Maybe Jenni wasn't the one for me, after all.

CHAPTER 12: ON THE RUN IN PRAGUE

By now, I'd had some experiences and some fun. However, I'd not really been out with anyone that I'd call my girlfriend. Most of the women I'd dated had told me about their experiences on the websites too. They said that many men had simply sent a photograph of their erect penis in their first post, with a tag line 'Wanna shag this?'

I was shocked at this at first but realised that not everyone had the same ideals and values. Obviously, it must've succeeded for some men as they kept doing it, hoping they'd get lucky. In reality, I wondered how many women simply messaged back, 'Great huge cock. Come around tonight and fuck me hard.' I couldn't guess the percentage. Other men just messaged, 'Show us your tits love!' and expected a reply or photo. I began to wonder what kind of people really used these sites.

Nevertheless, I knew that all different kinds of people existed and that there must be some like-minded people for me to meet. I did form a bond with one lady called Kat, who was younger than me by a good few years. She was a nice enough person, friendly with a wicked sense of humour. She was quite petite, though fortunately not a midget or dwarf. We kind of fancied each other, without being in love or having that special feeling. The X-factor was missing as they say. I mean, that spark that everyone wants – as I kept being told by those who rejected me. True, a spark was required to make it last. We had quite a few dates and appeared to develop a firm friendship, although it wasn't too exciting in the bedroom in all honesty.

I remember we had a day out at a Boar Park deep in the countryside, and it was about as satisfying as a vegetarian sausage. You know, not as good as the real thing. Like a pretend sausage; like sex with a thick condom on; like a warm can of pop or beer; like a rainy day at the beach; like eating a boiled sweet with a wobbly tooth. Anyway, you get the message. I was inside the farm shop about to purchase some speciality boar sausages when she whispered in my ear, 'It's not working between us, is it?'

I continued to buy the sausages, but a tear rolled down my cheek that night as I ate them, after I accidentally bit my tongue. In truth, I mean I was very upset of course. I'd been rejected again by someone who I thought was a lovely person. But Kat was correct – there WAS something missing and it wasn't working as it should've been. Maybe I just didn't fancy her enough, or maybe I wasn't ready for a relationship. Kat was more like my sister, rather than a lover. Although, that sounds rather bad as I'd shagged her. I mean Kat, not my sister. Yet, she knew that the physical attraction was missing between us and was looking to meet a future partner too.

I vowed to get back on the sites and try to meet someone else. It was then that I met another teaser. Or just another lady who didn't want to be with me for some reason. She was attractive, with short dark hair and a tidy body. After a couple of dates, I invited her to my place. A mistake I made here was not going to any trouble in terms of the meal I mustered up for her. It wasn't a frozen pizza or an old classic from university, faggots in gravy. I simply didn't have anything in my kitchen apart from fish fingers and mushy peas. At the time it seemed a good idea, but it went down like a bad fart in a small lift.

I was stupid and should have made more of an effort for her, by ordering a curry or Chinese at least. Mushy peas gave me bad wind anyway and so I was on edge all night. She was pleasant enough but had a pet horse and kept talking about it all night. I think it was called Ted. She was like, 'Ted this,' and 'Ted that,' if you know what I mean. By the end of the night, I was wishing Ted was fucking dead. I didn't mind horses at all, but there's only so much shit you can put up with about a horse. She clearly loved Ted much more than any man she'd ever met and certainly I was nothing compared to him. By the time she'd described every fetlock and how beautiful he was, I thought there was a possibility that she was into bestiality.

It wasn't a complete disaster, however, as she invited me round to her stable, I mean house, for dinner. She cooked me a lovely meal and said I could stay over that night. After dinner, which put my mushy peas to shame, I was feeling excited and began to get horny. Then, I suddenly realised I simply couldn't compete with Ted. He was hung like a fucking horse and I wasn't. I was having a panic attack in case she compared me to Ted. I didn't even kiss like him. After a while kissing on the sofa, she suddenly declared, 'I've changed my mind. I don't want you to stay. Please go home tonight.' I knew where I stood, rejected again. Maybe my breath stunk, maybe I shouldn't have stuck my tongue down her throat. Maybe Ted turned her on more than me. I never got to find out, in fact. Being rejected in this manner, with no explanation, was hard to take of course. I began to wonder if there was something wrong with me as a person and began to doubt myself a little. As I stared into the mirror, it seemed to shout at me, 'You're a sad lonely bastard and nobody likes you!'

Soon after, I got a text message from Kat out of the blue. We had remained friendly, without really seeing each other. She asked if I had any holidays planned for the summer period – which being a sad lonely git I'd not. We discussed going away together as friends, not partners of course. We considered the options and decided on the beautiful city of Prague. We just booked it and agreed to share a room as friends only. It made perfect sense as we just wanted to get away and knew each other. However, I secretly wondered if she still liked me in a romantic kind of way.

Prague was a lovely place and the Czech beer was amazing, the best I'd ever tasted. Our hotel was near the red-light area though, just off Wenceslas Square. The architecture was sublime and there was a great feeling about the place. We generally bonded well and visited the Royal Palace, a mini Eiffel Tower, a Torture Museum and took in a puppet show and a classical music concert. The concert was emotional for me, as my Grandad had died recently. As I listened to the beautiful music echo around the magnificent church, tears rolled down my cheeks. I hadn't cried publicly for as long as I could remember, but I couldn't help but weep. It was haunting music and simply made me think of the old man I admired so much.

One night we went to a bar in the narrow-cobbled streets of the Jewish quarter. It was fantastic, with a great band who played *On the Beach* by Chris Rea amongst other tracks. After a couple of drinks, I needed the loo and so I walked towards the toilets, down a long flight of stairs. They were deep underground and it was candle-lit only. It was a medieval setting, with big dark wooden tables and burning candles providing the only light. It was almost dark, very scary and made the hairs on the back of my neck stand up. There was nobody about at all – it was all very spooky. Feeling uneasy, I rushed into the toilets and into the cubicle, but having done so, I realised I was in the bloody ladies' toilets. There were no urinals, but it was so dark I couldn't see properly. I emptied my bladder as quick as I could and exited before any women entered.

I was about to rush upstairs from the abyss and tell Kat what had happened, when I heard someone at the top of the stairs. I glimpsed upwards and saw her white blouse. I then had a bright idea. I'd hide behind a wall and jump out and scare her senseless. It was extremely creepy down there anyway and I thought it'd be funny. I waited behind the wall until she got to the bottom of the stairs.

When I glimpsed her arm, I jumped out and made the noise of a warped monster. She screamed a deafening scream that could be heard at the other end of Prague. Then I realised, it wasn't Kat! Oh fuck, what had I done? I'd made some poor lady shit her pants. She was still fucking screaming as I legged it upstairs. I ran as fast as I could and grabbed Kat's handbag shouting, 'Grab your fucking jacket, we're off.' We scarpered as people ran down the steps to the aid of a hysterical woman.

The next night, Kat felt tired quite early, so I decided to stay out on my own. Like a gentleman, I walked her back to the hotel, wanting her to get back safely. Then, I made my way to one of the local bars near our hotel – in the red-light area which was a real eye opener. There were pole dancers next to the bar, all beautiful women with great toned bodies. They all looked distinctively Eastern European with high cheekbones and legs all the way up to their armpits. I had a great time, having a beer and watching them get naked. There was a menu that I perused which gave prices for all the drinks and then it said in big letters at the bottom, 'Blow Job 60 Koruna'.

I was tempted for a few seconds, but I'm rather tight and thought it was a little steep. Plus, I really didn't want to pay for anything like that. However, for just 20 Koruna I could get a show with all the women involved. I thought to myself, 'Oh fuck it, I'm on holiday,' and paid. I sat next to an Irish couple and noticed there were lots of women in there too. I had a real laugh with the Irish couple, who were married. We discussed all the famous sights of Prague, whilst scantily clad ladies served drinks.

We were sat in front of a table, which spun round, and the sexy ladies appeared and did a striptease routine in tune with some tantalising music. It was like the puppet show I'd watched with Kat, but these were real dancing ladies - with no clothes on. The finale involved them spreading their long limbs on the table in front of us, as it spun round. They sort of imitated sex with each other too, but it wasn't too convincing. A drink or two later, a few of them came over to me and started rubbing me all over.

One of the performers was certainly a goddess, stunning in every way. I was beginning to feel faint, with three partially clothed women gyrating and stroking me. One sat on my knee and one tickled my nipples from behind. One was rubbing the inside of my thighs and staring at me with her sexy seductive eyes. I realised if I came in my pants there and then, I'd save a fortune paying for their services. After a few minutes, I could take no more and got up and left. I was a fucking teaser - I wasn't going to pay for anything. The goddess sighed as I left, as she wanted me so badly. Of course, I mean she wanted my fucking money. Anyway, I was gone and went back to the hotel to change my underpants. Every now and then, I think about that gorgeous goddess. I sometimes wonder if she still works there.

CHAPTER 13: A TOOTHY TALE

I'd gone to Prague with Kat as a friend and came back as no more than a friend. I kept thinking something may happen and we'd try again as a couple, but alas it just didn't. Being away with her was fun on the whole – we certainly had a laugh and were relaxed in each other's company. However, the feelings were more platonic and the passion between us just wasn't there. It was an experience, but it made me realise that finding everything I craved would be more difficult than I thought. I wanted to do all the things I'd done with Kat in Prague with someone who fancied me and wanted me to be their lover as well.

As I continued to look online to find my perfect match, I was becoming obsessed with the process of trying to meet someone. After my evening meal, which tended to be a microwave meal for one, I would go online and stare at all those different faces. Lots of women appeared to be attractive and I had chats with quite a few. Mind you, I guess many of the photographs posted were at least five years old. Not all those I fancied replied to me, but then again, I didn't reply to all the messages I received either. It was like a game in a way and I was getting used to it by now. I did find the chats all a bit false at first and some women clearly were just toying with me or playing a game themselves. I did strike a connection with a few women, however, and this occasionally led to a date.

One woman I met was called Tina. She was also petite, like Kat, with a slim body and was quite a fitness fanatic. She also had a big dog so frequently taking him out for a walk kept her very fit. She was a lovely lady, but there was a big problem from my point of view. On the photographs, she had her mouth closed or didn't smile too much. When I met her, she smiled and exposed the biggest buck teeth I'd seen. They were gigantic and clearly her teeth were simply far too big for her tiny mouth. Put simply, she was small, and her teeth were fucking massive.

I'd always tried to select women with a nice set of teeth as it was something that I found attractive. But now, sat on a date with her I couldn't stop looking at those huge gnashers. However, the more I tried to avoid staring, the more I ended up gawping. After a couple of pints though, they didn't seem as big. Or maybe I was just getting used to them. I reckon her teeth would've been really handy and put to good use If I ever needed a drink desperately and there wasn't a bottle opener to be found. Then I wondered what those beasts could do to my cock if she ever gave me a blow job. I would certainly have to be on good terms with her, that's for sure.

We actually got on well and had a laugh, and I was getting used to her smile. She had a great sense of humour and was funny in many ways. I don't mean funny looking – I mean funny as in she was comical. And probably a bit funny looking as well. Okay, she wasn't the prettiest lady I'd dated, but she made me laugh and smile and that's what I needed in my life. Wasn't I just being shallow if I just kept thinking about those bloody enormous teeth? I tried not to be, but in all honesty, she could've eaten an apple through a tennis racket.

We took her dog out a couple of times and she almost ran along, leaving me behind at times. She was physically very fit and strong for a small lady. After one of these walks, we had a couple of drinks and began to cuddle up and get close. I'd never kissed anyone with such teeth and was slightly apprehensive as she straddled me and closed her eyes. By now, I was more relaxed because of the alcohol and made the plunge to kiss. I think she was slightly worried too, but we made it work and her large tongue was slipped into my gaping mouth.

I knew she had a big long tongue after we'd bought an ice cream one day. Whilst I was licking the ice cream at the top, her lick started from the base of the cone and she devoured it in double quick time. In fact, she could probably balance the whole cone on her tongue. I'd opened my mouth as wide as I could just in case those teeth came into contact with my delicate lips. I didn't want her slicing me with any of those fangs. She was actually a good kisser, until that lengthy tongue went down my throat and probably touched my internal organs.

Then, things progressed to a new level. She began to undo my belt and remove my trousers. Everything went through my head at this point. Would she be able to do it properly? What if she accidentally bit my cock? I was a tad nervous and struggling to become erect as she kissed my groin area. Then, she licked my hairy balls like a cat lapped up milk and my eyes shut in the anticipation of her giant gnashers biting through my testes. But I felt no teeth, and this was rather good. In fact, it was bloody superb. She was obsessed with my balls and kept spitting on them and sucking on them, taking each one in her mouth like it was a boiled sweet. I'm glad I had a bath the week before.

I was definitely aroused by this point and after about fifteen minutes my balls were soaking wet. Nobody had ever worked my gonads like this before, and it was eye-watering. I was anticipating the worse, however, as she moved on to my throbbing member and embraced it with her mouth. What was I concerned about? This was amazing – buck teeth or no buck teeth.

She carried on and on and on. Normally, I'd have probably come by now but when I looked at those teeth, I could sustain my staying power for sure. She was determined to make it happen though, as she wanted to satisfy me. After what seemed like a couple of hours, she was flagging and the sofa was soaking wet, but on she went until I came in an almighty climax. I fired my load so hard that it went half-way across the room and just missed the television. My explosion of pleasure was immense – just like those teeth.

I did see Tina for a while, but those teeth never got smaller unfortunately. It seems cruel I know, but despite the amazing oral sex, I just didn't have the hots for her. She was a sound genuine person, but after a while I ended it. I never mentioned the teeth of course, but I reckoned she knew it was the image. I felt guilty to a degree; I really did. She kept texting me and hoped to see me again – but I knew she wasn't the one I wanted to settle down with. I just didn't have the connection that I was craving. Additionally, by now I was becoming more and more intrigued by the dating sites I was perusing and kept wondering if I could find my perfect partner, or at least have more fun with someone who I really fancied.

Soon after finishing with Tina, I was messaging a nurse who was about ten years younger than me. Well, she told me she was a nurse, but people often embellished the truth. For all I knew, she may have been a lollipop lady or cleaner. She was called Daisy and was an absolute stunner on the photographs I'd seen. She was a brunette, with long wavy hair and dark features. I had visions of ripping off her sexy uniform and making love to her all night long. If she did turn out to be a cleaner, I'd make her wear nothing else other than those bright yellow marigolds. I was quite surprised she agreed to meet me, in all honesty. She had a child and probably wanted to meet an older man for some reason.

We met up in a chic bar and had a couple of drinks. My first impression was that she was far too good-looking to go out with me and I had the vibe that it wouldn't end well. This time, I was the one who felt a little uneasy. I had some self-doubt about my image, about the way I looked. I assumed this girl could go out with any man she wanted. She was wearing a tight dress that clung to her curvy body. At one point, she went to the toilets and disappeared for ages – I was beginning to think she'd left me all alone like a fool.

Thankfully, Daisy returned and looked radiant. Maybe she'd just put some more make-up on to impress me, or maybe needed a dump. Anyway, I tried my best to be funny and make some humorous conversation. She was responding occasionally, but it felt as though I was doing all the trying. Unfortunately, the conversation didn't flow, but I was determined to give it my best shot. I imagined her licking my balls, like Tina, but I needed to be careful as I didn't want to develop a visible bulge in my pants.

Eventually, we moved on to another bar nearby and got closer on some seats. We'd had a couple drinks by now and I was feeling more confident. As the time felt right, I went in for a kiss. Unbelievably, she responded by kissing me. This was fantastic, I thought, but the kiss itself fell flat. It was a little messy and didn't feel right – like she was going through the motions and didn't fancy me. I knew it wasn't real passion or genuine. Her expression made it plain too, as she pulled a slightly weird and disgruntled face. It was the kind of face that you'd expect, if I'd just told her that I'd had a big shit in her handbag.

It was probably a mistake to kiss her so soon. It was the beginning of the end as far as she was concerned. We parted amicably and I gave her a peck on the cheek – but it wasn't the cheek I'd wanted to kiss. My dreams of caressing her naked bottom were long gone. The next day she sent me the dreaded text. She'd had a decent night on the whole but saw me as a friend and not in a romantic way. I was expecting it to be honest – her body language was evident on the evening. So, I'd sent a similar message to Tina not long before meeting Daisy but now it was my turn. A girl I'd really fancied, didn't fancy me in that way. Boy, this was tough – I was slightly hurt but I knew rejection was to be expected. One thing I couldn't do was to give up trying to find love. I had to keep going – it was still early days.

CHAPTER 14: WHERE'S THAT SPOON?

One day I opened my profile and I'd had a message off a young lady who was in her early twenties, which was unusual to be frank. Most of the messages I received were from cougars or women of a similar age. They tended to be on the ugly side as well – not the type I'd go for most of the time and in the vast majority of these cases, I'd not even reply. It sounds rather cruel, I know, but my view was that I didn't want to lead people on or play silly games teasing them. If I didn't fancy them or have any attraction, what was the point? This girl was far different to all the others. She was not just young, but very attractive indeed. She had long blonde hair and a lovely smile in the photographs. She was also rather small, but curvy as well. Surely, this was a mistake on her behalf? I vowed to find out, with a hope that somehow, she simply liked older men and I was the chosen one.

Nervously, I replied to her message and we began to chat. I tried to play it cool and not be too pushy, even though I was desperate to meet up in the flesh. She was called Rosie and admitted that her last boyfriend was much older and for some reason she preferred the more mature male, rather than men her own age. This made sense to me, as everyone had different tastes. Age shouldn't matter anyway, as long as two people liked each other. I was obviously flattered, as she was a good-looking lady and seemed very mature and intelligent in her responses. After a while chatting online, we swapped mobile numbers and began to text. Eventually, we agreed to meet up in a countryside pub, beside a lovely canal.

When I first saw her, I was surprised how pretty she was in real life – even more attractive than her pictures, which was unusual. I was certainly lucky that she was in my company and we possessed a kind of electric chemistry between us. She was clever and had a great sense of humour too. I bought her a drink and we sat outside overlooking the canal barges and had an interesting chat. Then, she offered me a drink as well. We were both driving, so I asked for a shandy and she ordered half a lager. When she asked for the drinks however, the barman refused to serve her and asked for her identification. It began to spiral through my head that she may actually be underage, as she did look young – even with some make-up on. Thankfully, she produced her I.D. and was served accordingly – but it made me realise that there was a substantial age difference between us.

We continued to text and met up a week later in a local park. The plan was to go for a countryside walk and then go for a coffee or drink. We met up in the car park and I remember it being a lovely sunny day for once. Everything just felt right when I saw her, and she appeared to be in a relaxed mood. We went for a walk in the park and I suggested having a drink in a pub, about a mile down a country lane. It had a small beer garden outside, and we found ourselves a table in the sun. Everything just felt fabulous – I was finally with someone I really fancied, and we had some sort of spark too. The conversation flowed easily, and it was as though we'd known each other ages. The only problem, as such, was the fact that she was so much younger than me. But that would only be a problem if I made it one.

After the drink, we walked back to the cars and I suggested that she was welcome to come back to my house if she wished. Of course, being young she still lived with her parents, though she was training to work in the justice system. She agreed and followed me back in her car. On the way back, I was excited but thought it would be much too early to try it on. After all, being too forward may scupper my chances in the long run.

Having arrived at my house, she seemed pleasantly surprised that it wasn't a dump. I'd tried to keep it fairly clean for a single bloke, though I certainly didn't have OCD like some people. In fact, I was quite messy at times and left my cricket porn, I mean cricket magazines, lying all around the house, but tried my best to maintain a sense of decorum. My kids often complained that my washing-up skills were appalling, as sometimes they found bits of food stuck on the rim of their plate. My defence was that I didn't have enough hot water – as I only used hot water for a bath. In hindsight, I could've switched my hot water on more often than I did, especially when my children visited.

Anyway, we sat on the sofa and chatted some more. She declined a pizza but seemed keen on ordering a Chinese later on. I felt her body language was all positive and she snuggled right up to me. It was clear that she fancied me too, and so I went in for a kiss which felt rather natural. She was a lot more passionate than I'd anticipated and I said, 'Shall we go upstairs?' with my heart pounding and my trousers sticking up. 'Yeah,' she said, grabbing my hand and pulling me up. I really hadn't envisaged this at all – but that's why it seemed more natural, I guess.

We went to the bedroom and I gently removed her clothes and sexy panties, as we continued to kiss. Firstly, I noticed that she had a tattoo of a colourful butterfly or two on her back and a pierced belly button as well. It didn't put me off in the slightest, although I tried to make out whether the butterflies were symmetrical. I also examined her lady bits and noticed she was clean shaven and completely bald. Not a hair in sight and thus it made my scrotum seem even more hairy, as I hadn't trimmed in advance. Her clitoris was like a perfect baked bean, just right and ready to flick and lick. Most women I knew didn't admit to flicking the bean, but I reckoned that was all lies. At least men were more honest when it came to self-satisfaction. I didn't ask Rosie if she played with herself though, as that would've been totally inappropriate when I was attempting to get down to business.

I was certainly excited and was very tempted not to use a condom. Yet, I had one in my bedside drawer and it seemed the most sensible thing to do in the circumstances. I managed to get it on with a fumble and with all the finesse of a dog with three legs trying to sprint. The copulation was fantastic, and I tried to last as long as I could, being sober. The fact that I had a rubber on certainly helped in that regard. It was never quite the same wearing a condom, of course. It was like stroking a cat whilst wearing gloves.

When I finished, I pulled out and didn't actually realise that the condom wasn't on my willy. I went to the bathroom and let her have some privacy too. We got dressed and went downstairs to cuddle up and watch a film or some television. I ordered a Chinese takeaway too and it was all great as we snuggled up. Then, after a while and looking a little sheepish, she said, 'The condom is still inside me – I couldn't reach it,' quietly. I had completely forgotten about the fact that it wasn't on when I'd pulled out of her tight pussy. The fucking thing had got stuck inside her. 'Don't worry,' I said, 'I'll get it out for you gently.'

We went back upstairs, and she lay on her back, spreading her legs as wide as she could. Now, bearing in mind we'd only had sex for the first time about half an hour before, it may have been slightly embarrassing for her. I examined her pussy like a gynaecologist going about his business. I opened it wide and tried to reach the rubber with my fingers. I couldn't feel anything at all and after several minutes of rooting around inside, she became more anxious. Then, I realised I had the answer to the frustrating and concerning problem – 'I'll get something from the kitchen,' I stated abruptly.

I went to the kitchen and rummaged around in the cutlery drawer hoping I'd find a suitable implement to insert into her vagina. I discounted knives and forks immediately, as well as corkscrews and bottle openers. I saw a pizza cutter, which was no use and a spatula which was a no also. Then I saw a couple of long narrow spoons that'd been there for years – like one of those you use for a knickerbocker glory. I grabbed them and ran back upstairs where she waited, lying in anticipation. I said excitedly, 'Would this be suitable to try?' showing her the dessert spoon. Her face dropped in angst and worry, 'Okay,' she replied, 'As long as you sterilize it first.'

I boiled the kettle and poured boiling water over the spoon, removing the existing stains. It was spotless and ready for action. Carefully, with her help, we inserted the spoon into the requisite hole, and she felt around for the offending item. I didn't ask her what other items she'd shoved up there in the past. It just wasn't the right time for that sort of chat. I was concentrating so hard, like it was a proper medical procedure in the operating theatre. I was encouraging her to succeed with the words, 'Come on babe, you can do it!'

Eventually, after about five minutes of discomfort, she found it inside and began to drag it down. When I saw it, I became so excited and exclaimed, 'Yes, yes, you've done it!' getting ready to give her a high-five. She pulled the condom outside and we had a chuckle at the whole experience. To be fair to her, it was a really strange thing to happen and she was very open and honest about it all. Not long after, there was a knock at the door and the Chinese takeaway arrived. As we ate, I asked her how her fanny felt, and she was fine with everything. She appeared to be my type of girl.

I saw Rosie a few more times and I began to fall for her and enjoyed her company tremendously. Yet, as time progressed, I began to feel that she was fobbing me off a little too often and made excuses not to see me. Then, when she came to my house the next time, she said I'd been too pushy in wanting to see her all the time. I'd agreed that I wanted to see her more, but I knew that the age difference was probably putting her off. I was keen, probably too keen, and hadn't played it cool after all. She was a busy young lady with an avid social life, and I wasn't anything remotely serious to her. I understood that we were at different stages in our lives. She simply wanted some fun times with an older man, and I wanted to meet a potential long-term partner.

Rosie didn't break up with me as such, as we still saw each other occasionally for a while. But I knew the score and was certainly a little upset that she didn't want any commitment at all. Then again, I'd been the same with several ladies and knew what she meant and how she felt. The age difference was a big factor on the whole. She wanted to go clubbing, whereas I preferred drinking in pubs. She didn't like rambling or cricket of course – come to think of it she didn't like much of what I liked.

I guess it was inevitable that it wouldn't last and eventually, we stopped contacting each other. That is until, out of the blue, she got in touch again and wanted to see me. I was like a fucking lap dog and of course jumped at the chance to see her again. She came to mine and we had a fantastic time catching up. Then, she asked if I wanted to make her breakfast in the morning. The obvious answer was, 'Yes of course, whatever you like.'

She stayed over and we had a rather enjoyable time catching up in the bedroom too. But, in the morning she seemed a little off with me and totally different from the previous night. I really couldn't read a woman's mind – she was the one who'd instigated our liaison but now she was acting differently. My hopes had been dashed again and I felt somewhat empty inside.

This was a girl I had a lot of feelings for and who made my heart race, but now I was being abandoned like an empty of bottle of wine after a party. It seemed as though she wanted some physical fulfilment and her breakfast before casting me aside into the wilderness. I must admit I felt a little used that night, but it made me reflect and think how I'd probably treated some other ladies in a similar way. It was payback time in a way. She'd got what she wanted and left. We did message each other a little longer, but after that night she was a little colder with me for some unknown reason and in the end, we lost all contact.

I pondered this situation over and over in my mind but realised that I'd never fully understand women and how their brains operated. As an individual, I usually liked to be honest and upfront and always laid my cards on the table. I guess some ladies kept everything close to their chest and only revealed their feelings when the time was right. Others probably shared their feelings much more readily. The problem was, my cards at this time were always losing ones. I needed to choose a winning combination or have some luck if I was ever going to meet the girl of my dreams.

CHAPTER 15: WHAT D'YOU SAY?

My search for love continued and I trawled the dating sites I'd joined and eventually began talking to a lady from the Liverpool area, though she lived in Manchester. We appeared to have a few things in common and she certainly looked attractive in her pictures online. She was quite small and had long brown hair and a lovely figure. Her name was Denise and I remember speaking to her on the phone and noticing the difference in her scouse accent, compared to what I was used to.

I'm not saying it was my favourite accent, but I was prepared to give it a go. I'd never really considered accents before, but in hindsight it gives a clue as to whether you may connect. For example, if someone spoke in an accent I didn't fully understand, like one of my Irish friends, then it wouldn't bode well for long and detailed conversations. Come to think of it though, that may actually be better. I wouldn't have to have listen to them talking shit, as I wouldn't understand any of it anyway.

When Denise spoke with a scouse accent, however, it reminded me of a time I was sat around a pool on holiday surrounded by about 10 women from Liverpool. The matriarch of the family was like an elephant seal lying on her sunbed, looking around at her colony. She'd gone abroad to have her teeth sorted and kept smiling, displaying a massive white mouth – to match her massive belly overhanging her tiny bikini bottoms.

Her forehead was as flat as a pancake due to copious amounts of Botox and her lips had been pumped full of filler. Whatever, she looked a fucking mess – but she still believed she looked gorgeous and kept telling everyone that fact. She made a long phone call home and everyone around the pool could hear every detail about the process she'd been through to look such a mess. I knew more about her teeth than her own fucking dentist. I was trying to read my book in peace, but the seal and her colony had other ideas. In fact, they didn't care what anyone else was trying to do – which was to get some sun in a nice quiet and peaceful environment.

This family from hell kept rambling on in that accent, oblivious to everyone else. I thought it was scouse, but every now and then I couldn't make out what they were saying – it sounded foreign to me. I think it may have been some strange language from the elephant seal colony. This group also treated the waiters with disdain, clicking their fingers to get served and snatched drinks out of their hands in the same way that an elephant seal would devour a squid for lunch. Indeed, an elephant seal colony probably possessed more manners than this bunch.

Then, one of the cubs in the group started bouncing a ball and singing at the top of his voice. The elephant seals thought this was fantastic and encouraged him to do a full medley of the top songs they'd heard the previous night – whilst I kept reading the same page of my fucking book. I can still hear his bloody repertoire now, especially *Proud Mary, Rolling on the River.* I just wanted to push this irritating little fucker right in the pool. So, on reflection, I wasn't too keen on Denise's accent.

In some ways, however, the accent of a woman could be quite sexy and erotic to a degree. I remember using a sat nav once and being aroused by the really sexy voice of the lady telling me which way to go – 'At the next junction, turn left,' she said. 'Whatever you say baby,' I replied as I drove along. If a sat nav bellowed out in a scouse accent I'm convinced it wouldn't excite me in the same way.

I guess different people found different accents attractive and it became part of the overall package of a relationship. Just like the way ladies smelt. I found some perfumes very appealing, but others simply made me sneeze and my nose run. If I didn't like her scent, it put me off slightly but not as much as a woman with that sweaty body odour smell, however. You know, the smell when she'd just played badminton for an hour and hadn't a shower afterwards. Certainly, both accent and scent could be a passion killer or massive turn on for me.

Anyway, Denise's accent wasn't the sexiest in the world. Not like the lady on the sat nav for sure. However, one thing that appealed to me greatly was that Denise had a slight interest in cricket, unlike any other woman I'd met. We talked a little about cricket and she agreed that a good first date would be to watch a day of Test cricket at Old Trafford. We bought tickets to see England play and I was excited at the prospect of a day at the match. We met outside the ground and then queued to get our tickets from a kiosk inside the gates. Our first conversations took place in a queue and it seemed quite bizarre that our first date began like this. As we chatted, people around us gave us funny looks. It appeared as though I was trying to pull her whilst people were waiting for their tickets. One bloke nearly intervened and asked if she was fine.

Once in our seats, we began to relax, and she admitted that she'd never seen a live game before. That enabled me to explain all the rules over the next six hours, although I got a bit fed up of answering questions all day. At least I knew what to talk about, I guess. We were lucky that one of England's greatest ever batsmen, Kevin Pietersen, got a big score that day and it was a pleasure to watch him play. Well, whilst I enjoyed the technical brilliance of some of his shots, she was happy to drink alcohol and eat the picnic that I'd brought. What could be better than tuna sandwiches, a pork pie and crisps washed down with seven pints of lager?

To be fair, she could knock it back and she seemed to enjoy the food too. We walked around the ground a few times and found better seats towards the end of the day's play. By this point, the cricket was not the main focus for me. I'd decided after several drinks that I fancied her and wanted to try and pull her that night whilst in the city. We'd actually had a real laugh and the conversation seemed natural enough. I gave up trying to explain the laws of LBW though. She simply didn't understand about a ball pitching outside leg stump, especially after 5 pints. She kept getting confused about the different stumps – even the middle one. 'That's the one in the middle,' I made clear several times.

After a few hours, she asked a more difficult question, 'Why do batsmen keep leaving the ball and not try and hit it?'. I thought about this carefully and then responded, 'It's a five-day game. They need to assess whether it's swinging or seaming and assess the line of the ball. If it's likely to hit the edge of their bat, it could be caught in the slip region and they'd be out, and a new batsman would have to face a swinging ball. They must do their best to retain their wicket and tire out the bowlers, so they avoid any danger. They must be patient and wait for the right ball to hit, such as a full toss or half-volley or long-hop. It's about evaluating the risks of their shots and playing the percentages, with regard to the state of the game.' She never asked another bloody question.

After the play ended, we were well oiled and went into the city centre for more drinks. We ended up in a posh bar somewhere and Denise picked up the cocktail menu. My eyes nearly popped out when I saw the bloody price. It was about a tenner per drink. I was used to *Wetherspoons* prices and my local cricket club prices back home. This was a posh bar in a vibrant city, and I was facing a hefty bill bar. She must have realised I was surprised by the price, probably because I blurted out, 'For fuck's sake that's expensive!'

She bought the cocktails and paid on her card. By this point, I was well gone and hadn't a chance of making my last train home. In reality, I'd wanted to stay with her since the tea interval, when she started asking about the sightscreens. To be fair, she'd attempted to take an interest in the game and tried to enjoy it, but I'd made absolutely no effort to catch my train.

She agreed that I could stay at her flat in the city centre, however, when we arrived at her fairly plush apartment there was a terrible, ghastly smell coming from the kitchen. I was all excited and hopeful when we first arrived, but that smell was like a rotting decomposed corpse on the side of a canal. She'd forgotten to put her bin out, and it'd been a hot day. Talk about a passion killer.

We went downstairs to her bedroom and I eyed up the king-size bed. I started getting excited again, when suddenly she blurted out quite forcefully, 'I'll make you a bed up in the other room'. I was deflated to say the least. I had visions of making love all night, even though I was probably dribbling down my chin by this point. To be fair, I was rat-arsed as I'd been drinking for about 12 hours by now. I was lucky I had a bed for the night, and she'd been accommodating. We parted to our separate beds and I slept like a baby but woke up the next day with a throbbing hangover, rather than a throbbing cock.

In the cold light of a sober morning, she looked a bit rough too to be honest. It didn't put me off, when I saw her without make-up, and to be fair she saw me looking like I'd been dragged through a forest by a giant creature, who liked teasing humans by dragging them through forests for some unfathomable reason. I'd got used to seeing women in the morning, without their 'face on' and it made me realise that make-up made a massive difference for some women more than others. I didn't particularly like women who had to rely on a couple of inches of foundation and half the Debenhams make-up counter on their face to look decent. A more natural look appealed to me, unless they needed to shave their moustache.

I saw Denise a few more times and invited her to a party at my house. She met some of my family and friends and seemed to get on quite well with my sister and cousin. However, she didn't stop the night so one of my friends dropped her off at the train station. By now, I'd had a few snogs but not much more. I was wondering whether she was a genuine lady who wanted to take things slowly, or maybe just a huge cockteaser. A week or so later she agreed to stay at mine but slept in her pyjamas next to me and wouldn't let me progress past first base. My sister had told me that it was unusual not to want to move things forward by now, but Denise had hinted to me that good things come to those who wait. Of course, I wanted to be a gentleman so abided by her wishes.

The next time she came to my house, I was convinced she'd want some action. Surely, she had sexual needs as well, I assumed. We slept together again, but this time she was in her underwear. Again, we kissed and cuddled. Again, it didn't progress past squeezing and twisting her erect nipples. In a very romantic way, I hasten to add. I was beginning to think that there was something wrong with me, or maybe it was her mentality. I'd tried to be patient and remained open-minded. In the morning, she got up and had a shower whilst I waited in bed.

Suddenly, after her shower she walked slowly into the bedroom completely naked. She had a gorgeous figure, with a small Brazilian for her very tidy lady garden. She looked sexy and I felt like pulling her back in bed, but she began to get dressed in an evocative way. I felt it was some sort of signal, so leapt up and jumped in the shower too, to get nice and clean. I was showering with a semi, thinking about what we might do in a few minutes. Then, having finished the shower I began to get dried. For some unknown reason, my excitement dissipated quickly. My normally self-assured persona disappeared, and I felt limp and inadequate. I was trying to inflate my manhood in the bathroom before making a similar dazzling entrance to her. I planned to walk into the bedroom naked, with lots of confidence, showing her what I possessed.

I walked into the bedroom, with a towel wrapped around me tightly and sat on the edge of the bed. My cock was limp beneath the towel and my confidence was in tatters. I can't explain why my libido disappeared, why my self-confidence drained. This was my chance to impress her and I simply couldn't do it. She looked at my sagging moobs as I sat on the bed and I could see she was thoughtful. She was probably expecting me to take the bull by the horns and make a spectacular entrance by displaying my crown jewels in all their glory. But then again, she was probably just a teaser. She was fully dressed by now and wasn't exactly waiting on the bed in her underwear, or in the nude. Why had I not grasped the opportunity? I really don't know, in all honesty.

It'd been another chance that we'd had to take the so-called relationship further, but Denise didn't seem too bothered about the physical side. I'd wanted things to progress, but for some reason, it just hadn't. I was about to visit Manchester the following week to watch the Roses *Twenty20*, wearing fancy dress like everyone else in our group from the cricket club. Would she really want to meet up and see me dressed as a giant sausage? I'd already made myself look like a giant knob as it was. In fact, I did go to watch the cricket in fancy dress, but she was nowhere to be seen. I never saw her again. Like my sister said, every now and then you'll meet a cockteaser.

CHAPTER 16: SET-UP SURPRISE

As my dating life trundled on, I'd started going out with a mate from work on a more regular basis, although we'd had many nights out in the past with other friends from work. His name was Mart and he was a big lad from the Sheffield area of Yorkshire, with the biggest hands I'd ever seen. In fact, Mart's idea of a balanced diet was a pizza in each hand. He could put his food away for sure, but surprisingly I could keep up when it came to supping pints. We went through a stage of working our way through all the speciality beers in *Wetherspoons* such as the Czech and Polish beers and got suitably merry, usually on a Friday after work. Mart had been a great support for me at work when I'd separated and so he knew every detail of my dalliances and my quest to find love. He used to take the piss about my latest failings, along with another couple of friends called Ash and Dainty Dan.

Ash was another big unit, a rugby prop type of guy, who looked a bit like Santa Claus – except he wore garish shirts instead of a fur trimmed red suit and boots. If you're a fan of the BBC quiz *Eggheads,* you'll know the type of outrageous shirts that Barry wears. Put it this way, if you spilt some sauce down the shirts, you'd think it was part of the pattern. Ash wore those same ridiculous shirts – and thought he was as clever as Barry too.

He was a lot older than me and was a bit of a father-figure and mentor to me in a way. He did, however, tend to have a depressing view about work and the world and was a grumpy, miserable figure at times. In fact, if he ever went to McDonalds for a 'Happy Meal' he'd probably order either an 'Unhappy Meal' or maybe even an 'Old Grumpy Bastard Meal' instead. If you felt like you were having a positive and meaningful day, after a coffee with Ash you'd feel like shoving your head in a hot oven.

Dainty Dan was, as you can imagine, far from dainty. He was about 6 feet 3 tall and weighed 17 stone on a good day. He once tried to run the Manchester 10K race and was overtaken by a man dressed as a muffin. He had a great sense of humour though and was always keen to discuss current affairs and make fun of any gossip. He often took the piss out of us three too. When he spoke, the other side of town could probably hear his big booming voice, echoing in the distance.

You could say he was the life and soul of a party but was often the guy who became just a tad silly after downing ten pints. Put it this way, you wouldn't want to dance with him as your drink would end up all over you. The more alcohol he consumed, the louder and louder his voice would become too. One time he queued for fucking ages at the cricket to get served and brought back two beers each in plastic trays. Soon after, during celebrations when a wicket was taken, they all ended up splattered on the floor. You could say Dainty Dan wasn't a happy bunny.

Together, over a lunch-time coffee, they would all rib me about my exploits and try to give their advice about my latest situation. Well, I say advice – it was more like a constant teasing of the most recent disaster. Apparently, I often said I'd met 'the one' only for it to fizzle out soon after. They thought everything was hilarious – a bit like my friends at university, Nick and Gary, all those years earlier when I kept being stood up. They loved hearing about my latest conquests and all the gossip. I think my depressing situation made them feel so much better about their own lives.

As Mart was from Yorkshire, it allowed us to have some banter when it came to sport too. He was a keen Sheffield Wednesday fan and we always had a few bets between us about football, as well as plenty of discussions about the latest games. He was also a cricket fan and, of course, supported the White Rose of Yorkshire – rather than the Red Rose of Lancashire like me and Dainty Dan. We went a few times together to watch the Roses *Twenty20* at Old Trafford. There was always a fantastic atmosphere, with a full house of about 20,000 people.

I remember one game when we were sat on the second row and Yorkshire took a wicket. Mart turned around to the whole stand, stood up and shouted, 'Yorkshire, Yorkshire!' in that silly accent. Well, about five thousand Lancashire fans, me included, stood up and yelled at him to sit down. We then all started singing, 'Lancashire la, la, la, Lancashire la, la, la...' in unison. Being from Yorkshire, his wallet was full of cobwebs too and he seldom put those gigantic hands in there, unless there was a deal to be had of course. You could say he made me look generous.

Mart had been looking to meet someone himself and had finally had some luck with a girl called Leanne. I'd met her a couple of times in passing, but on one particular evening she was to join us later on. For some reason, that night we'd started drinking red wine - probably due to a pub promotion and the cheap price. As I said, Mart was a tight Yorkshire bastard from the wrong side of the Pennines so it must have been cheap, and I liked a bargain too for sure. We never usually drank red wine and it was going down so well we were buying rounds in bottles. A few other lads met us and had a glass or two as well. It was certainly a great atmosphere and we were all very merry.

Well, I say merry - I probably mean pissed. When Leanne turned up, she was quite shocked to see us all in this inebriated state. Nevertheless, she joined in and embraced the evening too, which was great, and we started chatting about all sorts of things. She seemed really nice and Mart told her I was single and looking for love. Suddenly, Leanne said her mum was single too and was only a few years older than me. It was then suggested that maybe I could meet Leanne's mum and go on a date with her. This was just so hilarious after a bottle or two of red wine.

Leanne then asked if she could take a few photographs, so that they could be sent to her mum for approval. Well, of course by now I'd have tried anything and agreed to have the snaps done. With all our group watching, she then proceeded to pretend to be a professional photographer and take pictures from various angles. I was just laughing all the time and making them funny, as I just couldn't be serious. But before she sent any of them to her mum, I wanted to look at them in fine detail and delete any bad ones. I wanted her mum to see the very best of me - even if I was blatantly drunk.

It then occurred to me that I hadn't actually seen Leanne's mum yet and I'd agreed to meet up. I was being fucking set up and they were taking advantage of my drunken state. What if she was single because she looked like a fucking donkey? I demanded to see Leanne's mum in a photograph and didn't agree to meet unless I found her attractive. Fortunately, she was actually a good-looking woman and so I agreed to meet up. Next, it suddenly dawned on Mart that if we actually met up and got on well one thing could lead to another. Ultimately, we could end up getting married and I could feasibly end up being his fucking Father-in-Law. He started having doubts about the plans and suggested that this was a bad idea, a very bad idea.

Yet, Leanne still fired off the pictures to her mum for her approval and we waited with bated breath. Well, in all honesty I was past caring by this point. She could've had no teeth and looked like a fucking gargoyle and I'd have still agreed to meet up. About half an hour later, she responded and said that I was a suitable match and the date was on. By this point, Mart was shaking his head in disbelief and Leanne found it all very funny. In fact, I found it all very strange. Maybe, just maybe, we'd hit it off and I'd meet the woman I'd been searching for.

The date was set for a couple of weeks later, but it was agreed that Mart would meet me before we made our way over to another pub to meet Leanne and her mum together. A sort of double date, if you could call it that. The big problem was that me and Mart arrived at the pub early after work and began downing a few pints, well before we were due to meet them. By the time we arranged to meet, we were both quite drunk again – and they were sober. I genuinely thought Leanne's mum was attractive when I first saw her. Then I asked that question you shouldn't ask within five minutes – 'So, how old are you?'

It was a silly question, because I'm sure Leanne had already told me her age previously. Maybe I was just making small talk, I don't know. She responded, 'I'm 41 now,' with a fake smile and over the course of the next hour I said, 'You don't look 41,' about 70 times. I honestly can't remember talking about anything else, other than her age. I was trying to flatter her – because she didn't look her age. However, that wasn't the point. I just kept banging on about it as I couldn't think of anything else to say. The body language wasn't there either, to be honest. Maybe she was a little unsettled that I was merry already, or maybe she just thought I was a dick. I certainly acted like one.

Needless to say, it didn't work out between us. Maybe a genuine date with the two of us could have gone better in hindsight. In all honesty, it all seemed a bit of joke at the time and I guess I saw it as that. At the end of the night Mart took me for a curry down some back street. It made me suspicious that we were the only people in the place. It was an all you could eat Indian for a set price. When we helped ourselves to the different vats of curry, they looked like they'd been there for about three weeks and the naan bread looked older than us. On top of that, most of the curries looked and tasted similar. We'd had a few drinks by now, but it still wasn't great. In fact, it was crap and was likely to give us the shits as well. Literally a week or two later the place closed down because of incidents of food poisoning, due to a complete lack of hygiene. What a great night though.

Another strange night out with Mart and Ash ended up with me getting a date in quite a similar way. We got talking to a group of girls and they asked if I was single. One of them showed me a picture of their friend, who was looking to meet someone. They said I'd be absolutely perfect for her and arranged it so that we swapped numbers. However, on the night in question I was more interested in the girl who started talking to me as she was a bit of a stunner. I tried to get her number instead, but she was rather insistent that her friend Mavis was more my type. I obviously disagreed, but knowing I had no chance with the beauty in front of me decided to take the number. In fact, I texted Mavis a few times and we agreed to meet up, half-way between our respective towns. Obviously, we both had to drive and remained sober throughout.

As soon as I saw Mavis in the flesh, I knew it wasn't meant to be. She was dressed like it was the 1970's, in a frumpy old-fashioned dress covered in yellow flowers. To make matters worse, she had a Kevin Keegan perm. I mean, a fucking perm! I'd have been ideally dressed for her if I'd kept those outdated brown cords my mum bought me for university. It was like she was living in the wrong bloody decade. She acted as though she'd never been on a date before and kept telling me that she wouldn't do anything with anybody unless she was married first. That was all well and good, but I'd only asked her if she wanted a fucking drink.

I must say Mavis seemed really sweet as a person, but she was a little reserved and incredibly inexperienced on the dating front. Her friends had certainly done me like a fucking kipper. The picture I was shown was misleading to say the least, and it was though this was a completely different person. It was obvious I guess, but often photographs didn't bear any resemblance to who was on the date. I couldn't exactly get it out and hold the picture I'd been given next to her to compare, could I? I may have stated that she looked different to what I thought, but I tried to be polite and pleasant. I genuinely didn't want to upset her feelings. There wasn't any point seeing her again anyway as it'd probably take me a year just to get a kiss on her hand, if I was interested. But I certainly wasn't interested, and it was a case of thanks, but no thanks. Indeed, she's probably still got that same sickly dress now and probably still a virgin. Each to their own, I guess.

CHAPTER 17: NO SEX ON THE BEACH

Having been blown out yet again and still desperately single, I suggested a holiday with my old mate, Big Col. We scoured the best deal and thought about a place we may enjoy, with plenty of nightlife and potential action. We realised that the best bet was probably Rhodes Town on the lovely Greek island of well, Rhodes obviously! However, prices seemed a little cheaper nearer to Faliraki, so we settled on a place in between the two - although walkable to Faliraki itself. I'd heard about its reputation as a wild party strip and fancied going back to my youth somewhat and giving it a go. In reality, however, I was probably better suited to the more laid back and cultural old town.

I'd not been on a lad's holiday since my trip to Torquay all those years before. I was excited, of course, and wondered what awaited us in the sizzling sun. The first thing I noticed was how incredibly hot the place was. I'd been abroad to Cyprus many years before when my friend from university, Nick, had shown me around the island. But I was younger then and didn't feel the heat as much. This was bloody stifling, reaching over 40 degrees Celsius one day.

The sand was so hot on the beach that you simply couldn't stand on it. I made a real tit of myself after only a couple of days, by burning my fucking feet. I didn't apply sun cream liberally enough and at the end of the day my feet were red raw and stinging like crazy. Luckily, I'd brought some after-sun but still had to wear my socks after that when we walked anywhere. I looked like a real dick, wearing socks when everyone else was barefoot. The pain of sunburn was not to be underestimated.

Our usual day consisted of lounging around the pool in the morning for a few hours and me getting burnt. Then, we headed off into the town to get some lunch and watch any sport, particularly cricket, which was on the big screens. We'd head down to the beach and check out the talent, but this only made me get even more burnt. It also made me feel slightly inadequate, as I was usually paler than anyone else. I looked at those bronze bodies with some jealousy and the young posers walked around with no hint of any excess fat or wobbly moobs. In this resort, I was beginning to feel incredibly old. Maybe Faliraki wasn't the best idea after all.

At our hotel, however, there were a couple of attractive mature ladies and they dared to go topless around our poolside. Me and Big Col obviously noticed this and wondered whether we should chat to them. In all honesty though, it's rather difficult to strike up a conversation with a stranger when they've got their baps out. Even someone with the best of intentions would start staring at their breasts in that situation. So, we pretended to read our books and stared at their breasts anyway over the top of the pages. They must have realised that every bloke around the pool would be ogling them. In fact, they probably enjoyed all the attention and got a suntan in the process. Unfortunately, the only thing I was getting was red patches over all over my skin, as I sizzled away.

Around late afternoon, we tended to have a couple of pints and then got ready for the night ahead. We headed out with excitement, first to a couple of pubs on the way to the strip or for some food. There was a really good bar which was themed on King Arthur and it had a large round table in the middle for some reason.

They had a couple of great bands on and we even got in touch with our feminine side and had a cocktail, complete with sparklers and umbrellas. At the strip, there were bars down both sides of the road, blaring music out and young girls trying to entice us by the promise of 'free shots' – even 2 or 3 of them. I mean shots, not girls. Of course, these watered-down shots had about 1% alcohol content and despite downing about 16 of the things, they made no difference. It was all part of the game, though, to get customers in. What I did notice in Faliraki was how bloody old I was compared to most other punters. Big Col and I looked around at the talent and felt we were up against it. It was similar to an old haggard lion trying to be accepted back into the pride.

Nevertheless, we vowed to have a good time and I tried to chat a few young ladies up, without much success. I was getting on well with a Bulgarian cleaner, but she had a night shift to do, or so she said. I tried my bit on the dancefloor too, thinking I was a babe magnet but really having the same impact as my mosquito repellent, only the ladies were the equivalent of the mosquitos. Mind you, I still got bitten a few times despite the repellent so maybe I could succeed if I didn't give up. Resilience was an admirable quality to possess when it came to the opposite sex.

Then, on the third night we got talking to two young Polish girls who were about early twenties. They were both incredibly tanned, both good looking with long dark hair and had their own teeth. I only say that because Big Col got so drunk one Christmas that he ended up snogging a rough, old bird, who had a solitary tooth. She entered the same pub a week later and he had to hide behind the jukebox to avoid her, whilst I was in hysterics. Anyway, these ladies were well out of our league, but seemed rather keen to talk to us.

We asked if they fancied a drink and they agreed to join us for a goldfish bowl. We asked what they wanted, and it was 'Sex on the beach', which was rather encouraging. We got the bowl and four straws to slurp up the cocktail. It was fun, having a chat and sharing the drink. We asked about their lives in Poland and they seemed equally interested about our lives in northern England. What I hadn't realised though, was that the cocktail was disappearing very quickly. Obviously, they were slurping away as quickly as they could. So, we ordered another goldfish bowl. Again, we were talking away and they were doing most of the slurping. Of course, when it came to pay the bill me and Big Col picked up the tab.

We then moved on to another bar and bought them another drink. We had a bit of a dance, but I sensed that they were ready to leave, and they made their excuses soon after. They did agree to meet us again, however, a couple of days later in the same bar. We honestly didn't think they'd show up. A couple of nights later, they were there again as planned. Wow, they must actually like us we thought. Again, we got another goldfish bowl. Again, they drank most of it.

We ordered a different bowl next, to try a different cocktail. They drank most of that as well. In fact, we realised far too late that they were simply using us for free booze. They'd supped the best part of four goldfish bowls on us, plus a couple of extra drinks. To be fair, we enjoyed their company and they were certainly attractive young ladies. Nevertheless, there was never really any prospect of taking things further. They were keen to make their excuses after those drinks and we didn't even manage a goodbye snog. It was all a bit of damp squib.

On one of the nights, we paid to attend a comedy gig with free unlimited drinks for about two hours. We thought that'd be fun and we also got to use a shisha pipe before the event. We were told that it was 'apple' flavour, but it appeared far stronger than that to me. I'd never smoked a pipe before and quite enjoyed it in all honesty. For sure, after using that shisha pipe we both felt high for some reason. It may have been a combination of the booze and pipe, but we were buzzing all night. The comedy gig was pretty good too and the unlimited booze meant the bars were crazy before the show and during the interval. If anybody went anywhere near the bar during the show itself, the comedian absolutely ripped into them causing wholesale laughter around the floor. Nobody dared to get a drink during the show after that.

During the interval, I remember going to the toilet. The reason I remember so vividly was that as I pissed long and hard into the urinal, a gigantic beetle type creature walked over my foot. Now, I'd seen a few cockroaches and beetles before, but nothing like this. It was about the same size as a rat, crawling over my foot with carefree abandon. It was like something out of a horror film. I thought briefly about squashing it with my foot but reckoned it may jump up and bite my nose off. I'd seen the film *Alien* when I was younger, and this creature looked like its son. If I left it alone, it probably wouldn't attack me, so I thought. I wondered if that shisha pipe had made my head go funny, but then I heard some bloke scream as I left. Maybe it bit his cock off. I've never seen anything like it since.

On a couple of evenings, we went to Rhodes Town itself, which was much more to my liking. The harbour was full of million-pound yachts and there were even some super-yachts there, worth far more than that. It really was a picturesque sight, especially lit up at night. The old town was also beautiful, and although not in my preferred price range, Big Col and I had a nice romantic meal for two of a 'Greek Plate' which consisted of lots of different Greek dishes on one large plate. Well, it would have been romantic if I wasn't with Big Col of course. It was one of those places that made me think It'd be great to bring the love of my life. Instead, I was stuck with my big hairy mate and lots of feral cats, who seemed to roam around everywhere. We still had a good night, but it did make me think that it would be fantastic to have a romantic break somewhere with a new love. I was determined to keep trying on the dating sites when we got back.

The nights in Faliraki all tended to mingle into one eventually. The place was meant for the young generation, who had a whale of a time downing free shots with no alcohol inside and becoming lairy after a couple of pints. The young ones were getting pissed so quickly and me and Col were feeling our age, looking at them and thinking they were just being knobs. We looked at the young ladies too, all dolled up and wearing next to nothing. For some reason, they didn't seem that appealing to me anymore, compared to the more mature dirtier ladies.

I wanted to meet a lady of a similar age to me, who had some life experience and a story to tell. I didn't just want a cheap shag anymore or something that wouldn't last. It made me think that actually I wanted to meet someone to settle down with. I wanted to meet a lady I could take on a romantic city break, or someone who'd appreciate the beautiful harbour and ancient relics, rather than someone who just wanted to get drunk and probably thought I was an ancient relic. In fact, I wanted to fall in love again. Sometimes at night, I dreamt about what it would be like to meet my soulmate, but a dose of reality made me wake up in a hot sweat and all alone. There was nobody to cuddle, there was nobody to talk to. It would be difficult to find the special person I was looking for, but I was determined not to give up.

CHAPTER 18: SCRATCHING THE SURFACE

My intentions may have been valiant, but I was still finding it difficult to meet the right person. My strategy was, therefore, to keep dating women and hope that I'd know when I'd met 'the one', so to speak. I got talking online to another woman, who was a similar age to me, and had some common interests. We arranged to meet for a drink locally and she duly turned up on time, which was always a good start. She'd tried to impress me with her dress sense and had a fairly trim body to display. However, her face was not how I'd imagined it, if that makes sense. I'm not saying she was ugly, but the pictures online must have been taken from a very good angle, with amazing lighting. She looked a bit like the once famous northern comedian Les Dawson in his prime.

We had a few drinks and went to a dingy club, down some back street. I tried to walk around, but this proved difficult as my feet were sticking to the floor. I looked at the other clientele in this gloomy place and felt that no man on earth could fail to pull in this jungle. Many of the women had several piercings through each nostril, plenty on their ears and probably half a jewellery store through their clitoris.

There were tattoos galore, with lots of birds of prey on view and every jungle animal you can imagine. I saw tigers, jaguars, monkeys, parrots and hummingbirds. David Attenborough would've been in his fucking element. Not being a big fan of tattoos, these were not the sort of women that appealed to me, but it didn't matter of course because I was on a date with Les – I mean Valerie.

Valerie was trying to be funny and cracked a few jokes, which I appreciated. Not only did she look similar to Les Dawson, but she was almost as funny as him too. When I first saw her, I felt like making my excuses and leaving. Now, I was having a ball and a riotous laugh with this comical lady. She certainly had a face for radio and would have been fantastic presenting her own comedy show. When she took to the dancefloor, her giant earrings were jingling about, and her contorted face was looking so happy. I started to have a bloody great time and carried on dancing in carefree abandon. I was surrounded with all my favourite animals and it felt great.

Whilst in the club, Valerie bumped into one of her friends – or they'd potentially arranged to meet in case I'd turned out to be a complete nutcase. Her friend wasn't much better looking either, and she kept putting her arms around me and flirting somewhat. Valerie didn't seem jealous at all and we all carried on dancing and had another drink. At the end of the night, we shared a taxi together. I was sat in the back, in the middle of these two beauties and things started going through my mind. They were both rubbing my thighs and giggling like naughty schoolgirls. I simply wondered where I was going. Surely, I had to get out of this situation and get home?

Then, Valerie asked if I wanted to go back to her house. I was fairly drunk, but still in two minds what to do. I was hoping she may invite her friend back too, and then I'd try my luck with them both despite feeling a little nauseous about the situation. That idea was blown soon after, though, as the taxi stopped, and her friend got out. I'm sure she tried to pull me out the car too, unless I was mistaken. Maybe I should have followed her – but that would've been so cruel on Valerie. The taxi set off and headed to her house. Part of me wanted to scarper, part of me didn't.

We got to her house and Valerie opened up, I mean her door. From what I remember, she had the biggest fish tank known to man. It was bigger than the main tank at Blackpool's Sea Life Centre – it seemed like there were fucking sharks swimming in there, manta rays and giant eels. It was an amazing aquarium, and I was mesmerised. Whilst she wanted to get amorous, I just wanted to watch the fish. I told her about the solitary goldfish I'd once won at the fair, but she didn't seem too impressed. My kids had also had a small aquarium in the past, but this was something else. I could've watched the fish for hours it was so relaxing. Having asked about two hundred questions about her fish, she began to get friskier and suddenly pulled me off the sofa and to her bedroom.

We got to her room and she began to kiss me, quite passionately. I must say that I winced slightly at that prospect but shut my eyes and hoped for the best. She wasn't missing any teeth, but it just looked that way at times. It got much better when she took her top off and I could play with her sizeable knockers. In fact, I was surprised about how shapely her body was and thought that it could be good, if I couldn't see her gurning face. I couldn't really suggest that she should put a bag over her head, but maybe if she turned around, I'd get aroused a bit more. Surely, it would be wrong though to shove her face deep into the pillows or ask for that paper bag.

As usual in these situations, we started in the missionary position. She smiled at me with that lovely big round face and it was a bit of a turn off. Nevertheless, I vowed to keep going and have a bash. After a minute or two, I felt a real pain on my back and cried out like a whale. The fish downstairs probably thought I was trying to communicate with them. 'What the fuck have you done?' I exclaimed. In fact, Valerie had dug her bloody long nails into me with some venom. How could I carry on, after that? She was a fucking lunatic in bed and had hurt me.

I jumped up sharply and moved over to the full-length mirror, twisting to have a look at the damage. There were visible scratch marks covering most of my fucking back. I wasn't happy and told her so, with some shock. This had never happened before, and I reckoned she'd done it on purpose. She was apologetic, though, and said she'd just got carried away because it was just so good. That was bollocks, I'm sure. Nevertheless, I was in a tricky situation now as I had a naked woman in front of me and she was gagging for it.

As I stood there though, I was a little petrified she wanted rough sex and would try to maim me further. I remembered a story that a friend of mine had told me years before. He said that he'd had a one-night stand and as he was about to climax, the lady had forcibly inserted a couple of fingers up his arsehole. He'd winced in pain, but she thought it would turn him on. For his sake, I hope she'd cut her fingernails that's for sure.

Anyhow, Valerie promised not to do it again and I was thankful she hadn't slipped her digit inside me. Then, it occurred to me that I could kill two birds with one stone. If I asked her to turn around and do it doggy style, I wouldn't have to look at that fucking face and she wouldn't be able to physically assault me. She readily obliged and I gave her a good pounding from behind. I felt like shoving her head into the pillows and slapping her arse hard to get my own back, but maybe that's what she wanted. Maybe she wanted me to use my belt on her and cause some physical pain in the process. Whatever, she seemed to enjoy it and made a fair bit of noise too. I was pretty sure that I'd never let her near me again. Those fingernails could be so deadly.

The following week, she badgered me a fair bit to meet up with her. I was tempted to ask if she wanted me to bring some rope so that I could tie her up and maybe buy a whip or other implements. I reckoned she was into sadomasochism for sure. Yet, I wasn't into anything like that at all. I was also hurting for several days and had to have a few baths to try and soothe my back. The situation had shocked me for a while and I definitely didn't want to repeat it. I also thought about that face, the contorted face that I'd wanted to cover up. I couldn't take a bloody Morrisons bag to her house, could I? I vowed never to see her again.

A couple of weeks later and I was back in that jungle of a club, out of pure desperation. My potential dates had dried up or let me down yet again. Unfortunately, Vicious Valerie was there again with her tattooed friends. By this point, my back had healed properly, and I felt ready for anything – apart from Valerie that is. I was hoping I'd score with someone else or maybe even meet one of her friends, such as a fit girl with a jumbo-sized eagle tattoo on her back. She'd given me some romantic signals and I began to consider if we'd fly off into the sunset together.

Unfortunately, *Eagle Girl* flew off with a man sporting a mammoth mythical dragon tattoo. I simply couldn't compete with that. Whereas many of the younger guys displayed complete works of art on their bodies, my level of manliness extended to three small chest hairs sticking out of the top of my cheap shirt. As the beer goggles began to kick in and my chances of success dwindled, I began talking to Vicious Valerie once more. She was very apologetic about making me bleed and promised it wouldn't happen again. Was I really prepared to give her another chance to maim me? Of course, I was. By this point in the night, I didn't care anymore. I was living life right on the fucking edge.

Alcohol was becoming one of my best companions and affecting my judgment on nights out. After drinking all night, I was making big mistakes, but I certainly wasn't alone in this respect. I knew Valerie wasn't for me, but I still went for it. What was I doing? What was I thinking? You could say my head was mashed on many of these nights and I was becoming heartless. I had no feelings for Valerie but was still being physical with her. But did she care about me? Probably not, as it appeared to be a mutual understanding and no more than that. It was all rather weird and just a little bit sad. It wasn't what I envisaged when I signed up to internet dating. It didn't seem to be working as I expected, and my depressing love life continued to exist.

CHAPTER 19: OLDER AND WISER

It amazed me how many women actually had a tattoo. I remember that one lady had a tattoo of a red rose on one of her breasts, another a picture of a devil. Mostly though, the women who I had carnal knowledge of, had either flowers or butterflies, or maybe animals on some part of their body. It was definitely the case that more and more women were getting a tattoo or having their naval pierced. Or maybe even their lip, nose, nipple or clit. I wasn't really into it myself, but hey, each to their own. Body adornment had become big business and some people just loved it.

Whilst searching online, many women also mentioned their tattoos and piercings and wanted someone of a similar ilk, who had lots of the same. It was the look they were searching for, which was understandable, I guess. Everyone had a different attitude to body adornment. I wouldn't have minded a small discreet tattoo, but not a massive one. Some of the tattoos that looked good in the present, may look rather ridiculous in twenty years' time, when they'd put five stone on, and everything had started to move south. My preference was none at all, just like my preference would be a non-smoker.

When it came to beliefs like religion, I stayed away from those who had a strong faith and wanted to practise their religion regularly. I'd been brought up as a Christian and had even been a server in my local church as a youngster, during Holy Communion. As time progressed, I'd done some reading about religion and found *The God Delusion* by Richard Dawkins a fascinating read. I respected other people's views, of course, but now I'd realised I didn't really believe in God and religion didn't mean much to me anymore. Having said that, as the amount of body adornment increased, I found that those who didn't have a religion had also increased. I certainly wasn't alone in questioning my beliefs. It just didn't seem that important to most people on the sites I visited.

As time progressed and the lack of opportunities became apparent, I agreed to meet up with an older lady once again. This seemed to be more in desperation than anything else. Desperation to get my end away, I guess. Gloria said she was five years older than me, which didn't sound too bad. We agreed to meet up in a familiar pub chain, which we duly did. When I first laid eyes on her, I wasn't sure if it was her or not. The reason being was that she looked at least fifteen years older than me and not like the pictures on the site. This was disingenuous of her, as she was being untruthful to say the least. Those bloody photographs were about ten years old.

It was difficult to remain unflustered in such a situation. I thought she was still attractive for an older lady, but she must have been in her early fifties now. But then, I realised that age shouldn't be a barrier at all. I'd dated a few younger ladies and so a much older lady would provide a different challenge. She had dirty blonde hair and was wearing bright red lipstick, to enhance her large lips. After a drink or two, I decided to broach the subject of her age. I knew that I'd have to be careful because many women didn't like to discuss their age, but I guess asking her weight may have been below the belt.

I realised that I'd have to tactful and mindful of her feelings, so I said in my most tactful and mindful manner, 'How old are you then?'. She nearly choked on her straw that I was so direct, but I felt it was better to get it out in the open. Her response was, 'Fifty-two, although I look much younger, don't I?' she said smiling. I only had one option at that point in time – 'Of course, you don't look a day over fifty-one!'. The date went well enough, I guess, though there wasn't the type of chemistry I was searching for. However, she appeared to be a pleasant lady with lots of commendable values.

In all honesty, she looked about her age, but was still attractive in many ways. After a couple of dates, she invited me to her house to accompany her in taking her dog out for a walk. She had a large detached house, in a nice area and a respectable professional job. We took her dog out on a long walk and got some great fresh air on a lovely meander around, in the local countryside. Then, we went back to her house and had a quick brew. Gloria was certainly a likeable person, but the age factor was in the back of my mind. She had a pretty enough face and a good sense of humour, but at the end of the day she was a lot older than me. Despite these concerns we were getting on well, so we stayed in touch and decided to meet again.

On the next date, alcohol was consumed in vast quantities and we ended up back at her house in quite a drunken state. We kissed and then made our way into her bedroom. I'd never slept with someone so much older, though there was a first time for everything, I guess. How could I describe it? Well, it was dissatisfying if that makes sense. I seemed to be going through the motions, in a drunken sort of way and it meant absolutely nothing. I just didn't feel any sort of proper connection and even the lustful element seemed to be missing. It was all a bit of an anti-climax and probably ruined the friendship between us. Indeed, that's all we were really – friends. There was no proper sexual chemistry and hence it just didn't seem right.

I'm not saying that older women couldn't be sexy, because I knew some cougars would be fantastic in bed. Yet, Gloria was not that type of lady and on this occasion, I actually regretted taking that step. Maybe her age was at the back of my mind, I don't know. I think the feeling was probably mutual in actual fact. Needless to say, we kept in touch a little longer being polite with each other, but I can't remember seeing her too many times after that. Yet again, alcohol had affected my judgment and yet again I felt somewhat empty inside and unfulfilled. I was making some bad choices and it was beginning to get me down.

So, that experience was a little underwhelming – but it made me realise that I was probably better trying to find someone a little younger than myself if possible, or not too much older. The next person I met for a date was probably of a similar age, but much more butch than me. She was a prison officer called Sam, and I remember asking her lots of questions about the job. For sure, I reckon she could've beaten me in an arm-wrestle and I'd not say that about many ladies.

She looked like a Turkish powerlifter, with quite a bit of testosterone inside her to be honest. She could've probably pushed a mini over by herself and rolled it across a car park. We had a friendly enough chat, but there was to be no bed gymnastics. I certainly wouldn't want to get on the wrong side of her, for sure. She'd probably have picked me up above her head and tossed me across the room, like a caber.

After Sam, the next lady I met was called Pamela. Now most men have been familiar with a different Pam from a young age. But with this lady I'd moved from 'Pam of me hand' to the real Pam – this Pam was a very shapely woman, with a large bum and bust. She was younger than me and told me she had a young daughter too. She was naturally attractive and didn't need much make-up at all to look good.

We had a night out at her local quiz and had fun, trying not to come last. I enjoyed a pub quiz and particularly excelled at sport and geography. My general knowledge was quite good, but I couldn't stand those cheating bastards who used their mobile phones. I'd rather come last and not cheat. Well, I'd probably cheat just once not to come last. I certainly tried my best to impress Pam. Some men used pictures of their cock or their car to get some sex. I wanted to use my brain instead. I could tell by the look on her face that she was assessing me and my intellect. Every time I got an answer correct, I felt it was one step closer to her love tunnel. Step by step, I was progressing from general knowledge to carnal knowledge.

A couple of years earlier, me and Big Col used to take part in a quiz every week at our local pub. I was also a fan of the BBC quiz *Eggheads,* which had a cult following, and also *The Chase* presented by Bradley Walsh. I found the challenge of a quiz both stimulating and rewarding, if we avoided the wooden spoon.

In our local, there was one particular team that won every bloody week. They cheated or had some dudes as clever as the Eggheads themselves, who were renowned as probably the best quiz team in Britain. I'd have loved to have walked in the pub one week with Kevin from *Eggheads* and seen the look on their fucking faces. He has legendary status as a quiz player and has won the British, European and World Quiz Championships. Not only would we win the quiz, but we'd wipe that fucking smirk off their faces.

After a while, when Pamela went to the bar, I noticed she had an arse like Kim Kardashian. It was very big, but very shapely and I was quite fond of it. I played it cool that night and definitely wanted to see her again. We carried on messaging each other and went out a couple more times in the local area, which was enjoyable. After several dates she invited me to her house for a curry and a few drinks. As I had to drive to get there, I was hoping that this would imply I could stay over at hers. Her curry was really tasty, and we had a few drinks on her sofa, before progressing to the bedroom.

Things seemed to be going well as we kissed and caressed each other and then I took her sexy white panties off. Her bum was certainly sizeable and shapely, just as I'd imagined. I felt like giving it a good slap, but thankfully refrained. If I'm honest the sex was nothing special and nothing too extraordinary. It was though I was going through the motions again and copulating for the sake of it. Pam didn't seem too confident in bed and didn't ooze sex appeal. But she probably thought the same about me at the time. Maybe it was the chemistry that was missing. Maybe it was the smell of the curry and my fear that I'd let rip with a stinky one, whilst pumping away. In my experience, stuffing my face with curry was not very conducive to passionate sex soon after.

Despite the lack of excitement in the bedroom, I still wanted to see Pam again and tried to maintain the contact between us. She was still an attractive lady and we'd made a bond over a curry and a quiz. She knew I could name most capital cities in the world, was knowledgeable when it came to current affairs and that my expert subject was sport and cricket in particular. Again, she invited me to her home, and we ended up in bed, after some strained conversations. Again, it must be said, the lack of real passion between us was evident. Something was definitely missing. At the time, I couldn't put my finger on it, but my heart let me know things weren't right.

Not long after, Pam ditched me citing a lack of spark between us. I could understand what she meant - we were friends, but the sexual chemistry didn't grow between us. It was unfortunate, I guess, as I liked her as a genuine person. Nevertheless, I knew I'd have to resort back to the old Pam and continue my search online. By now, I was used to rejection and though it still hurt, Pam was right. There was something missing between us. I felt it would be a long time before I could truly give my heart to someone. Negative experiences were mounting up and though I appeared confident, my bravado was wearing thin. Of course, my feelings were hurt as I looked in the mirror and just saw failure. I was doomed to be single and lonely and the black dog wasn't far away.

Where did I go from here? It seemed I couldn't sustain a relationship or even find a proper girlfriend. I'd met a lovely, attractive lady and yet I didn't find her sexy or passionate. I began to question my own sanity and my low moods became more apparent. The more I was rejected, the more I sulked and became a moody bastard. I wanted to fall in love like people did in the movies. I wanted fulfilment and companionship too. It just seemed I was getting a few shags with women who didn't want much more. They certainly didn't want it with me anyway. Of course, lust was one thing, but not everything. Internet dating was meant to be all fun – but it was becoming almost addictive and causing me angst and hurt. Maybe I needed to relax more and take it all in my stride. Maybe it was just the state of my mind at the time. But I realised I had to pull myself together and remain positive to have any chance of meeting someone I cherished.

CHAPTER 20: THE DOG'S BOLLOCKS

Despite another knockback, I continued to talk to women online in the hope of success. I was becoming more adept at spotting who the timewasters were and who may be genuine. What I hadn't come across yet was any dirty talk by women – well, they may have made some rude jokes as part of the banter associated with the chat but nothing more. I'm sure I'd made plenty of jokes whilst chatting to see if they had a sense of humour, or not. If women took offence too easily, I reckoned they wouldn't have been able to put up with my childish humour at times, so stopped messaging. Take farting for example. Even though I was an adult, I still found it funny to a degree, whereas some ladies would've found it disgusting and disgraceful. I wanted to find that lady who'd maybe let one rip in bed and not be too embarrassed by it. If a sneaky trump escaped, I'd hope they'd laugh it off.

You get the point – I wanted to find someone with my sense of humour, or at least someone who could put up with it. The next lady I met was called Sharon and unlike the others she liked a bit of dirty talk. I was talking to her online and she told me what she'd want to do to me if we met up. This was all new to me at the time, as all the previous ladies had been different.

Sharon must have been feeling horny, or maybe this was simply her style. Part of me found it exciting, but part of me thought she was just full of hot air. She was a lady with a fuller figure, with large breasts and a big bum in the photographs – but she was curvy. She had long blonde hair, which looked bleached and wore bright red lipstick. I gave her a bit of dirty talk back but felt slightly awkward about it as my daughter was sat next to me. Only joking, but it just didn't come naturally to me.

Nevertheless, we had a connection online and it played on my mind about what she'd been saying to me. I did want to meet her, and I did want to find out if she was all talk and no action. Or rather, would she follow up on her dirty fantasies. That's if she wasn't a teaser and if I actually liked her. She lived on the coast, so I agreed to meet her half-way between where we lived. I had to get a train and remember sitting there, wondering what I was letting myself in for. Before I met a new lady, I always had some nerves and set off in anticipation of what may materialise. It was exciting too, but often there'd be an anticipation of disappointment or a feeling of inevitability that it was doomed to failure again.

I met Sharon in a pub, near the train station. My initial impression was that she actually looked like her pictures – which was often unusual for the women I'd met. She was quite large, but shapely and her magnificent boobs were on display. Well, not literally, but she had a low-cut top on and was certainly flaunting what she had. To my surprise, however, she didn't seem as confident as I'd assumed and was quite quiet in real life. She'd been the one initiating the dirty talk, but now she was the shy one. I guess it was easy to flirt online and maybe say stuff after a glass of wine or two. The reality could be very different. I'd like to think I was usually confident, but now and again, everyone had their quiet and shy moments.

We had a drink in the pub and the alcohol got to work again. She began to loosen up and have a laugh, which made me feel more comfortable too. We then headed to a few more bars and the booze flowed as usual. Towards the end of the night, we had a sloppy kiss and I expected to catch my last train back. I'd told her I had a dress-rehearsal for a musical I was in the next morning, so couldn't stay out too late. To my surprise, she suggested catching a train to hers and stopping the night. I really needed a good sleep to perform my role for the dress-rehearsal, but hey, I'd had some drinks now. I decided to accompany her on the train back home.

We got on the last train, which was to take longer than I thought. Everyone was well pissed on this train; it was bloody carnage. People were singing, some were struggling to stay awake and some could hardly stand up. I felt relatively sober compared to this lot. What a bunch of pissheads they were. A drunken couple were making out opposite us. I think he was slipping her the finger and she had her tongue down his throat. I half expected him to get his cock out, they were that tanked up. I looked at everyone and wondered where this fucking train was going to end up. I really felt like downing a few tequila shots, just to catch up with this ridiculous rabble as most of them looked like they were in a fucking zombie movie. You could say it was like being on the set of *Shaun of the Dead*.

After that journey I was ready for anything, then she said there was another fucking train to catch. I'd assumed there was only one, but we had to wait on a freezing cold platform for another. By this point, her tits were shrivelling up and looking half the size they once were. Her lipstick was smudged, and she was looking the worst for wear. I just wanted to get some sleep and was beginning to regret my journey into the abyss. Thankfully, the last train arrived, and we caught this one near to her house. At this time of night, I felt like I'd travelled to the other side of the country.

We finally got back to her house, which was a semi-detached down a quiet street. When she opened the door, a little scratty dog ran to her and began barking loudly at me. It was a funny looking creature compounded by the fact that it had some sort of skin disease and so patches of his hair were missing. She told me his exact condition, but I can't remember. What I do remember though, was that this little dog stunk as well, and she explained that was part of his illness. Basically, it was an unkempt scruffy dog, who smelt and had a serious skin disease. It began licking my hand as I sat down on the sofa.

Sharon offered me another drink. I was tempted to have a cup of tea but decided to have one more, after seeing this little smelly dog. Then, Sharon sat next to me and we began to kiss again. She went for my belt and I assisted her by removing my jeans rather quickly. To be frank, I was quick to get her baps out as I'd been staring at them all night. She'd wanted to flaunt them and now I had a chance to have a play. They were very nice, but as I licked her nipples the diseased dog jumped on the sofa and tried to join in. It kept licking my hand and generally annoying me – I mean the dog not Sharon.

Next, she pulled my boxer shorts down and exposed my erect manhood, ready for her use. She went down on me and it was rather good to be honest. I watched her bright red lips around my cock and then closed my eyes for a moment. This felt good, I thought, and it was amazing how she could also lick my balls at the same time. Suddenly, despite my intoxicated state, I realised that the sensation wasn't normal and wasn't right. I opened my eyes and that little bastard of a dog was having a lick of my balls and joining in with us. I yelped and pushed him away in some horror. I'd always wanted a threesome, but not like this. This was all wrong and that fucking smelly disease-ridden dog was all to blame. Sharon thought it was hilarious and began to laugh, but I didn't see the funny side at first. I kept saying, 'Oh my god, what's he done!' repeatedly. Then, I suggested we make our way to the bedroom away from this stinky thing. It looked like some strange alien with a body odour problem.

We went upstairs and thankfully the mutt remained downstairs. I removed Sharon's dress and panties and exposed her large arse. To be honest, the sex was alright – but nothing more. Her body shape didn't turn me on, like some others had in the past. It sounds a little cruel, I know, but I didn't feel the connection and it seemed as though I was doing it for the sake of it. I really hadn't wanted to go back in the first place, but almost felt compelled. The smell of the dog, the distant location and that bloody journey had all put me off in some way. Of course, she didn't live up to her dirty talk like I expected.

In the morning, we had a quickie at her instigation, which was no better really. Then, I made my excuses as I had to get two trains back home. On the way home, I knew I wouldn't be going back there again. She was sound enough as a person I guess, but sexually I wasn't turned on and she wasn't my type of person. During the rehearsal, I kept thinking about that bloody dog. I actually felt sorry for it. I was trying to remember my lines and it kept popping into my mind. Unfortunately, Sharon didn't enter my head much. We did communicate online and by text for a while, but I had to be blunt in the end and tell her my true feelings. I felt bad in a way, but I had to be honest and let her find someone else. She deserved that at least.

Once more, I'd had a night out that had culminated in a one-night stand to forget. Men had always told me in the past how great and exciting one-night stands could be. Around this time in my life, I was beginning to disagree with their sentiments. The actual thought of it was turning out to be much better than the reality. Maybe it was the women I was choosing. Maybe it was just me and not what I was really searching for. I guess I had to get it out of my system and play the field a little in order to find that special person. Ultimately, however, I knew deep down that these single nights of passion were not making me truly happy and not what I wanted. I wanted much more than that. I was looking for a deeper bond. I was searching for true love. Why on earth couldn't I find it?

CHAPTER 21: CANNIBAL CRAVINGS

Even though Chris Rea was my musical hero, I'd always liked Meatloaf's music and once sang *I'd Do Anything for Love, (But I won't Do That)* when doing karaoke. His song *Bat Out of Hell* was an absolute classic and we'd sung it countless times on nights out. Although I admired his music, I wouldn't say I fancied him. In fact, I knew I didn't fancy Meatloaf. Yet, I ended up seeing a woman who looked a bit like him. Why on earth would I meet her? Why would I bonk her? I really don't know – I should have remembered that song *I'd Do Anything for Love...*

Sometimes, you just did silly things that normally you wouldn't do. I met her on a night out after talking online for a while. Needless to say, she wasn't a looker and wasn't like the pictures I'd seen online. I discovered that people always found a way to post a couple of great photographs of themselves. I was more often than not disappointed, but equally some women were probably disappointed when they met me. But, at that stage in my life I must have been down on my luck and just went with it. She was a nice enough person and talked openly about her children when I met her, so I told her about my kids too. Her name was Marvin, I mean Marion.

On the night we met, we both got drunk though so I can't really remember everything that we discussed in detail. Maybe we talked about our favourite bands and the music of Meatloaf. Anyway, at the end of the night I invited her back to my house. Obviously, I was thinking with my knob at the time and she also had similar thoughts. Despite having a few one-night stands in the past and feeling empty afterwards, I obviously thought differently once intoxicated! Having said that, the sex itself was much better than with Sharon, who was far better looking. It was all rather weird actually. I simply didn't fancy her, but we had what proved to be a good night of passion. Maybe it was all down to how desperate I was at the time or my state of mind, but there was something about her that I liked. She was a lovely person on the whole and I invited her around again about a week later.

Marion came to mine and brought a couple of DVDs to watch if we wished. She looked more attractive the second time, but I knew I was using her for sex. Having said that, I'd made it clear that I wasn't after a relationship with her. So, I was honest and upfront before she came around. I didn't want to be cruel and lead her on, I didn't want to give her the wrong impression.

In some ways, I did feel bad. It was probably pure lust and the physical need to copulate. Then again, she also had physical needs and knew the score before she came. She was equally aware of the arrangement. It was friends with benefits. Was this what I was looking for? No, not really – I genuinely wanted to meet my ideal match and fall in love. But sometimes, beggars can't be choosers. I know it sounds wrong, but Marion knew the arrangement – or so I thought.

Without feeling any pressure to perform, or be amazing in bed, I think we both relaxed and enjoyed the physicality. I'd slept with some really attractive ladies, yet the sex hadn't been as good as with Marion. After the act, we had some food and watched some television. A programme came on about a cannibal killer in Germany. I don't know why we watched it, as it was quite sickly to be honest. It was a true-life documentary about the issues of consent and killing, and of course cannibalism.

Basically, the documentary was about a man called Armin Meiwes. He had used internet sites for cannibals, I think. I don't know the names of the sites, but I suspect it wasn't 'Cannibals R Us'. Unbelievably, he asked on the site if anyone wanted to volunteer to have their penis cut off and then be killed and eaten. I really wonder what he thought when he posted that question? Honestly, he must have thought it was a bit of a long shot. He must have assumed that nobody would reply, 'It's always been my fantasy to have my cock sliced off. You can cut my penis off and eat it, then eat me as well if you wish!'

Incredibly, another sick individual had that very fantasy and did want to be eaten. I really can't work out who was the most depraved out of the two. Anyway, the bloody programme showed a reconstruction of the whole event. He tried to cut his knob off, but at first the knife was too blunt. You'd have thought he'd have bought a fucking machete to make a proper job. Eventually, though, after trying a few attempts he cut it off and placed the victim in a cold bath. Meiwes then took the severed member, chopped it up, like a bloody chorizo, and fried it in a pan with some garlic and herbs. It really did put me off my hot-dog.

Apparently, he didn't eat it all, however, as the fried penis was over-seasoned. So, after all that effort he'd only eaten a tiny morsel of cock. Let's be honest, he'd have been no good doing the eating challenge in *I'm A Celebrity Get Me Out of Here* would he? Ant and Dec would've been disappointed with his efforts and his campmates would have been worried that he might eat them instead. Hopefully, the show has a thorough vetting process to rule out cannibals anyway.

I usually enjoyed watching those cooking programmes on television and in particular, *MasterChef.* Now, I'd envisaged Gregg Wallace giving Meiwes some feedback on his rare dish, 'Well, it's certainly different, we've never had this dish to taste before. The presentation could be better as your fried cock in garlic lacks some balls on the side. It's also too chewy and requires more salt. In fact, I'm not too impressed on the whole. You may struggle to get through to the next round with that dish, unless you do well in the invention challenge...'

You never know, he may have pulled it out the bag with his invention dish of roasted brains, served with liver and kidney chunks and a couple of fingers on the side. Anyway, the sick bastard then slit the throat of the victim who had consented to everything. He then chopped him up into pieces and hung him up, like a piece a meat at the butchers. Over the following days, he ate his flesh. He was only discovered when someone called at his house and smelt something rancid. Like I said, I really don't know why we watched this romantic programme together. I looked at her and she seemed a little uncomfortable. Maybe she thought I was a closet cannibal.

In fact, Meiwes tried to argue that he'd done nothing wrong as the victim had consented to be killed. This brought into question what people could lawfully consent to. Obviously, in England euthanasia is still unlawful, but the defence of consent is still allowed for various activities such as recognised games and sports, surgical interference and some harmful sexual activity. With regard to the latter, there had been cases when high risk sexual activity had caused injuries to eyes, when the victim had consented to a bag being placed over her head. In hindsight, I'm glad I didn't suggest a bag over the head with Valerie previously. People had also been burnt and hurt badly in bondage sessions. I knew all this stuff went on, but it really didn't appeal to me. I couldn't get turned on by someone using a cheese-grater on my gonads.

I'm sure Marion had wondered what I was going to suggest next. Maybe she wanted hot candle wax dripped all over her, but I'd just be happy to drip my hot bodily fluid over her. Then, out of nowhere she started questioning me about my feelings and how I really felt about her. Bearing in mind this was only our second date, I was taken aback by the direction our conversation was taking. She fired question after question at me. I thought I'd already made it clear that she wasn't really my 'type' of person, but it seemed now that, after all, she wanted far more than just friends with benefits. She wanted far more indeed and made it clear that just shagging in future was out of the question. She wanted to go out with me properly, to be my girlfriend.

I was in a quandary now, as I liked her as a person and didn't want to hurt her feelings. She said, 'What type of woman do you go for then?' looking into my eyes. I thought about it for a few seconds and then replied, 'Looks and body usually.' She knew by my response, that I was rejecting her. Not only that, I'd rejected her on the grounds that she was fucking ugly and a bit fat. I honestly didn't mean it to come out like that at all. She was putting me under pressure, and I didn't choose my words wisely.

Despite watching *Shallow Hal* and learning lessons, I was still being bloody shallow. By this point, the dating game was turning into a series of short-term sexual liaisons and I was beginning to turn into some of the men I'd been told about by my dates. I was becoming a knob and it wasn't something I was proud of. I liked her as a person, but yet I was treating her shabbily. In my mind, however, I was just being brutally honest and candid. I didn't want to hurt her feelings at all. The whole episode had been a misunderstanding, rather than a mutual feeling between us.

I thought she was a nice person, but just didn't fancy her like I should've done. Another female friend had once told me about an occasion when she started falling for a so-called fuck buddy and started developing feelings. She made the fatal mistake of telling him her feelings. That was what women often did I guess, but men could sometimes be more clinical with their feelings and just enjoy the sex, nothing more. My friend realised that she was sending out the wrong message and their liaisons came to a rather abrupt end. This situation with Marion was replicating that very episode. Looking back, I reckon that a friend with benefits arrangement can only last a certain time, before one party develops stronger more intense feelings.

Sometimes men just wanted a 'no strings attached' relationship. I was now, however, beginning to doubt the fuck buddy thing altogether and did actually want something more. I had to try harder to find a proper girlfriend, someone who I actually wanted to spend time with and do other things with, rather than watch documentaries about sick cannibals. I'd found some lovely ladies, but I just didn't fancy them. I wanted to find that 'spark' that people talked about. At this point, I thought about playing some Meatloaf and considered the song I should play. Of course, it had to be *I'd Do Anything for Love (But I Won't do That)*.

CHAPTER 22: SALAD DAYS

I sat in the town centre bar and nervously waited for my next date. She walked in, smiling and looking happy and gave me a hug. This was a positive start as I liked ladies who smiled a lot, even though I was a grumpy bastard at times. Her demeanour was very likeable, as was her toned and trim body. Her name was Lucy and she had long dark hair, with dark features. When I saw her, I wouldn't say I was 'head over heels' about her, but she was really nice, and we seemed to click rather more than most of my previous dates. It was all very encouraging as the conversation flowed easily.

At the end of the night, we hugged, and she gave me a peck on the cheek. I'd had a few pints, but she was driving so had stayed sober. I walked home with a smile on my face and was hopeful that things may progress. I reckoned that she liked me, by her body language and the fact that she told me she'd had a lovely evening. Having said that, I wasn't always the best at reading signals and some ladies were like poker players on a first date. A couple of times in the past, I'd been convinced that they'd liked me, but I got the dreaded text – I wasn't their type, or there hadn't been that spark they were after. It really was a lottery at times. I just needed my numbers to come up, or at least get three or four out of six. The bonus ball probably equated to getting my end away.

I texted Lucy quite a few times over the next week and we also had a couple of chats on the phone. It was, as they say, good to talk and we seemed to gel. Well, what I mean is she laughed at my shit jokes, which proved that she liked me for sure. We agreed to meet in the same bar in town the following weekend. When I saw her this time, she was more dolled up than previously and had a tight-fitting dress on. Wow, she looked hot and as we chatted, I could feel my whole body getting slightly flustered and a little horny.

We ended up staying in the same place all night. We didn't move seats or go to another pub, which looking back seems strange. But then again, it probably signalled the fact that we were getting on really well and didn't need to go anywhere else. This time Lucy was drinking and so she was even more chatty. As she lived a fair distance away, she told me she'd booked into a local hotel for the night, so she could have a few drinks. That was a great signal to be honest. It meant that she'd gone to a lot of effort to see me and be with me. As the night progressed, I was in two minds whether to ask her back to mine. I didn't want to ruin anything, and she appeared to be a classier lady than some of the others I'd met.

Towards the end of the evening, she talked about going to her hotel but didn't invite me. As the hotel was probably further away than my house, I then interjected and said she could stay at mine if it was easier for her. I never put any pressure on her at all, but just mentioned it. In fact, I was surprised that she agreed to come back with me immediately. To be honest, I was gagging to rip her sexy dress clean off and get her in between the sheets. Although, I reckoned I had to be a little more romantic than that. Maybe, I'd offer her a glass of wine first, then rip it off.

When we got back, I didn't ask if she wanted a frozen pizza. I didn't ask if she wanted another drink. I didn't buy her a bunch of flowers on the way home either. I just wanted to get down to business, hoping she felt the same. Thankfully, she did feel the same. We kissed passionately on the sofa and she made it clear that she wanted more by saying, 'I really want you...'. This was just what I wanted to hear, and I replied, 'I really want you too!'. This was fantastic and my heart pumped hard, as I removed her sexy dress.

As I removed that dress, she grabbed at my belt too and tried to get my jeans off. I was ready to go by now and felt like satisfying her there and then. But first, I had to remove her sexy matching red underwear. I struggled a little with her bra strap in all honesty. Time and again, I couldn't take these bastard bras off in one motion like they did in the movies – obviously they must use some magic camera trickery. It was all rather fiddly and took about five minutes but was worth it in the end when her lovely breasts fell out. Then, I removed her panties and wasn't disappointed with what I saw in front of me, as she certainly knew how to look after her delightful lady garden. She also had a lovely toned body, but unfortunately the wheels fell off when I discovered that she was a fucking vegetarian.

Not long after, I didn't mind she was a vegetarian when I was giving her my very own sausage to eat. The sex was great, and I gave it my best shot from several positions before nearly collapsing, with sweat pouring from my brow. It'd been a serious work-out and probably the best I'd had for some time. I sat there all content and she seemed satisfied too. I obviously expected her to stay over after our marathon session, but she wanted to go to her hotel for some reason. All I did know, was that I'd met someone who I wanted to see again and hopefully she felt the same. Things were definitely looking more positive.

Soon after, Lucy came to see me in a musical with one of her friends, which was a nice touch that I appreciated. I was only an average singer and part of the chorus, but I had some lines to say and tried to make people laugh. It seemed to go well, and she even bumped into my parents who had come to watch too. Over the next few weeks, we saw each other more and more and she stayed over at mine a fair bit. One thing that surprised me was that she still lived at home with her parents, despite being in her early thirties. Nevertheless, she had a decent job and was totally independent otherwise. It did mean, however, that I couldn't stay at hers at all – it always had to be mine.

It was great to have Lucy stay over on a regular basis, although meals could be problematic at times. As I said, she was a vegetarian, and this made things a little awkward as I loved all meat. I often craved a juicy steak, pork chops, bacon butties, roast beef or chicken dinners or even barbeque spareribs or duck pancakes. I was also a fan of a burgers and kebabs – but she couldn't eat any of it.

I tried my best to be accommodating when I made meals, and even tried some popular vegetarian dishes, such as salad. I also made more vegetable dishes such as vegetable curry and a curry with vegetables in it. I even tried that meat substitute stuff, which didn't taste much like real meat to me. And of course, salad and more fucking salad, typically with some feta on top.

I'm not saying it was a major problem, but I tried my best to break her ways and tempt her with a bacon butty. The only thing she liked though was my own special sausage. Her pet name for me was 'big boy' which implied she either thought I had a big knob or was a bit tubby. Maybe it was the latter, but hopefully she reckoned my manhood was big too. Fortunately, she also had extremely small hands – which made my tackle seem much bigger. In addition, she was the kind of lady who'd only require an extra small tampon if they were sold in different sizes, if you know what I mean. Because of this, Lucy introduced me to the wonderful world of lubricants for our sex play. I'd never really considered these before, but she said they helped in the bedroom and I didn't disagree. In all honesty, my normal lubricant had been a good handful of spit – but maybe she was too classy for that. As long as I didn't have chafing, I was happy to use anything to increase the pleasure. Nevertheless, despite having access to plenty of lube, she still wouldn't give up her chocolate hole easily. There was more chance of the UK winning the Eurovision Song Contest than me winning that argument.

I still hadn't introduced my children to any woman I'd dated – but with Lucy I became tempted as time progressed. Of course, I spoke about her and they knew I now had a proper girlfriend at last. They seemed happy about this, but I was still reluctant to introduce her just yet. My kids were still pleading with me to get a cat around this time, simply because my cat flap still existed. They said the flap wasn't utilised and if I got a cat, the flap would be used regularly.

The only flaps I knew about were on the women I'd slept with. They were all varying sizes and shapes – probably a bit like cat flaps, I guess. The kids said if I got a cat, they'd play with it and look after it. That was complete bollocks, of course. I knew I'd be the one to look after it and pick its poo up if I got one. But the pressure they put me under had some impact on my mind and I was seriously thinking about trying to make them happy.

Anyway, Lucy took me to see some cats at a local cat sanctuary. I walked in and saw all these puny scruffy cats looking at me with their sad eyes. They were almost pleading with me to pick them and take them home. However, the more I looked around, the more I felt bad and the more I realised that a cat was for life. Did I really want an animal to look after for that long? Did I want that responsibility? I reasoned it would be stupid to choose one just because my kids had pestered me. They'd pestered me about lots of things in the past, but I hadn't conceded.

Jeez, I hadn't even let them have wi-fi access at times as I'd turned it off, much to their angst and consternation. They told me that not having access to a digital device was almost child cruelty and they would rather go without food and drink. It was simply incredible how much youngsters relied on their phones and devices. Nevertheless, they'd have to forget the fucking cat. There was to be no pussy.

CHAPTER 23: PISSING IN THE WHITBY WIND

After a few months of seeing each other, we decided to book a few nights away. Lucy fancied the East coast and so we looked at possibilities in the region. I suggested the small seaside town of Whitby in Yorkshire. I'd been to Whitby once before, whilst in the Sixth Form doing my 'A' Levels. I'd studied Geography, so we went to the area to study rock samples near Robin Hood's Bay and research the coastline, as a sort of field trip. Whilst there we stayed at the well-known youth hostel at the top of the formidable 199 steps, made famous by being referred to in the novel *Dracula* by Bram Stoker. At the top of the steps was the ancient Whitby Abbey too, which many visitors walked up the steps to see. It really was a lovely spot, with fantastic views.

As most of us were 17 at the time, our teacher Dr Richards, had made it plain that there had to be no drinking on the trip. Well, this was the worst thing he could have said. We respected him on the whole, as he was generally a decent bloke, not like one of those teachers who spent all day yelling at the students. After our busy day walking the beautiful coastline, he allowed us a few hours free time before our curfew began. We went into the town and found some lovely pubs, down the narrow-cobbled streets. We really didn't know if we'd get served, but I guess they were happy to get some punters in, so we didn't get thrown out as soon as we walked in. Amazingly, we all got served too.

Well, we were young lads who'd only just started drinking alcohol. After literally two or three pints of beer, most of us were well gone. I remember a couple of lads being sick down the narrow alley and the vomit rolling down the street, as onlookers tutted in disgust. I left the pub, and everything looked blurred to me. I looked at the boats in the harbour and they were rocking about on the water, making me even more dizzy. Then I remembered we had to walk back to the youth hostel, up those fucking 199 steps.

I guess it was a rite of passage that lads around this age engaged in this sort of behaviour. The first time I got drunk was at the age of sixteen at my Grandad's 65th birthday party. My uncle had given me a few cans to drink and despite not enjoying the taste of lager, I vowed to drink four or five. It felt quite good until I slumped in the chair back home in the lounge. About an hour or two later, I suddenly awoke with a pool of vomit in my mouth and throat. I was choking but did my best to hold it in, as I made a dash for the kitchen sink. I grabbed at the door handle of the lounge and for some unfathomable reason it came off completely in my hand. So, I was now holding a pool of sick in my mouth and was stuck in the bloody room.

I was using all my might to dig my nails in the wooden door in order to open it. I banged on the door too, hoping my mum would come to the rescue. By now, I was fighting a losing battle. I couldn't hold on much longer. Then, as my mum opened the door, I couldn't contain myself anymore. I let rip to empty the vile vomit from my throat all over our pet Cocker Spaniel who'd decided to jump up at me. My mum didn't know whether to laugh or cry. I made it to the sink but left a trail of sick across the kitchen floor too. I felt really bad about the whole episode and took our dog out for endless walks after that, in order to rehabilitate myself.

The walk back from Whitby to our hostel was also just a blur to me. As we walked up those steps, most lads tried to count them one by one. Except, we couldn't actually count by this point and kept repeating the same numbers. When we were near the top, we were still on step 44! However, the walk did allow us to sober up a little, before encountering our teachers. We'd tried to suck some mints and share chewing gum on the way back, but I had a feeling that a few mints wouldn't hide the fact that we were still pissed.

As we entered the youth hostel most of the girls gave us a dirty look and Dr Richards looked at his watch. We were only about an hour late, that's all. Of course, he'd been concerned about our wellbeing as he was responsible for us, which was understandable. We apologised and said we'd got lost, although it was quite a small place and we stunk of booze.

He knew we'd been to the pub, I'm sure. He told us to go to the dormitory and get to sleep, which clearly wasn't going to happen.

We talked for a long time and had a few laughs, obviously a lot louder than we thought. Dr Richards was in the dormitory next to us and after a while, he came in and let fly. He gave us a volley of abuse and told us we'd let him down. To be fair, he had a point, but I'd never seen him like this. He was almost incandescent with pure rage and most of the lads sunk their heads under their duvet in fear. He said he didn't want to hear another word and that we'd better get to sleep soon.

Then, when he left the room it fell silent, apart from a few whispers saying we'd better keep quiet. About an hour later, I was absolutely dying for a piss. Everyone was now asleep and there was silence, apart from a drunken snore every now and then. It suddenly dawned on me that I couldn't use the toilet though, as to get there I'd have to walk through Dr Richards' dormitory and probably wake him up. Oh shit, what was I going to do? I couldn't risk waking him up, he'd probably kill me. Thankfully, I saw a tall window that I may be able to get to. I reasoned that it was the only possible option.

I found a wooden chair in the corner and stood on it to try and reach the window. It was still a struggle, but I managed to pull myself up on the window ledge, which was a considerable height. I forced the window open and knelt on the ledge, with a colossal drop below. I held on tight as I moved my crotch towards the open window and emptied my bladder with a gentle sigh. It felt so good to finally get rid of it and I felt that I'd achieved my goal. I stepped down gently on the chair and went to get back in bed, when I heard a voice pipe up, 'Did you piss out the window?'

It transpired that all the other lads were in the same predicament and needed to empty their bladders urgently. Jonny went next and then it was Graham. Just to make them feel more at ease, I told them to hold on tight as there was a mammoth drop down below. Unfortunately, as Graham tried to get up on the ledge, he sent the wooden chair flying making a loud crash on the floorboards. Everyone turned and looked at him, but at least he was hanging on for dear life and hadn't fallen out the window. Just as he started urinating out of the window, the big light went on. For

Fuck's sake, it was the Doc. He was apoplectic, snarling, 'What the hell is going on here?'

Graham nearly fell out of the window in fright but had to carry on pissing. I mean nobody can stop mid-flow after a session on the pop, can they? I just pulled the covers over my head and tried to drown out the shouting. Dr Richards couldn't believe we'd risked our lives just to have a piss. 'Why didn't you use the bloody toilet like everyone else would've done?' he asked. Then some brave soul piped up, 'Because we didn't want to wake you up sir,' nervously. He then paused and said, 'But you fools have woken me up twice now. You lot aren't allowed out tomorrow night. Get to sleep now and don't make me come back in here or we're going home tomorrow.'

I recalled that story to Lucy, as we booked a few nights at a Bed and Breakfast in the town. The journey was fine, but parking became more problematic, as in most towns. Eventually, we found somewhere to park and walked the extra mile to our digs, lugging a suitcase. Luckily, it wasn't at the top of the 199 steps this time, but I vowed we'd have to walk up them so I could reminisce. When we got to the old-fashioned terrace, it reminded me of that place Del Boy and Rodney had stayed in an episode of *Only Fools and Horses* called *The Jolly Boys' Outing.* Yes, it was like the *Villa Bella* where an old scary lady had greeted the Trotters in Margate.

In much the same way, an old couple greeted us and welcomed us to their haunted house. Well, they never said it was haunted, but it felt a bit spooky. It was like going back in time. I brushed past the cobwebs and we got to our room. It was quite small, but to be fair it was clean inside and there was a tiny en suite. I was looking forward to our mini break for sure. We dumped our stuff in the room and, not wanting to waste any time, went out to see the sights on offer.

You can't go to Whitby and not have fish and chips – it's a must. There were just so many chip shops and the queues were vast in many of them. It was all fresh fish, caught in the North Sea according to the billboards. We found a nice little place on the seafront and devoured cod and chips. It was one of the best I'd tasted for sure and from what I remember Lucy had the fish too. This made her a part-time vegetarian I think, or maybe a pescatarian. Anyway, I thought it was odd that she wouldn't eat meat but would eat fish. Why did she think it was okay for a fish to die for her meal, but not a pig? I still couldn't tempt her with a pork pie though.

As we walked around the town, there were kippers hanging up and others being smoked. The smell of fish was all around, and it was a fish-lovers paradise. I told Lucy that I wanted to visit the Abbey and walk up the 199 steps. We made our way up the steps and counted one by one, like most people. This time, I wasn't drunk and enjoyed the lovely walk and great views. From what I remember, the very window that I'd pissed out of all those years ago was still there. However, the building was no longer being used as a youth hostel like in the past. It certainly brought memories back though of our geography field trip and our stay there all those years before.

Me and Lucy then saw the whalebone arch and had a drink in a few of the old-fashioned pubs. We went on the beach, had a cliff-top walk and visited some mansion house on the last day. On the whole, it was an enjoyable break away which brought us even closer together in many ways. She was a real lady and very sweet too. Things were certainly looking more promising for once. Maybe this was it, maybe Lucy was destined to be mine.

CHAPTER 24: RED SPOT

Having had a pleasant time in Whitby, me and Lucy saw more of each other and things were going great. She was very lady like and tried her best to laugh at my attempts at humour. However, the more I saw of her and the more serious we became, the greater the doubts began in my mind. I don't know why, but I began to look at her faults and began to wonder whether I actually fancied her enough for a long-term relationship. I mean a relationship that could progress further into something more meaningful. Maybe the fact that we were getting more serious put more pressure on me and my views changed. Maybe I still wasn't ready to commit to someone, say, to live with them. I can't fully explain why I had doubts, but I did. It was a feeling inside my heart, I guess.

One night, after we'd been together about six months, we went to my local pub for a few drinks. We were sat in our usual spot and after a couple of drinks, she mentioned she'd like to have children. She wanted to start a family and had always dreamed about kids, that sort of thing. Well, I was taken aback because I thought I'd told her early on that I'd had the snip and didn't want any more kids. Three was enough for anyone in my eyes. I told her how I felt, and she looked a little crestfallen. I didn't mean to upset her, but I had to be completely honest. I noticed that she was a bit tearful and I really did feel bad at the time. Here was a lovely, honest women with a likeable personality and I'd just upset her by being truthful.

Around a week later, we were sat on my sofa when I had to have an extremely difficult conversation. I'd been thinking about what she'd said, and my views simply hadn't changed. I didn't want any more kids and I'd decided that it had to be the end. I told her that I didn't want to stop her meeting someone else, to prevent her having a family of her own. She was so nice she deserved that chance. I couldn't give it to her.

It had to be the end between us and as I told her my voice was creaking, I was shaking slightly, and my heart was racing. It was so difficult, but I had to do it in person. I couldn't just fire off a text, like some people did. She deserved a proper explanation. To be fair to Lucy, she was very upset at the time, but she still understood what I was saying. I was upset too and the week after at work was so difficult, as I kept wondering whether I'd made a big mistake. My heart was racing for a few days and I had a terrible feeling inside my body. I'd been searching for love and now I'd pushed it away. It was almost as though I was pushing a self-destruct button and hurting myself. But part of me knew it was also the correct thing to do for our long-term future.

Lucy was undoubtedly the one I'd developed the greatest feelings for so far. Now, I'd ended it and I felt like shit. For a few weeks I really missed her too and my head was all over the place. I was hurting, and she probably was too. Would I really find anyone as remotely nice as her? She was such a lovely person and I'd let her go. Once I'd started seeing Lucy, I'd not been on any of the dating sites at all. Now, after ending our relationship I didn't start using them for a few weeks. I needed to stay single a while and try to enjoy my own company. I tried to have a few nights out with Mart, Big Col or the cricket lads just to let off some steam. I wasn't interested in meeting anyone for a while, so vowed to have a break from the dating game for a few weeks.

As time progressed, I began to get an urge to see what was out there so logged back into the dating sites and all those lovely desperate faces appeared in front of me again. Maybe I could meet someone, I thought, as I scrolled through all the attractive ladies once more. I hadn't been online for a while, but now I was ready to play the game again. I fired off a few messages hoping for a response or two. I thought about changing my profile or updating it but when I read it, I couldn't really add to it that much so left the same photographs and write-up. It'd been partially successful so far anyway.

Shortly after, I received a message from an older lady called Lolita, who looked fairly hot in her pictures. She had long brown hair, a nice tanned skin and had long legs that went all the way up to her thighs, funnily enough. During our conversations she'd told me that her husband was over in Iraq or Afghanistan somewhere, as part of the army. I didn't like the fact that she was married but she told me unequivocally that their relationship was dead, and they were getting a divorce. To be fair, many women online were still legally married or going through a separation of some sort. I guess I had to trust her and hope that she wasn't doing the dirty on him.

I mentioned this situation to Mart, Dainty Dan and Ash over our lunchtime coffee one day. For a start, they reckoned she was playing dirty. Secondly, they reckoned that her husband was an elite sniper like Rambo who'd take me out when he got back to the UK. They both told me to keep eyes open for a 'red spot' just in case. They thought it was hilarious that I'd be assassinated by a sniper in the near future. I must admit, they put some doubts in my mind. He may not have shot me but could've found out and just stabbed me instead with his army dagger.

Anyway, by this point I'd not done anything other than talk to Lolita. She was adamant that their relationship was over, but I pondered what my friends had said. When it came down to it, my personal safety took a back seat to my knob. I'd not had sex for a while and was beginning to miss the feeling. I agreed to meet her despite any reservations I'd had. I told Mart and Ash that I'd look out for a 'red spot' but was confident Rambo wouldn't shoot me. I told them that if I was killed, they'd know who the culprit was.

I met Lolita in a local bar, and she was fairly attractive for her age. She said she was 42, I think, but didn't look any older than 45 so maybe this lady was telling the truth. She had a few wrinkles on her forehead, but apart from that she was tidy and well presented. During the evening, she told me that she possessed fake boobs too. Well, I mean she probably didn't use the term 'fake' but rather 'implants' instead. I'd never seen a fake pair before, but I obviously alluded to the fact that it would be nice to squeeze them. I think I asked about a hundred questions about them. At least it gave us something to talk about, although she probably got a bit fed up with it. I hoped that she didn't have a fake pussy too.

Despite all the questions about her boobs, Lolita wanted to come back to mine at the end of the night. I'd not seen a 'red spot' all night and I was looking forward to a play with her silicone. When I finally removed her bra, they were something of a disappointment. I'm sure they weren't even symmetrical, as one seemed to sag a bit more on careful inspection. Maybe she'd got them done on the cheap in Iraq when she visited her husband. When I finally squeezed them, they were quite solid and dense. It was a bit like squeezing a firm orange. I don't think she appreciated me analysing them, like I was going to give her marks out of ten. I much preferred the natural version myself. But hey, if they made her happy, it was her choice. Maybe she needed a divorce to pay for all the other work she wanted doing.

After fondling them for ages, it was time to get down to business. Lucy always had some lube to assist us, but Lolita needed no such thing. Let's just say she was already waiting for me, so much so that it slipped in like a really slippery thing. She was so wet I was worried about my bed sheets. I'd only washed them a couple of months earlier and didn't want to wash them again for a while.

From what I remember, that night I kept pumping and pumping and pumping, but it just didn't happen for some reason. Try as I might, the climax just didn't arrive for me. It wasn't as if she was ugly or anything. Maybe I had her husband in the back of mind, or maybe I was worried he'd chase me down and assassinate me. In fairness, it was probably the amount of booze I'd supped that night. She was probably a bit disappointed, but we had to give up in the end.

I didn't know whether I'd see Lolita again after that night. However, we stayed in touch and she came around about a week later. This time, she came after work and we were both sober. She looked very smart in her business suit and ponytail. She had a brew and then I was going to suggest moving to the bedroom. Yet, for some reason I was now very nervous. I didn't feel that comfortable even though it was my bloody house. Did I really need booze to shag her? It seemed that way, though she looked even nicer in her work clothes.

Eventually, and rather bluntly, she instigated the deed instead. She just blurted out, 'Shall we go upstairs to bed then?' blowing me a kiss. I didn't feel ready to perform at all, but I simply couldn't turn her down. We went up to the bedroom and she seemed keen to give me a blow job, without me even asking or pleading. I nearly released there and then over her fake boobs, but I gave them another squeeze and tried to think about oranges instead.

Last time with Lolita, I simply couldn't eject, but now it was over just all too quickly. I just didn't have my usual self-control for some reason. Of course, I was sober, but I could sense she was rather disappointed by my efforts. She was probably expecting another marathon session. Instead, it was more like the sixty metres sprint. I'd tried my best, but this time I'd failed. I simply couldn't compete with an elite soldier like Rambo. That was the last time I saw her. Maybe Rambo had her knocked off or, more likely, she simply moved on to her next target. At least she didn't leave any red spots around my genitals as a parting gift.

CHAPTER 25: A HAIRY TALE

One night, I was introduced to a woman in a bar, by a mutual friend. She was, to put it bluntly, rather obese. As a younger guy, I'd tended to fancy the slim and athletic type. As I got older, I'd found myself attracted to more curvy ladies with a bit of shape. To be fair, I liked most women and most body types appealed to me. But I wasn't a feeder that's for sure and Alice was bigger than the 'curvy' that I liked.

That night though, I found myself spending large amounts of time talking to her. She had long dark hair and a great sense of humour. Nevertheless, she still had a body like a darts player, and I wasn't really attracted to her. I knew some men loved really big ladies – but I wasn't one of them. Each to their own, though, I reckoned. There really is someone for everyone out there, I'm convinced. Even if someone fancied a large bedridden lady and wanted to feed them pizzas all day, that was their prerogative.

I'm not saying Alice was one of those women – far from it. But I reckoned she'd struggle to run the 100 metre hurdles in less than a minute. The hurdle I was considering this particular night, was whether I would bonk her given the choice? It appeared that she seemed desperate to talk to me, in fact, she just seemed desperate. The thing is, she actually seemed a really nice person and I thought she was funny. I actually found myself warming to her, in fact I'd say we really hit it off.

At the end of the night, after copious amounts of beer and therefore my willy starting to do all the thinking, it all boiled down to one thing – did I fancy some sex? As the drinks flowed, she kept grabbing hold of me and we even had a cheeky kiss at one point. I was in two minds as to which direction to walk as we left the last bar, accompanied or on my own, but given that I was human and of the male variety I couldn't say no. I'd heard that saying that very big ladies were like mopeds – everyone wanted to ride them, but generally not be seen or known for doing so. On the night in question I invited her back with me, and she was in the taxi before I'd finished my sentence. I put my arm around her, and that seemed to be her cue to try to kiss me again and so dived straight in, slipping her tongue in my unexpecting mouth. I'd not envisaged this at the start of the night, but sometimes they could end up the best.

When we got back to mine, I refrained from asking if she fancied a pizza. I didn't want to sober up too much and wanted to get on with it, so to speak. I tried to take off her dress, which I managed with her help. Having removed her tights too, it became obvious how big she was with her belly hanging down far enough to make her belly button disappear. In fact, her fanny was nowhere to be seen either. What the hell? My knob took a definite decline at this point and became totally flaccid.

I hadn't seen a lady this large before and it certainly wasn't turning me on. I then began to worry that I wouldn't be able to get an erection. I'd never struggled before, but there was a first time for everything. I knew some fellas suffered from erectile dysfunction, but I'd been lucky enough to always be able to perform my duties. This was now a challenge I had to overcome, if I wanted to stand hard and tall. I didn't possess any blue pills so I couldn't cheat in this respect. Everything had to be au naturel as they say.

However, with her pussy hidden and my knob shrivelling up further by the second, this wasn't going well. I nearly suggested just putting a pizza in the oven instead and just giving up. It may have been the better option at the time. Instead, I tried to find her clitoris. The problem was, it was like trying to find a lost coin in a farmer's field full of sheep. What I didn't want to do, however, was go down on her. For a start, she'd had those tights on so there may have been the female equivalent of 'Betty Swollocks', shall we say. I tried manual stimulation in the hope that some miracle would occur.

This was becoming an embarrassing situation, for both of us. I simply couldn't get hard and she probably felt bad about it. I tried to put a condom on but failed miserably. I then suggested that we go upstairs to bed and try again in a different position. She laid down on the bed sideways and stuck her voluptuous backside out. This had more of the desired effect, and I was able to find wood at last. I managed to perform, but it felt more like one of those *Tough Mudder* challenges, rather than an enjoyable experience. In fact, I'd have probably preferred to wade around in mud for an afternoon, at least you got a free cider at the finish line! I was a little deflated and realised I'd made a mistake in inviting her back.

I didn't think things could get much worse. Then, for some bizarre reason, she pulled her hair out. I was gobsmacked as her thick head of long hair disappeared in front of my eyes. Alice had been wearing bloody hair extensions and had ripped them out! Now, she had short hair, not a look I really went for in a woman. I wouldn't say she was bald, but it was fairly short to say the least. For fuck's sake, this whole evening had been a fucking disaster. I didn't know what to say or what to do. I'd never seen anyone do this before and it changed her looks completely. So, I turned over, looked the other way and closed my eyes.

In the morning, I didn't even contemplate a quickie. The only quick thing I wanted was for Alice to leave. I looked at her and wondered what the hell I'd done. I guess most of us had been there at some point. Most of us had regretted a night of passion at some time. To be fair, it didn't change the fact that she was a nice person and she made her excuses and left. We both knew at that moment that everything had been a big mistake. What was I doing?

I'd spent the evening having a lovely time with a woman who, though I didn't fancy her, was great company. At the end of the night, I could've just given her a quick kiss on the cheek, thanked her for a lovely evening gently letting her know that the spark just wasn't there for me but instead I'd typically let my other 'brain' do the thinking and most likely given us both a night that we wanted to forget. When would I stop being a complete knob?

A while after my experience with Lolita, I was still a little concerned that a 'red spot' would appear on my forehead and that would be the end for me. Nevertheless, I continued to search for my ideal partner and was determined not to give up. I began talking to a lady named Carly, who told me she was half-Indian. She had a nice tanned skin and a decent body, though she was quite short and a tad dumpy. Her hair was dark, and shoulder-length and she possessed a nice smile with a good set of teeth. In fact, she seemed to be my type in many ways. In a way, it was nice to go out and meet different types of women as I found most of them attractive. I didn't go for clones or a certain look all the time, like some men. I found it refreshing and a tad exciting to meet up with ladies from different races, different hair colours and different body shapes. I tried not to be judgmental, but I guess sometimes I didn't have much choice who I could meet. Of course, I was still being rejected at times and it was a shame when a woman I truly fancied rebuffed my messages.

Anyway, I met Carly in a countryside public house, and we had a friendly chat about current affairs and other important issues, such as the price of bread. I sort of fancied her, even though she told me she had a few tattoos on her back. About a week later, we met again and did something similar. Again, we discussed what horrible shit was going on in the world and then how the price of milk had gone up due to inflation. Jeez, these were tough times. Okay, the conversation was somewhat strained at times, but Carly was pleasant enough and we had a little chemistry. There was something intriguing about her for sure.

We continued to text and spoke on the phone a couple of times, so I suggested she could come to mine for some food or a brew. Carly agreed to visit, but she lived a fair way from me so had to drive. That meant, of course, that we couldn't drink and in all probability that meant that we were unlikely to move things to the bedroom. Sometimes, I needed alcohol to relax me and give me some extra confidence. But then I realised that I wasn't driving at all, so I had a couple of ciders before she visited.

When Carly arrived, I offered her a cup of tea or a stiffer alternative. I mean a stiffer drink, of course. Surprisingly, she plumped for a bottle of cider, so I had another bottle too. We got chatting again, but thankfully this time the price of bread or milk wasn't mentioned. After a while, I jokingly asked if she'd show me her tattoo. She seemed quite pleased I'd remembered her tattoo and was equally pleased to lift up her top and show me her back. She asked if I wouldn't mind giving her back a quick rub and, of course, I obliged. She said it was nice, because she felt a bit stiff. I may have mentioned that I felt a bit stiff too.

This show of intimacy extended further when we kissed on the sofa. I really hadn't anticipated anything happening, but things were progressing nicely. Then, as her back was a little sore, I suggested a full body massage upstairs. She accepted the invitation willingly and we made our way to the bed. In a flash, she whipped off her clothes, apart from her knickers and laid on her front. I certainly liked her slightly dark skin and the tattoos weren't too bad either. I rubbed her back for a while and tried to be erotic, by digging my thumbs into her pressure points. She was groaning already, and I hadn't even got my cock out.

Then, with some trepidation, I began to remove her knickers. Thankfully, she arched her hips to allow me to remove them and expose her rather cute arse. I massaged and kissed her bum for a while but noticed a dark mass of hair between her legs. I then suggested she turned over. She slowly turned over and my eyes popped out in total disbelief. She simply had the hairiest bush I'd ever seen. Now, I'd seen old-style 80's porn movies full of hairy bushes. But they had nothing on this. Most women had started removing all pubes or leaving a well-pruned lady garden down there, but not Carly. This was natural, all natural. She was one hairy lady and proud of it!

I considered whether to go down on her and continue our extended foreplay. I thought, why the hell not, but it was a big mistake to say the least. I ventured into the abyss and fought my way through the jungle. It was the equivalent of working your way through the Amazon rainforest with a blunt kitchen knife. I felt like an explorer in Jules Verne's novel *Journey to The Centre of The Earth*. Hair after hair got stuck in my mouth as I fought my way to her clit. Then, just when I thought things couldn't get worse, I saw some toilet tissue embedded in her folds. It was all there waiting for me to lick and swallow. I now had a combination of pubes and bog roll to contend with in my mouth. This was making my erection vanish very quickly indeed, but I endeavoured to persist, just like an explorer would.

From finding Carly a sexy woman during the massage, everything had changed. Now, all I could see was an enormous hairy bush and not much else. She moaned and groaned as I tried my best to satisfy her, but occasionally she saw me spitting a hair out of my mouth. I could swallow the bog roll, but not the hairs. I couldn't even eat an ice-cream with a hair on top. Her pussy didn't taste like ice-cream either. It was more like an old tin of tuna.

After that, I tried my best to carry on and enjoy it. However, the copulation was only satisfactory and no more than that. I know it sounds rather cruel, but the shock of the bush had put me off somewhat, even though she still managed a few groans throughout. I tried to groan a little but had a pubic hair the length of a skipping rope lodged in my throat. At the end, we cuddled for a few minutes before she covered up her immense bush once more. Needless to say, I never got lost in that jungle ever again. I discovered that I was now making excuses not to see some women, if it didn't feel right. However, Carly understood and was of the same mindset. It just didn't happen between us and something was missing. Ultimately, men and women were looking for the very same thing – that spark and chemistry and sexual compatibility. It was sure difficult to find, but I couldn't give up. Not yet, anyway.

CHAPTER 26: NYMPH RIDES AGAIN

In my experience, Christmas is a time that single people feel a little more lonely than usual. It's a great family time if you have kids, but after separating all those years previously, it was still really difficult not to see my children on Christmas Day. When we split, we'd come to an arrangement that my day with the kids would be Boxing Day. In fairness, this worked out really well as I could spend some quality time with them. This meant I had the full day with them, rather than a fleeting visit. It meant my most precious time over the festive holiday was Boxing Day, as seeing the kids open their presents was just fantastic.

The Christmas period could be difficult, however, if you were single, lonely and a tad depressed like me. Festive films on television always showed happy couples together and happy families. This particular year, it looked like I would be spending it on my own again until I arranged to meet a lady called Steffi.

I'd established Steffi had a couple of children and maybe she too was feeling a little down about being lonely. That was evident as she'd told me it was difficult to be alone at Christmas. I guess dating sites were ideal for bringing people together at this time of year. Anyway, I think we first met on a pub car park and went for a drink. She was tall, rangy and athletic with long legs and long dark hair. She was fairly attractive, without being a stunner. She wasn't the easiest to talk to but spoke with quite a posh accent and carried herself well. She seemed very intelligent, sensible and had a decent job. Steffi didn't set my heart racing, if truth to be told, but I liked her enough to keep in touch and arrange another date.

On our second date, we met for lunch in a popular bistro type place. It wasn't the cheapest place, but as it was Christmas time I offered to pay. I was hoping that she might offer to 'go Dutch' and split the bill. But she thanked me and was gracious enough to let me pay. Not that I was fucking bitter about it. At the end of the meal we went for a short walk around the grounds and then got into our cars. I was just about to set off, when I wound the window down and said, 'You're welcome back to mine to watch a film or something,' anticipating that she'd rebuff me. 'Oh, thanks, that sounds very nice,' she said, then adding 'I'll follow you back then.'

She followed me back and I started to get a little excited at the prospect of more sex. I drove back with a semi on, but then remembered it was only our second date and the chances were we'd simply watch a Christmas film together. When we got back, I made her a brew and we looked at the TV guide. Luckily, there were a couple of great films to choose from and we agreed on a thriller type movie. I banged the fire up nice and high and got it lovely and warm. I then got some chocolates out and we snuggled up on the sofa, watching the film, which was a belter. It was all rather cosy, and I felt quite happy.

After the movie, I thought it was time to kiss and so made my move. Luckily, she responded, and we kissed for quite a while. I didn't want to push things too much, but I didn't have to. She went for my belt and undid it, with some ease. She pulled down my jeans and unveiled my sexy chequered underpants from the market. I was definitely ready for her and she knew it. I must admit, I was expecting some oral stimulation as she'd taken control but that wasn't forthcoming. Instead, she took off her own jeans in double-quick time and sat astride me in a hurry. She was obviously a woman who liked to take control. In no time at all, she was riding me like a cowgirl riding a stallion. Well, I wasn't exactly a stallion, but more like a Shetland Pony if you know what I mean.

She rode me and rode me, until I could take no more and expelled my love juice. Boy, she could go like the clappers. It was all fantastic at that moment in time. By now it was getting late, so I asked if she wanted something to eat and made some sort of snack, like cheese and biscuits. Unfortunately, she still didn't fancy anything else in her mouth, but fancied another go on the sofa after her supper. Again, she instigated everything, but made me go on top this time. Wow, Steffi was one horny lady that was for sure.

Of course, she didn't want to go home on this night. She stayed over and first thing in the morning was demanding more sex. We did it in several positions and most of the time she was also playing with herself with her fingers. I didn't know what to make of this, because it seemed that my knob alone couldn't possibly satisfy her. The more I pumped, the faster her fingers went. In my experience, women were reluctant to flick the bean in front of a man - but Steffi had no qualms about this. Most times we had sex she would play with her own clitoris until orgasm. It was all very bizarre - surely it would've been better if I could help her climax. It was the equivalent of her just sitting there, whilst I tossed over her tits and gave her a pearl necklace.

Nevertheless, I'd enjoyed our night of passion, although my knob was feeling rather delicate after what seemed like hours inside her. We met again a few days later and went for a countryside walk. This time, she invited me back to her house, as her kids were out. She'd made some sort of stew, which was really tender actually. A bit like my cock after the pounding she'd given me. But I was ready, if she wanted more action.

On this occasion, she stripped me down and I was standing to attention, ready for a blow job. But Steffi teased me by kissing my thighs and going nowhere near my manhood. Nobody had been a teaser like this before. I piped up, 'Go on, do it baby,' expecting her to take it in her mouth. Her reply was somewhat startling to me. She growled, 'Not now, I'll do it when I'm ready to thank you.'

Okay, it appeared that she wasn't keen on giving oral sex. Every woman was different, I guess. Some enjoyed satisfying their partner in that respect and which bloke didn't enjoy it? Others were far more reluctant to engage in a bit of oral. I usually didn't mind giving oral sex, but I was reluctant to do so now. If she wanted to tease me, I'd fucking tease her. Without much hanging about, she pulled her panties down and opened wide. I wasn't tempted to go down now, so I just rammed it inside her. We'd had little foreplay; it was just pure copulation. It seemed that she liked it this way - little or no foreplay at all. She just wanted the old-fashioned in and out.

I was with Steffi when we went to a local pub on New Year's Eve too. It was a great atmosphere, buzzing with lots of drunken punters as you'd expect on such a night. I knew a few others in there and wanted to mingle a little and have a chat. However, she was all over me like a cheap suit and wouldn't let me out of her sight. Obviously, I was seeing her and liked her, but she wouldn't give me any space. It was all consuming and she followed me around like a puppy follows its new owner. I was kind of embarrassed when she kept kissing me in front of others I knew. I wanted to talk, but she wanted to shove her tongue down my throat all the time.

Soon after, she came around to my house and again she instigated sex. By this point in our relationship, I was beginning to think that Steffi was some sort of nymphomaniac. I'd never met anyone who'd taken such control of me, in the bedroom. She certainly liked control and liked to be the one on top, most of the time. I remember another occasion when she stayed over at my house. We did it all night and then in the morning, before work, I was shattered. I was a spent force and simply had no energy. I felt like I'd run the London Marathon the previous evening. Yet, when we woke, she started rubbing my cock again trying to get me hard.

I just wanted to get up and get ready for the day ahead. I mean, I enjoyed sex tremendously, but this was just ridiculous. Nevertheless, I felt compelled to try and satisfy her insatiable appetite. Again, there was no or little foreplay – I just gave her my tired tool whilst she pleasured herself again. It just wasn't enjoyable and there were no feelings at all. I wanted to make love with someone, not just fuck them all the time at their request.

Granted, there were moments and times when a quickie could be amazing, if both partners were ready for that. Sometimes, just ramming it in was so exciting. But, to insist on that all the time was just copulating for the sake of it. Actually, it made me realise that sex without any feelings was sometimes worse than not doing it all. I wanted to find a partner who was compatible with me, which Steffi clearly wasn't. I was having plenty of sex, but the quality of it wasn't great. It was like watching a 3D movie without wearing 3D glasses. In fact, it was probably preferable to have virtual sex on a 3D platform rather than be used by Steffi for her personal gratification. Mind you, if you had sex wearing 3D glasses how would you know if you were coming or going?

I'd not encountered anything like this before. I felt that Steffi was beginning to take over my life and that I was losing control of my own personal freedoms. She was also stopping over at my house more and more often, mainly at her request. Maybe I should've spoken to her more, but I found her quite a difficult person to communicate with. As a single guy for so long, I needed my own space. I needed to be able to go out with my cricket mates and let off some steam. I needed to go out for a few beers with Mart and Ash or go for a curry with Big Col. At that time, I just felt a bit trapped with her. I'm not saying she was totally controlling, because she wasn't. However, I felt that she liked to be in control of most things that we did, and I was beginning to miss doing some of the things I enjoyed. I was beginning to think that she wasn't for me – either in the bedroom or otherwise.

CHAPTER 27: DIRTY DANCING

I simply didn't develop the connection with Steffi that I'd anticipated, after that first night of passion. She definitely liked to be the leader and was the dominant partner in our relationship. She dominated me in the bedroom and also dominated me by her domineering personality. I didn't mind a strong, independent woman at all. But I didn't feel that our sex life was conducive to a long-lasting partnership. In simple terms, I was wondering whether to dump her.

Then, one day she surprised me by saying she'd got tickets to see *Dirty Dancing* in Manchester. She told me it was her treat and wouldn't take no for an answer. Being a bloke, I wasn't really a fan of *Dirty Dancing* and had always turned over if it came on TV. I knew it was a famous chick flick, but I'd much preferred the other classic dance movie, *Saturday Night Fever*, with John Travolta strutting his stuff. Now, that was a great film and the Bee Gees' music was just sensational. I'd blasted their biggest hits many times and had tried to show my moves to *Night Fever* and *Stayin' Alive*. Big Col and I had been blown out many times after making a dick of ourselves to those classics. However, I was aware that *Dirty Dancing* was a firm favourite with the ladies.

Steffi explained that she'd also booked a cheap hotel after spotting a super deal, so really, I didn't have much fucking choice. In my mind, I was ready to give it one final chance to see if things could improve. Maybe I needed to have a chat with her and tell her my feelings. Yet, men rarely talked about their feelings and I hadn't done so up till now. I'd not felt comfortable enough to actually speak to her properly. I guess I was worried about what sort of reaction I'd get if I told her how I actually felt. It wasn't a good sign that I couldn't share my views and opinions.

We arrived at the hotel and dumped our stuff ready for the night ahead. I remember having a snack and pre-theatre drink too, before the show. Our seats were as high up as Blackpool Tower. It seemed like we were sat just below the ceiling, in the clouds so to speak. As I suffered from vertigo, my legs wobbled slightly. When the cast came on stage, they were the size of fucking matchsticks. Even Steffi seemed slightly disappointed with the views. We may as well have watched it on TV. The music was okay I guess, and when the main song, *(I've Had) The Time of My Life,* came on there were women screaming and screeching. The problem was, I wasn't having the time of my life. I was sat there watching all these stupid women screaming thinking another song would be much more appropriate right now. It'd have to be called *(I've Had) The Shittiest Time of My Sad Fucking Life.*

Well, it wasn't quite that bad to be honest, but you get the point. It really wasn't my thing, even though I'd appeared in a couple of productions and liked a theatre show. Maybe if I was with the love of my life, I'd have felt differently – but I seriously doubt it. All I was thinking about as the show progressed was that I was dying for a pint. I couldn't wait to get out of there and get to the pub. I was determined to get merry and try and make the most our night away.

At the end of the show all the women went barmy and screamed even louder. There was another bloke near me. We looked at each other, nonplussed and shrugged our shoulders. We felt the same and he gave me a little wink. I motioned with a hand signal that I was now ready for a drink. He nodded and gave me the thumbs up. All this as the women were going crazy around us, including Steffi. Thankfully, after about twenty minutes the applause stopped, and we could get to the pub and get pissed.

We soon ended up on Canal Street, the well-known gay hub of the city. I'd enjoyed a few nights here before and it was very welcoming place for both gay and straight people alike. We went to a bar, which was buzzing with lots of people. There was a DJ dressed in drag, wearing a colourful dress and a huge wig. He was caked in make-up and wore high heels too, walking with a swagger. He played some fantastic songs and did some crude jokes between each tune. I was downing pints for fun and thought he was hilarious. It was a great atmosphere, and everyone was having fun.

At one point, the DJ walked over to me and pointed to his cheek for a little kiss. Being drunk, I went to give him a peck on his cheek and he turned around so that my lips met his. I squirmed as his bright red lipstick ended up on my lips too. Steffi thought it was hilarious and actually began to have fun as the music was cranked up. He played some great hits and the whole place was rocking in carefree abandon. The atmosphere was just electric, and Steffi was getting turned on again. I'm surprised she didn't force me to do it there and then on the bloody dancefloor.

After a while, the DJ called a man over to the microphone whose name was Steve. He looked quite sheepish and shy but stood on the little stage in front of everyone looking embarrassed as people cheered. Then the DJ asked him, 'Are you gay Steve?' with a suggestive look on his face. Steve nodded in front of the gawping crowd. Without pausing at all the DJ asked the crowd, 'So, who wants to shag Steve tonight?' laughing. I looked around and about ten men put their hands up. Some were jumping up and down trying to gain his attention too. The DJ shouted over the microphone, 'Fuck me Steve, you'll have an arsehole like a wigwam at the end of the night.'

I was laughing most of the night and we even had a dance or two. Steffi had also let herself go for once and seemed to be enjoying it. Generally speaking, she was quite a serious person but here and now she showed another side to her character. Very late into the night there were no proper restaurants open, so we had to get a chicken kebab, on the way back to the hotel. This reminded me of my university days, but I tried my best not to slop chilli sauce all over my jeans. Eventually, we got back to our room and ended up naked. Well, I guess most people didn't sleep fully clothed.

Yet again, she didn't go down on me. Maybe it was a good thing this time though, as I wouldn't want chilli sauce licked into my bell-end. It was all very predictable, as usual, and I just shoved it in and pumped hard for as long as I could, before passing out. After the disappointment of *Dirty Dancing,* it had actually been a good night. But as we travelled back on the train, I still thought that there was something missing between us. I think it was known as chemistry.

A couple of weeks later, she'd stayed at mine a few more times and had almost demanded sex first thing in the morning, every single time. I was struggling to cope with her demands. I'd made my mind up by now; she was a fucking nympho. Maybe I should have told her she was being unreasonable and expected too much. But I just couldn't bring myself to tell her. I was also getting a bit pissed off with the fact that she was beginning to stay over too often and affect my independence. I didn't want her to take over my life and suffocate me. That's how it felt at the time. She was basically starting to get on my fucking nerves and control my movements.

When I'd finished with Lucy previously, I'd done it face to face, as it was the proper way to do it. Lucy deserved that. I couldn't do that with Steffi, as I was slightly scared of her and wondered what she might do to me. So, I sent her a rather abrupt text telling her things weren't working out anymore. I tried to be honest, in a diplomatic sort of way. Well, Mart and Ash never thought I was diplomatic or subtle. Once, on a night out a big thug looking type with tattoos down his neck came over to me and shouted, 'Are you staring at my girlfriend's arse?' in a rage. I paused slightly and then replied, 'Yes, it's fucking fat isn't it?' No, diplomacy wasn't my strong point for sure.

In hindsight, finishing with Steffi by text probably wasn't the brave or correct thing to do. Steffi wasn't happy at all, as you can imagine. In fact, she went ballistic in some of her responses and then tried to arrange another meeting so we could talk things through. I really didn't want to see her again. I was worried she'd cut my knob off with a machete. She kept firing texts at me and wouldn't take no for an answer. For a while, I was getting slightly concerned that she'd just turn up at my house and stalk me.

I'd seen *Fatal Attraction* all those years ago and now it all came flooding back. Luckily, however, I hadn't bought a cat like the kids wanted me too and I didn't have a bunny to boil either. In hindsight, I can laugh about it now but at the time there was a part of me that was genuinely worried about her obsessive behaviour. She appeared to become somewhat unstable and lots of thoughts went through my mind about what she would do to me.

That's why I couldn't face meeting her again. I felt it would best to keep at arm's length and try to limit any confrontation. I'd heard others had been dumped by text and thought it was wrong and heartless, but now, in this situation I thought it was the best option. The difference in personality between Lovely Lucy and Strange Steffi was immeasurable. It made me think about Lucy again and what I'd done. Maybe I'd regret ending that relationship for the rest of my life.

I tried to explain yet again some of the reasons I wanted to end it, but she wouldn't accept any of it and was determined not to let go. By now, I was getting genuinely concerned but as time went by, she texted me less and less. I accept now that she must have been hurting and wanted to talk about things. Maybe I was too rash in sending that last text saying, 'FUCK OFF AND LEAVE ME ALONE!' Did I regret it though? Not in the slightest. I knew she wasn't 'the one' for me, so I was back to square one. If at first, you don't succeed...

CHAPTER 28: DIRTY TALK

Maxine said to me online, 'I wanna smother your whole body in chocolate and lick it off. I'll even lick your arsehole.' My eyes popped out! How could I respond to that? I thought carefully for a moment and replied, 'I'll lick every inch of your body too – without the chocolate.' She was the dirtiest woman I'd flirted with online, without question. She loved telling me what she'd want to do to me, if we ever met up. So, in the spirit of flirtation and fun – I went along with it and talked dirty too. In fact, a few times it even got me turned on, but not to the point of masturbation. Maxine, though, regularly informed me that she was playing with herself, as we chatted. I never saw this, of course, but she did her best to explain in sordid detail what she was up to.

Our dirty talk went on for a few weeks on a sporadic basis, and then I suggested we cut out the talk and re-enact the words in real life. Was it all bravado? Was she just an online teaser? All would be become apparent, if we did actually meet. She could've just been playing games, of course. She may even have been married and looking for some extra excitement, on the side. I wasn't that naïve that I didn't realise these things happened. Maxine's photographs were quite nice; she had a short dark hair and was tall and fairly slim too. She was, however, a couple of years older than me and had a sort of lived-in face. I wasn't convinced that I'd ever see her in the flesh.

After finishing with Strange Steffi, maybe I should've taken far more care of who I actually met. I'd managed to escape her clutches so to speak – but in reality, you never knew who you were meeting up with. It was probably a far bigger risk for women really. There were all sorts of weird characters out there and some of them would even be dangerous. In a way, it was a risk if people met up without much contact first. It was much better to get to know someone a little and speak on the phone a few times. But sometimes, people liked to live life by taking chances, here and there. You never knew what that meeting could lead to. Obviously, it was always best to meet in a busy public place and let others know, especially for women.

Eventually, I agreed to meet Maxine in a countryside pub half-way between our respective towns. I was in two-minds whether to meet, as I was looking for a long-term partner and a woman like this clearly just wanted some fun. Then again, I hadn't had any physical intimacy since I'd been with Steffi and my manhood was fully recovered by now. You could say I was getting a bit desperate myself.

Some of the women I'd fancied online had either failed to respond or after chatting a while, they'd reneged on meeting up. Rejection was all part of the process and I was used to it by now. My initial hurt and despair at rejection had now become a mundane shrug of the shoulders. That's internet dating, I guess. Though I wanted a girlfriend, I still had physical urges and Maxine clearly had the same needs.

As I pulled into the car park, my heart fluttered a little. It was a bit different this time because of all the dirty talk we'd had. Nearly every other lady I'd met had been preceded by normal, run-of the mill banter and some serious conversations to show them I was an intelligent and decent guy. But now, I was meeting a woman who'd already told me she'd lick my arsehole. I must admit, there was a bit more excitement than normal – even though it was only teatime and we were both driving and sober.

Maxine pulled up in her car and got out. She stood next to me and was actually taller than me, without heels on. I'd never been out with anyone this tall, but she looked like her pictures and had a bright smile. Indeed, she was slightly better looking than I'd anticipated and was fairly easy to talk to. We had a couple of glasses of coke and chatted away. Not once did we mention the dirty sex talk. It was as though the online banter had never happened at all. The two women seemed totally different. It was as though she had an online persona, maybe after a couple of drinks, and a normal educated persona. She had a good job and seemed intelligent, with a thorough knowledge of current affairs. Yet, this was the lady who had told me only a few nights previously that she was caressing her clitoris whilst we chatted.

After a couple of hours talking, it was time to go as we'd not ordered food and I was getting hungry. Believe it or not, I asked her if she wanted some food at the pub – or wanted to come back to mine for pizza. Unbelievably, the pizza worked a treat again. Who doesn't like pizza? Of course, it was my code word for, 'I wanna shag your brains out,' but it often worked. She followed me back in her car, and I was thinking what types of pizza I had in my freezer. I *always* had a couple of pizzas, as they were a staple food for a single bloke. You could say pizzas enhanced my whole fucking life.

When we got back to my house, we didn't say a word. We were ready to re-enact our dirty fantasies there and then. Fortunately, she was up for it and her persona changed again. This time she became like the Mucky Maxine online, but this time it wasn't dirty talk – it was dirty action. She kissed me with her incredibly long tongue, and I was stiff before she'd taken anything off. All the previous dirty talk had made me horny, really horny. She had an unbelievable tongue – like an anteater – and licked my shaft like it was a 99. After that, it was a 69, although she didn't lick my arsehole as promised. It was amazing how this was really happening – almost like she said online, but not quite.

I then bent Maxine over the sofa and pounded away for as long as I could, before pulling out, so we could continue from another position. I had a good go from all angles and every conceivable position. She was on the floor, on a chair, on the sofa, standing up, sitting down, on the stairs, over the table, under the television, over the sink. We made the Kama Sutra seem like a tame picture book.

This went on for a while, but I couldn't last too much longer. I tried to be like a porn star and maintain my wood for an hour or two, but I'd not taken any Viagra, like porn stars did. Maybe I should've thought about BREXIT again, so I could last longer. Anyway, the inevitable happened and it was all over. We sat on the sofa and smiled at each other – we'd only met a few hours ago and had enacted our very own online fantasy.

Maxine enjoyed the pizza too, after having my own version of a meat feast. We got talking about all sorts of things. She had kids but had split up from her husband a long time ago. She told me that her husband had been into dating sites and had cheated on her by using them. I guess dating sites made cheating much easier and a marriage more difficult to maintain, if people were unhappy. She said he was now into threesomes and used a certain website, whereby couples actively sought a third party to join in their sex play. He would meet them and be sucked off by the female partner with a gob job, before watching the couple have sex – or maybe joining in. It was all very weird, but I knew all this shit happened. There was something for everyone out there. There was no limit to people's sexual fantasies.

Swingers parties were all very common too. I couldn't attend one of those, as I didn't have a partner. But maybe Mucky Maxine would attend one with me? I knew a lady who was once duped into attending one of these parties by her first husband. She assumed she was attending a normal party, with maybe a few board games and some dancing. She even took a quiche with her.

When she realised the games involved swapping sexual partners, she sneaked out the bathroom window and ran for her life due to sheer embarrassment. She said they were all old and ugly. At the very least he should have discussed it with her first. Did he expect that she'd just agree to join in? Each to their own, I guess, if it's all consensual fun but I reckon partners should discuss all this stuff in advance surely. It's not like swapping cakes is it?

I liked Maxine – she was fun to be with, for obvious reasons. I invited her around the following week and even cooked for her. I'm not talking a frozen pizza, but something proper like egg and chips. Of course, we tried to replicate the previous week's encounters. It was still good but didn't have the same intensity or excitement. The first time always had that extra buzz. We couldn't reach those heights again. It was like climbing Mount Everest one week and then Ben Nevis the next.

She visited my house a few more times – for basically one reason only. It wasn't my cooking that's for sure. Yet, our liaisons were based solely on sex and nothing more. We connected fairly well but didn't actually leave the house. We never went to the local pub or even a walk in the woods. It was all based upon lust – and that could never make a relationship last.

Of course, it wasn't ever going to progress further. It was sort of a mutual understanding though, and we both sort of accepted it should end.

It was all friendly and it was all very mature. We'd had our fun, but deep down we both still wanted a lot more than that, but probably not with each other. I was beginning to wonder if the dating sites I was using were all they seemed. To me, most people appeared to be after one thing only – and it wasn't love. Maybe I was chatting to the wrong types, maybe I gave out the wrong signals. Sex could be great, but love was much deeper, and it was what I craved. I was making some bad choices again and still felt some emptiness in my heart. What the hell was wrong with me?

CHAPTER 29: VOYEURS R US

I'd enjoyed the excitement with Maxine for a while – but I wanted more. I wanted feelings and wanted a deeper more meaningful relationship. Despite wanting this for ages, it was still difficult to find. I was frustrated that I couldn't find the answer. Maybe the women I was choosing to meet were just not my type, or maybe I was thinking with my knob too much. Most decent women wouldn't sleep with someone on the first date, would they? I doubt it. In fact, I was looking for a woman who didn't want to do things like that. I was being dragged into a sordid world of instant sexual gratification, with absolutely no feelings attached. I was genuinely looking for love, but lust always seemed to come out on top.

The next lady I met was called Diana, but she was no fucking princess. Diana was quite petite, with a tanned skin and dark features. She had a shapely body – but her lips were slightly lop-sided. I mean the ones on her face, not down below. Nevertheless, she was still attractive, and I was happy when she'd agreed to meet me. I thought again that she may be 'the one' – although Mart, Dainty Dan and Ash continued to take the piss at every available opportunity.

By now, Big Col had met the love of his life – although not online I hasten to add. He loved her so much that'd he actually left home to move in with her. I bet his mum and dad were so thrilled. They'd been trying to get rid of him for fucking years. No longer did his mum have to wash his soiled underpants. I was really happy for Big Col, but of course I was now seeing him less and less – which was understandable. He'd found his true love and was happy. I'd not found mine and was still eating fucking *Fray Bentos* pies for one.

I met Diana in a coffee shop one lunchtime, and we had a decent conversation on the whole. Well, it was the same kind of chat that often occurred on my dates. You know, the same standard lines that I usually asked, 'So how long have you been single? How many dates have you had? How many blokes have you shagged?' That sort of thing. I sort of fancied her, without being excited.

She was nice enough – although there wasn't an amazing spark. In fact, I was beginning to wonder if this thing called a 'spark' really truly existed. Nobody had made my heart truly flutter, nobody had made me feel tingly all over. What was love anyway? I was questioning everything by this point – maybe being single should be my lifestyle of choice, after all. Albeit, a forced choice.

After our first meeting, I wasn't sure if Diana would want a second date. Some women I could read – but not Diana. I looked for signals in women's body language, like fluttering eyelashes, stroking hair or pursing of lips. Eye-contact was also important – but Diana spent half the time looking at her phone. She didn't exactly stare deep into my eyes. In fact, looking back, she was a miserable lady who looked like she had the weight of the world on her tiny shoulders. She didn't quite look like a slapped arse – but Mary Shelley's monster in *Frankenstein* probably had more expressions. Maybe it was all the Botox injected into her face.

About a week later, after texting a bit more, we agreed to meet up on a Saturday night in town. I wasn't too enthusiastic, as our first meeting had been lukewarm. I'd fancied some ladies a lot more – but she wasn't that bad either. Actually, after some of my previous experiences, she was positively gorgeous. We met in a bar and she actually smiled a bit – as much as her face would allow. She was one of these women, who couldn't accept growing old gracefully. She'd obviously been on a sunbed for hours and looked as if she'd been on holiday to Greece for three months. Either that, or it was fake tan applied with gusto. Her lips had been done, as well as her knockers. Her hair was streaked, and she turned up dressed as though she was 21 again. Her fake nails were so long and sparkly I'd have to be careful that she didn't poke my eyes out.

There was a great atmosphere in town, though, and it soon became apparent that she was out to get pissed. I supped a pint and she knocked back a large glass of white wine in double quick time. We had a couple of drinks in one pub, then went to another and another. After about 5 drinks, we had a sloppy kiss and it became apparent that she was drunk already. The conversation flowed much better with alcohol taking over and she opened up a bit more - although she still had that annoying tendency to keep checking her fucking phone. When out, I strongly believed that couples should talk to each other. They should make eye-contact and communicate with their mouths. So often though, you'd see couples both staring at their phones - oblivious to each other. Obviously, they were either unhappy or couldn't stand each other.

I couldn't exactly tell her to put her phone away though - she may have poked me in the eye with those dangerous nails. So, I got mine out too a few times, which was unusual for me. We looked like we'd been married for years - playing on our phones and ignoring each other. I'd caught a train to meet her and my last train was imminent, so I asked what her plans were. I was prepared to get a taxi home if she was staying out all night - but she just blurted out that I could stay at hers, as she lived closer. This was turning into a top night - so I bought us another drink.

We staggered into the taxi sometime later and went to her house, a few miles away. It was a lovely big house - detached with four bedrooms. She'd told me she was some sort of administrator, so I wondered how she could afford it. But, hey, it was none of my business. We went into the large lounge and she wasn't slow at coming forward. She took my shirt off in no time and loosened my pants. I helped take her top off and her big fake boobs flopped out. They were similar in some ways to Carly's, as they felt like a hard orange with nipples on them - although they were far more tanned than hers.

Afterwards, she exposed her lovely shaven pussy and said she wanted me inside her. Despite being drunk, I easily obliged and took her as she lay on a Persian rug. Well, I think it was Persian - but it may have been Chinese. After a while, she got on her knees and spread her tidy tanned rear as wide as she could, exposing a sizeable chocolate hole which reminded me of a large walnut. I was going to take her from behind as normal, when she demanded, 'Take me up the arse,' with some authority. Well, this shocked me big time. Not many ladies offered these goods so quickly - and some never at all. I'd heard from the cricket lads it was usually a birthday or Christmas present when they got lucky. But Diana was now insisting on this, right here, right now. I really didn't have much choice.

Of course, I wasn't going to decline such an offer - I mean instruction. I expected to have some difficulty getting it in and considered using my regular handful of spit as a form of lubricant, or maybe raiding the fridge for some butter, as in *Last Tango in Paris.* However, my tool slipped in the chocolate hole all too easily. It did make me wonder just how many other men had fucked her rather loose poo tunnel recently. Jeez, I began to wonder if maybe she was a fucking porn star on the side. We tried a couple of positions - but after a while I still hadn't come and maybe she was getting bored. She pushed me off and I looked down at my throbbing cock. It was covered in chocolate, but not the kind you'd want to eat.

Down both sides of my shaft, the brown stuff was stuck to it. She told me to sit on the sofa, which I did. Then, as though she'd been prepared all along for this eventuality, she produced a wet wipe as by magic. She gave my willy a good wiping, up and down, and the shit was removed with such aplomb it was as though she was wiping wax from a candle. Having inspected it further and checked there was no sign of poo, she then began to give me a gob job. Jeez, this was a horny lady. I felt like I was in a fucking porn movie. She licked my balls for ages too and after what seemed like an hour or so, I came all over her Persian rug. Or Chinese rug, whatever.

In the morning, we had a quickie too - but it was nothing like the night before. It was like going from the set of a porn film, to being me again. In her bedroom, I noticed a computer screen and some equipment opposite the bed and casually asked why it was there. Without hesitation, and to my surprise, Diana said she used to perform video-cam shows with her husband. I wasn't sure what she meant by this, so asked lots of questions.

It transpired that they basically had live sex over the internet and other voyeuristic people watched them online. I wasn't sure if they made any money from it - or if they were just pure exhibitionists. Indeed, I wasn't sure about anything at this point. At the time it was all pretty weird to me, but they clearly got a buzz by broadcasting their sexual exploits over the internet for others to watch. They were probably the kind of couple who'd go dogging at their local dogging site, allowing others to watch as they had sex in a car with the windows steamed up.

Then, it crossed my mind that they may still be together, given the size of the house. She assured me that they had split up a long time ago – but I began to think there was something fishy going on. Diana had been all dolled up for a reason. She'd had Botox and implants for a reason. She was tanned all over for a reason. It then crossed my mind that she may have had a hidden camera downstairs too and been filming us the previous night. Maybe she was testing me out as a potential member of the cast? Maybe, she wanted another partner, so that she could live-stream her sexual performance? No wonder I'd felt that I was taking part in a porn film – she was basically a fucking sex performer. No wonder her arsehole was so loose. She was probably known as 'Dirty Diana' on all the websites. Oh shit, what had I done this time?

Once dressed, I made my way downstairs and went back into the lounge. I scoured the room for any cameras or computer equipment. I wondered whether she secretly filmed all her conquests. But thankfully, I couldn't see anything like that at all. Then, on the coffee table I saw a wet wipe. It was still there from the night before – smothered in poo. For some reason, my eyes were transfixed on it. I stared at that wet-wipe and thought about my life. It seemed that, after all, my love life at the time was summed up by that wipe – rather shitty.

I was beginning to get sick of waking up in a stranger's house. I was beginning to regret some of the things I was doing. The night before was now all a blur and I just wanted to get home. I wanted to meet a proper partner - someone who I loved and cared about. I wanted more than just nights of fun – I wanted something other than this. I never thought I'd feel this, but one-night stands were becoming too monotonous, dull and tiresome. I wanted someone to share all my intimate thoughts with, to cuddle and care for. I wanted to meet a lady who cared about me, who wanted to be with me night and day. I wished for all those things and more. I wished for a chemistry I'd not yet felt, that spark, that feeling that's hard to describe. Jeez, I was hoping for the impossible, the implausible, that thing called love. From where I was stood, it was totally out of reach and I was beginning to give up in my quest.

Dirty Diana walked into the room and looked at me sat there on the sofa. She was now completely different from the previous night – both in looks and personality. It was though we didn't actually know each other at all. It was so cold between us and as though a switch had been flicked. Maybe her husband was coming back that day – maybe she'd regretted the previous night. Maybe she just wanted me out of her house and her life for good. Who knows? Quite abruptly, she offered me a lift to the train station – which I accepted. As I sat in her car, there was silence between us on that journey. The atmosphere was one of regret and remorse. For some reason I felt empty inside and fucking rotten. I just felt sadness. I almost felt like crying. What the hell was I doing? What had my life become? I desperately had to try and turn things around – I just wanted to be happy again.

CHAPTER 30: HOPE ON THE HORIZON

Having had another empty experience so to speak, I felt that I should take a little more time chatting online before I made the plunge to meet someone. I tried to look at the options and dismissed those who appeared to be solely after some fun. After all, I'd not been too selective so far and had just gone with the flow. I'd also sought some excitement in the past - but now I tried to be a little more selective, although sometimes it didn't work that way. If nobody was messaging me back, then there simply wasn't much choice to be had. In many ways it was like a lottery - would that special person be the one to get in touch this time?

I began chatting to a woman named Wendy. She seemed rather pleasant during the conversations and was nothing like Dirty Diana or Mucky Maxine, in that respect. She came across as a genuine lady, who'd split from her husband and was now looking for a relationship. After a considerable time chatting online and a few phone calls, we agreed to meet in a town between our respective homes. In the photographs online, Wendy had shoulder-length dirty blonde hair and was quite curvy.

When I first saw Wendy in the pub, I was filled with some hope as she had a genuine lovely smile and a pretty face - though again I would suggest the pictures online were slightly flattering. The one thing I was struck by was her size. She was bigger than I'd anticipated. Not hugely fat or anything - but just taller and broader than I thought from the photographs. However, I was determined to see how it went. Within an hour or two, I thought this lady was different. She was on my wavelength and we just seemed to have some spark. She certainly seemed to like me too - I could tell by the way she stared at me and made lots of encouraging comments.

166

As the night progressed, we had more drinks and went from pub to pub holding hands. All the body language suggested a mutual attraction. Towards the end of the night, we had a long passionate kiss too. But then, she made it clear that wanted to go back home alone. For once, I didn't mind at all – in fact I thought it was a really positive thing. Instead of just wanting a shag, maybe she really did want a genuine relationship. I was fed up of just shagging anyway. I never thought I'd say that – but I wanted some emotional feelings for once. I even considered becoming a tad more romantic. My idea of romance thus far had been to offer a frozen pizza back at my bachelor pad.

Wendy agreed to meet up again and we went for a walk in the countryside. We talked about lots of things and the conversation flowed easily. She actually appeared to be the sort of person I'd want to be with. We didn't rush into bed at all and this was a positive thing, as far as I was concerned. We went to see a musical at a local theatre, *The Little Shop of Horrors,* and had a great laugh at a fantastic show. After the performance, we went back to my house and things progressed. By now, we'd seen each other quite a few times, so the sexual tension had built up more than usual. During sex, she seemed reluctant to show me her body and it dawned on me that she lacked confidence in herself and her self-image. I tried my best to be understanding and gentle.

Unfortunately, the wait was somewhat of a disappointment on the whole. I'd got to know her and liked her, for sure, but I could tell it felt awkward for her. Maybe she hadn't had sex for a while. In fact, sometime later when we went downstairs, she opened up to me and admitted it was a while since she'd done the deed and found it uncomfortable, as she had concerns about her body shape. She told me she'd lost weight in the last few weeks too. She wasn't fat in my eyes – but was big-boned and shapely. I didn't know how to react to all this – but was honest enough to say that she had nothing to worry about, as I liked her. I thought the sex would improve in time, if she felt more relaxed and disinhibited.

As time went by, one thing that became apparent was that Wendy had a liking for giving blowjobs. She offered me one on plenty of occasions and in a variety of situations. In contrast, she seemed to try to avoid actual intercourse on a regular basis too. It was all rather strange, as I was a big fan of the act of copulation itself. I just wasn't satisfied with regular gob-jobs. I wanted more than that. Having said that, boy, could she give a cracking blowie. Maybe she'd been practising on bananas and cucumbers while she'd been single.

Anyway, she liked to pleasure me whenever she could. Not many women had a penchant for gob-jobs like Wendy. On any occasion that she could whip my cock out - she would. Going for a walk in the woods - it was out; parked up in the car - it was out; down a back alley after a few drinks - it was out; mending something in my shed - it was out; cooking a nice supper - it was out. I had to draw a line at a McDonald's drive thru and a changing room at Primark though. It was actually great that a lady had taken the initiative at times and instigated this sort of thing. The problem was, we were hardly having intercourse in bed, as she was reluctant to get her kit off. Just noshing me off wasn't as fulfilling as I thought.

Although I was getting on well with Wendy and she was a lovely person - she also drove me slightly mad talking about her ex. She just couldn't let go and went on and on about him - despite my interjections that actually she should try to forget about him. It was, 'Jim this and Jim that' all the fucking time. I was trying to help her get over him, but I didn't want to be just a marriage counsellor. It was becoming increasingly apparent that she hadn't got over the split and still had feelings for her ex-husband.

I'd been through the same stage a lot earlier in time - so we were at totally different stages in the healing process. It'd obviously been a traumatic experience for her and her children - and I'd sympathised throughout. But now, all this was getting a bit too repetitive and harmful for our future prospects.

I mentioned this a few times to Wendy, but she seemed oblivious to the fact that she was probably still in love with him. She had tried a reconciliation, but this had failed miserably - like many couples, I guess. I knew how she felt, but now I'd moved on in my head - and she clearly hadn't. I suggested that we could go away for a few nights and see how things went. Luckily, my parents had a caravan in Pembrokeshire in South Wales, and I asked if we could stay there for a few nights. It was a long tedious journey, and I didn't particularly like driving, but I thought it would be a nice break for us.

When I'd been going through a similar stage after my split, I was lucky that mates such as Big Col, Mart and Ash were there for me. Big Col was my main drinking partner at this time, and he gave me so much advice over a few beers. I was glad to have someone to talk to and share things with. Of course, Big Col was also my pulling partner and we had some fantastic nights out – just what I needed at that time. In fact, it was essential to have those nights out for my own state of mind. Getting my end away was an added bonus and was positive for both body and mind. Mart was also extremely supportive around this time and prevented me from having a major meltdown one night, after I'd got suitably drunk whilst considering my shit situation. Alcohol and depression were a bad combination for anyone.

As I said earlier, Ash was considerably older than me and he'd been through a messy divorce too. He'd been there and done it, so was able to give me the benefit of his wisdom around this time. However, though he became amicable with his first wife after the divorce, I vividly remember one night when we were out drinking in town. He saw her walk into the same bar as us and promptly hid behind a large post. He simply didn't want to see her. It seemed rather odd to me that a middle-aged man was cowering behind a post, so he wouldn't be spotted. I had to give a running commentary about her position in the bar – I felt like I was an undercover agent, spying on her. Eventually, when she went to the loo, we made our escape.

Ash once took me for a day out to Cartmel Races in the Lake District, to help me clear my head. He tried his best to make me feel better – which I appreciated. It didn't help that I'd never been to the races before and didn't study any form guides before placing a small bet. After one race, in which my horse barely made it around the course, I took a glance at the guide. The horse hadn't had a placing in seventeen previous races and had failed to complete in most of them. I may as well have backed a horse with three fucking legs. Thankfully, on the last race I won all my money back – through pure luck that is. I just went for a horse's name that sounded funny or a jockey's colours that looked rather jazzy.

Although Ash cheered me up on this day – he was fucking miserable as he didn't have a winner all day and lost all his money. He'd studied the form in great detail and was confident of winning his bets whereas I'd basically chosen a horse because I liked its name and won some cash. On the way back, I ended up having to cheer him up a bit. At least he didn't see his ex-wife lurking in the beer tent that day. Having friends like this, and supportive parents too, made a huge difference to my mental state at that tough time in my life. Everyone needs to talk to others and get things off their chest. Too many blokes fail to share their feelings and ask for help if they need it. Suffering in silence would be the worst thing I could've done. So, I understood how Wendy must have felt at that time and tried to be sympathetic.

CHAPTER 31: TENBY TURMOIL

As we set off on the long drive down to South Wales, I was in good spirits and full of optimism for the few days ahead. Wendy appeared to be happy and the journey down, though long, was mostly pleasant. I'd never been a big fan of driving on roads in our country – particularly motorways such as the M6. It seemed that everywhere I travelled, there were numerous roadworks. I often used to sing, 'Everywhere you go there's always fucking roadworks,' to the tune of *Weather with You,* by Crowded House. I bet you'd recognise the song if you heard it. There were just too many bloody cars and not enough roads. And the roads that existed were often in a terrible state, full of potholes that councils couldn't afford to fix.

Getting to Pembrokeshire from northern England was not an easy journey. Having said that, the journey through Wales itself threw up some fantastic views along the way. We saw lakes and mountains and the countryside was amazing at times. Wendy tried to keep me occupied by asking me quiz questions about sport and we had the radio on too.

As always, we got stuck in a traffic jam at one point because of roadworks and I duly sang my song again. Then, on a few narrow 'A' roads we got stuck behind a fucking tractor travelling at 20mph. On some occasions, I felt like taking a major risk and overtaking – but Wendy was adamant that she wanted to arrive at the caravan alive. After the monotony of driving for over 7 hours, we finally made it to Tenby. You could fly across the Atlantic Ocean in a similar time frame. It really was quicker to fly to anywhere in Europe than drive down south from northern England.

When we arrived at the caravan, there was a huge sense of relief that the journey was over for both of us. We decided to go out on the town and get pissed. The pub crawl started off well and we started knocking them back in some lovely little pubs, which were full of life. We also ordered some burgers to line our stomachs and carried on drinking. Then, as time went on, Wendy started talking about Jim again - her ex-husband. I was already sick of this but had tried to be sympathetic in the past. But now, I was drunk and had developed a tendency to just say what came into my mind. This was not good. In fact, it proved to be a disaster.

As she rambled on about him again, I let rip with what I thought about the situation. Obviously, I should've been diplomatic and told her my opinions whilst sober, in a proper, thoughtful, adult conversation. In other words, the complete opposite of what I did. She denied still being in love with him - but clearly, she was rattled by my attack. I didn't mean to be so abrupt and offensive, but it was too late now. The horse had bolted.

Next, for some incomprehensible reason, I referred to her weight. Well, this was even more of a howler. I made the factually accurate point that she'd put some weight back on since we'd met. The very thing that she was uncomfortable about - the thing that made her feel awkward in the bedroom. It was a low blow and I was out of order. It'd been on my mind and now I was drunk - I'd said it.

Wendy came back strong with a few comments and opinions of her own. Nothing about small cocks thankfully - but it was clear I'd riled her big time. I tried my best to back-track and to reassure her that she was not such a fat fucker after all. I tried to think of every escape route I could, to get myself out of the huge crater I'd dug. Try as I might, she now didn't listen to anything I said. In fact, she started crying in the middle of the pub with embarrassed families looking away from us. It was cringeworthy for us too - and it was all my fucking fault. I'd ruined everything after downing several drinks in a hurry and not thinking straight. I'd been a dickhead, without doubt.

We argued all the way back to the caravan. Again, and again, I tried to apologise and re-word what I'd said from a different psychological perspective. I tried to fix it all with some smooth talking but failed miserably. At that point in time, I'd never experienced any weight problems myself so couldn't comprehend how she felt. I was ignorant and foolish. She was a lovely person, but I'd been so fucking shallow. What the fuck was I doing? I'd blown it yet again.

Back at the caravan, it was even more tense between us. I didn't want to sleep with her, and she certainly didn't want to go anywhere near me. In fact, she went outside and tried to call her mother to tell her what had happened. I told her she was over-reacting, as she'd been drinking too. She stated categorically that she was going to leave there and then and get a train back to Manchester. It was ridiculous – we were miles from anywhere in the middle of the countryside. I eventually persuaded her not to leave, as she was drunk, and I was genuinely concerned about her. I offered to drive her back home the following morning.

Wendy remained outside, however, and I was beginning to worry about her state of mind and well-being. She was very emotional and still trying to call her mum. The signal was very poor, but eventually she got through. I could hear her telling her mum what had happened, and she was sobbing down the line. By now I felt fucking awful about everything and my heart was pumping hard. I just didn't know what to do but if I'd tried to cuddle her, she may have punched me. With my usual tact and diplomacy, I used delicate and soothing words such as, 'Stop fucking crying, you're waking everyone up,' to calm her down and make her see sense. She couldn't just walk home or catch a train at that time of night. Somehow, I persuaded her to come back inside the caravan.

Sometimes, making up after an argument could result in rampant sex and tons of passion between the sheets. But on this occasion, there was more chance of me being sucked off by 85-year-old Doris in Caravan number 92. Not that I suggested it, by the way. However, Wendy had finally calmed down after speaking to her mum and we actually had a civil conversation. Well, it went along the lines of, 'You sleep in the main double bed. I'll sleep here in the lounge. I'll drive us back home in the morning.'

To say that 7-hour journey back home was tough is an understatement. Actually, driving down to South Wales when we were a relatively happy couple was bad enough, but this was a fucking nightmare. Imagine the tension and sheer hatred between us. She looked at me as though I'd killed her pet parrot and then shagged her sister.

This time there was no sports quiz, though turning the radio up was a wise move. It broke the silence between us. The mountains and lakes just looked innocuous this time. It was probably the longest 7 hours of my life. I just wanted to click my fingers and transport us back home by magic. But there was no magic. There never had been any magic between us, in all honesty. We were more like good friends than lovers. Between the sheets, it just didn't happen between us. And now it looked like we weren't even friends anymore.

Finally, we got back to our destination and the relief was palpable for both of us. I saw her smile at last and she seemed altogether happier. When she got out of the car, however, I was beginning to get a tad upset. I knew she was a pleasant person, who I usually enjoyed being with – until our massive barney. I could feel my throat getting dry as I went to say goodbye. I'd truly fucked up this time and I knew there was no going back. I'd crossed the line with my comments, but it was actually true that she wasn't fully over her ex. She wasn't emotionally stable enough to begin a full-time serious relationship. I'd been in a similar situation, but I was further ahead in the process.

A few days after we got back, I texted Wendy again and made my apologies once more. I'd decided that it wasn't meant to be, but I was totally wrong for upsetting her in the way that I did. She deserved much better than that. I tried to be friendly – without leading her on at all. Surprisingly, after a couple of weeks or so, she offered to come around to my house for a chat, as friends only. I didn't want things to end as it did, after that journey from hell so agreed to see her. I'd missed her a little too and thought about her quite often. Even though I'd decided that we could only be friends from now on, we'd had some enjoyable times together and I wanted to remain on platonic terms. After all, I'd been to Prague with Kat as friends in the past and there was always a chance that something similar could happen again – not with Kat but with Wendy.

When she came around to my house, we talked a while and even cuddled a few times. She knew it was over really, but we were friendly to each other and it felt satisfying that we could smile in each other's company again. I made sure that I apologised for what had happened and stated it was all my fault. She did concede, however, that maybe she talked too much about her ex. I think she realised that deep down she was still hoping for some sort of reconciliation.

Afterwards, after all we'd been through recently, she got my knob out again just like old times. I couldn't resist of course - nobody turned down a blow job, unless it was from toothless Doris, from Caravan number 92. Wendy satisfied me one last time and then, soon after, disappeared into the sunset. Despite several more messages between us over a number of weeks, we never saw each other again. She actually told me that she'd met someone else who she really liked, and I was genuinely pleased for her. She was a decent person who'd had a rough time and I hoped that she'd found happiness at last.

CHAPTER 32: HEN PARTY HIATUS

After my experience with Wendy, I decided to try the big city again and go to Manchester to meet my next date. She was a trim black lady who looked stunning in all the photographs online – very similar to the supermodel Naomi Campbell. Unfortunately, when I met her, she looked nothing like Naomi. If she'd have been like Naomi, I would've been excited for sure. Instead, meeting Cassandra made me feel as though I'd let rip with a wet fart – a little uncomfortable and slightly wary. The pictures online were just so different. I was hoping to meet up with a model type, but Cassandra was older than anticipated, with wrinkled skin and an expression that made her look like she herself had followed through on the way to meet me.

Nevertheless, I'd caught a train to meet Cassandra and so I was determined to have a good time. Although initial impressions were very important, I was also experienced enough to know that you should never judge a book by its cover. Cassandra was not like the pictures online, but she had a nice big smile and a real sense of fun. I'd initially been disappointed as I didn't have an attraction to her – but as time went on, I grew to like her personality. She had a great sense of humour and possessed a bellowing laugh too.

We had a few drinks around the Deansgate area of the city and swapped stories about dating online. Cassandra told me about all the blokes who had simply sent her dick pics right from the off. Others had simply asked her to get her tits out for them. I'd been told all this before, of course, but it still shocked me why men would want to initially approach ladies in such a crude way. Obviously, it must have been successful for some men – but I reckoned most ladies would simply have deleted the users, like Cassandra did. She told me that if men sent photos of them cooking a lovely meal or baking a cake, then they'd have much more chance with her. What turned a woman on more – a picture of an erect penis, or a strawberry cheesecake? No contest!

We had a conversation about knobs, in actual fact. She, like lots of others, thought that willies were very unattractive on the whole. I couldn't exactly whip mine out on the table and beg to differ, could I? Rather childishly, I then began a spate of knob gags which most men probably knew, and Cassandra had probably heard before. It really was a little infantile, but she laughed a few times. Disappointingly, she never responded with any fanny gags though. However, we seemed to build more of a bond over our dating history and had some fun discussing it.

After a while, we proceeded onto Canal Street and sat on a table outside. It was surprisingly quiet outside and so we considered going inside instead. Yet, at that moment a large group of ladies arrived wearing black T-shirts with sexual slogans emblazoned across the front in big letters. They were clearly from Newcastle. I could tell that because at first, I thought they were foreign, then realised they spoke with a strong Geordie accent. They were on a hen-do for a lesbian couple getting married in the near future. They all disappeared into the pub only to re-emerge a minute later – saying they weren't allowed in wearing the so-called obscene T-shirts.

I looked carefully at these T-shirts. They were hilarious in my view, albeit obnoxious to some people, I guess. They said phrases such as, 'Tit wanker; fanny licker; rug muncher; bum rimmer; finger blaster and cock-stroker,' amongst others. There were about twenty women in total, and all had a unique, rude message on their T-shirt. I was just in stitches and Cassandra saw the funny side too. The women surrounded us and told us that they'd been refused entry but were, 'Not coming all this fucking way not to get in.' So, in full view of both of us, they removed their T-shirts and turned them inside out. As they chuckled and laughed, the ladies from Tyneside effectively got their baps out. Well, most of them wore bras of course, but I tried to focus on the tits that were on display – albeit only for a few seconds. Being surrounded by lovely knockers was heaven for me, pure heaven.

Cassandra could see me looking intently but didn't seem to mind as she was having a gawp herself. A few of the ladies got talking to us and told us that they had come to Manchester for a couple of nights for their friend's hen do. The couple getting married were lesbians, although the party comprised of a mixture of gay and straight women. I thought one of the straight women was giving me the eye – she was wearing a t-shirt with 'Jizz-swallower' on it and now she was winking at me.

Cassandra got talking to one of the lesbians too, who was displaying a 'Rug-muncher' message. It seemed that she'd hit it off with the lady from Newcastle and there was some chemistry between them. I obviously didn't know if Cassandra was bi-sexual, as I was unaware of her sexual history but maybe she enjoyed a bit of fanny herself. As the drink flowed, I began to get excited at the prospect of those two putting on a show just for me. The 'jizz-swallower' was also licking her lips and pursing them in my direction. This was turning into a fantastic and amusing day.

After a while, however, the 'rug-muncher' and 'jizz-swallower' followed their friends inside the bar and we remained outside. I was really tempted to try and pull either, 'jizz swallower, cock-stroker, or knob-licker' but it wouldn't have been fair on Cassandra. I didn't ask her if she did any of things on the T-shirts at that point – but it made for more amusing conversations later in the night. It was all good-natured fun and it added to the date for sure.

Indeed, this episode on Canal Street reminded me of a night out with my friend Ash a few years earlier. We were having a drink in a rough bar in town when a youngish girl began dancing on the dancefloor on her own, with a few men staring at her – including us. She had long dark hair, a great body and some sexy moves. As she was the only girl dancing, she knew she had the attention of the whole pub. As she continued to dance, her dress started riding up slowly. I'm sure she knew this was happening, but she let it ride up and up until it exposed her perfect pussy. That's right – the girl in question wasn't wearing any panties at all and she knew every man was staring at her beautifully trimmed bush.

As I looked around and saw every bloke staring at her with their tongue hanging out, I realised I was normal. Then, after giving everyone more than an eyeful – the sexy dancer pulled her dress down quickly. After more dancing, it began to ride up again exposing herself and every bloke was watching with their eyes popping out. Ash cleaned his glasses to get a better view and I ordered another pint. We'd only intended to have a quick pint in there but ended up staying half the bloody night. It was a free show and we didn't want to miss it.

On another occasion, I was out with my cricket mates after a match. We ended up going to a club and having a good dance. Some women started dancing with us and for some bizarre reason, one of them started undoing the buttons on my shirt. I thought she may have liked me but as she tried to remove my shirt, she exposed my bloody white vest underneath! Now, why on earth was I wearing such an embarrassing hideous thing? The only explanation I can give is that I liked bowling in a vest as it soaked up all my sweat and I'd not taken it off after the game. So, here I was wearing my sweat stained stinky vest in the middle of the club.

The girl in question laughed when she saw it and it made her more determined than ever to remove my shirt. I was now trying to resist, but a few of her friends grabbed me and I was absolutely powerless. So, as I protested, they managed to get my buttons undone and take off my magnificent shirt. I was crestfallen as the laughter kicked in. Of course, they ran off with it. This meant I was now in the middle of a club chasing them, wearing my sexy vest.

People were in fits of laughter as I ran around the club, making a real tit of myself. The bouncer then approached me and threatened to throw me out unless I covered up the offending vest imminently. Luckily, one of my mates managed to retrieve my shirt just in time. Unfortunately, this was after plenty of unflattering photographs of the incident had been taken but, being part of a cricket dressing-room, I was used to the piss being taken on a regular basis.

As the night progressed with Cassandra, we became fairly merry and decided to go for some food. We settled on a Chinese buffet, somewhere in the city centre. By this time of night, however, the buffet was rather empty and hadn't been re-stocked with piping hot food. We were left with vats of food that were dry and food that'd probably been there for bloody hours. I picked up some spareribs but struggled to find any meat on them. There was probably more meat on a vegan's breakfast. The food was also lukewarm, verging on cold. Eating cold rice and beef in black-bean sauce, minus the actual beef wasn't great. In fact, it was so bad that we actually had to laugh about it. Never before or since, it has to be said, has a Chinese buffet fallen to such depths. I'd have probably eaten some cockroaches or crickets to have some protein at that point – maybe dipped in some cold sweet and sour sauce. I'd even had better vegetarian meals when I was with Lucy – but that was through sheer desperation to please her. In fact, a bowl of bloody salad would've been better.

During the starter of duck pancakes, without the duck, Cassandra told me a little about her family and friends. She said one of her friends was marrying her own cousin and that it was very common in some communities for cousins to marry. I knew this was lawful though – but that you couldn't actually marry your sister or brother, for obvious reasons. She told me that marrying cousins could lead to genetic problems, however, if any child was subsequently born. Apparently, in Iceland as the population is only about 340,000, people have to be very careful who they actually date. Before setting out on a date, many Icelanders checked on a national database to see whether they are swimming in the same gene pool. This was to prevent them shagging their own sister.

I guess there were some regions in England where the population was more closely connected. If men had a few children with different women, it was a real a possibility that two half-siblings would meet and even fall in love. But their children may have genetic deformations as a result. Unlike Iceland, though, it would be almost impossible to check if someone was shagging their own cousin or brother. Surely, there were enough people in the world to avoid such an eventuality. Maybe dating apps should introduce another section to check a family tree. It may lead to a few less dates but educate a whole new generation of people in genealogy.

As far as my family tree was concerned, I knew it wouldn't extend to Cassandra. She was actually a pleasant enough lady, who enjoyed a laugh. We bonded well throughout the day and over our dry, tasteless Chinese. She didn't want to marry her own cousin, but it was clear she wasn't going to marry me either. As we departed, I gave her a little peck on the cheek and thanked her for a nice time. She did the same too and we gave each other a big hug. I knew that the spark and chemistry that I was craving was missing and knew that I'd probably never see her again. After all this bloody time searching for the perfect partner – I was back to square one again. It seemed to me as though using dating sites was a fruitless activity. I was beginning to doubt myself and doubt the whole fucking process. Why couldn't I meet someone? What was wrong with me? To say I had some self-doubt would be an understatement. It appeared as though my life as a single man was meant to be. I'd had another enjoyable day, but the outcome was by now all too familiar. But then I thought, don't give up just yet - keep trying a little longer. I simply had to remain positive in my pursuit of love and happiness.

CHAPTER 33: IN THE DARK

A week or two after my date with Cassandra in Manchester, I went out with a few lads from the cricket club. Towards the end of the night, we ended up in a weird bar in town which was known for its eclectic mix of strange characters. The DJ was a man in drag and there were a few transvestites in there too. The music was mainly from the brilliant 80's and lots of ladies were dressed as if they were still living in the 80's too. There were also quite a few gay people and probably loads of people who didn't mind who they slept with – men or women. I'd been here a couple of times previously, but the vibe on this particular night was fantastic.

For some reason, I ended up in the beer garden at the rear. It was a bit of a haven for cannabis at that time of night – with hippies passing around joints to anyone who fancied a drag. I bumped into a woman who I knew, and she introduced me to her girlfriend. They were both merry to say the least and introduced me to a few more lesbians who they were out with. I sat in the middle of them, having a conversation which made absolutely no sense at all. I didn't understand what was going on by now – but remember just laughing at everything. Everyone was just stoned, and the beer garden crowd were fucking mellow.

I did consider whether my charms would work on any of the lesbians I was with. Maybe I could turn them? Maybe they would change their sexuality at the drop of a hat, when they saw me? Of course, that dream of taking several of them back home was just that – a dream. However, I then got talking to a Polish girl called Olga. She was wearing a long leopard skin coat, had long dark hair and was wearing bright red lipstick which emphasized her sexy lips. There was something erotic about her that I liked – but by this stage of the night I probably thought that the transvestites were sexy too, apart from the one who looked like Boris Johnson wearing a dark wig.

Anyway, after a while talking, I just blurted out to Olga, 'Do you wanna come back to my place?' in a really romantic sort of way. To my surprise, she simply said, 'Yes, let's get a taxi,' quite abruptly. We'd not kissed or held hands in the beer garden – it was quite a surprise that she'd agreed so readily. As we got the taxi back to mine, the conversation became even more strained. Well, you could say that we didn't really talk much. She was Polish but seemed to understand my northern accent. Not that I could understand everything that she was saying. This was developing into a strange situation.

When we got to my house, the first thing Olga said was, 'You don't live here do you?' in some disbelief. I responded, 'Of course I do, this is my house. Look, there's a picture of my kids,' grabbing the frame from a shelf. She still didn't believe me for some baffling reason. I was hungry by now so simply said, 'Are you hungry? I can put a pizza in the oven for us to share,' rather stupidly. She agreed, but I had a good-looking Polish girl sat on my sofa and I'd not made a move yet. What the hell was I thinking? More about my beer munches and rumbling belly obviously.

Then, as the pizza was in the oven – I tried to kiss her. I moved towards her and she pulled away in some disgust. 'I don't do kissing,' she said rather bluntly. 'What, you don't kiss at all?' I replied in some bewilderment. Then, I had a rather horrible and repugnant feeling inside me. We'd not had any physical contact whatsoever, not even holding hands. She was cold with me when I tried to kiss her. She was dressed provocatively, like a lady of the night. Oh, my word – was this lady a fucking prostitute? Of course, I was not known for my subtlety and usually called a spade a spade. I looked at her and said, 'You're not a hooker, are you?'

This was not a good thing to say. I could tell she was angry by the way she snarled at me. But she didn't seem to deny it either – she never said no at any point. This had all been a huge misunderstanding. I reasoned at that moment that she wanted paying for any sex that took place – but I thought she was an attractive lady who'd wanted some fun. I didn't know if she still wanted some pizza, but after a couple of minutes she said, 'I better go, but I need some money for a taxi back,' almost pleading with me. I was understandably confused and somewhat pissed off. The truth was I didn't have much money to give her – apart from my change from the night out. 'I've only got my loose change from tonight,' I told her. 'That's not enough – I need more,' she shouted. This was developing into a fucking stand-off. But she was in my house and I now wanted her to leave quickly. She wasn't having any fucking pizza either.

I ran upstairs and looked in my money drawer, which was full of change. I grabbed another few quid and ran back down – as I didn't trust her being in my home anymore. She could've stolen my Chris Rea CDs for god's sake. When I got downstairs, however, she was already outside the house waiting for a taxi. I gave her the money, and she stared at it like I'd just shoved a fresh turd in her hand. What did she expect? A twenty quid note for just coming back to my house and sitting on my sofa. I'd even offered her a fucking pizza. Talking about the pizza – I went back inside and devoured the lot in double quick time. It was delicious and she wasn't there to have any of it. Yet, in the morning when I woke up, I could feel the heat in my kitchen. It was like being in the fucking Sahara Desert as I'd left the oven all bloody night. She'd probably cost me about twenty quid in gas, after all that.

Olga reminded me of another lady I'd seen a few times, who was from Greece. Thankfully, however, she wasn't a prostitute. She was very pretty, with long dark hair and a lovely complexion. After meeting for coffee on a couple of occasions, she agreed to come back to my house. She brought with her some salad and feta cheese to make a salad. I'd offered to cook, but she was insistent that she'd make me this speciality, Greek Salad. As I've said, I wasn't a big fan of rabbit food. However, what she rustled up was quite simply the best salad dish I'd ever tasted. It went down so well with some crusty bread and a bottle of wine. I was beginning to feel romantic and get in the mood to take things further. Her sexy Greek accent was also turning me on.

As we sat on the sofa after our salad, she blurted out that not all Greek women were hairy, as if I'd made those accusations. I'd done no such thing, of course, but it seemed strange that she'd said it. It made me think that I'd find out very soon. We kissed passionately on the sofa and began to get horny. Then, out of the blue, she jumped up and moved away to the table. It wasn't to finish her salad or feta cheese that's for sure. She sat on a chair beside the table and then, quite emotionally, blurted out, 'I can't do this sorry. I'm really sorry, but I've got a boyfriend.'

I didn't know how to react at this point. Of course, I was shocked and dismayed that she'd not been honest and told me the truth. I'd seen her a few times and assumed she was definitely single. Now, as I questioned her, she almost broke down in tears and confessed that her relationship was faltering, but she didn't know what to do. She did, however, tell me that she liked me a lot and was rather confused about everything. But she also told me an awful lot about her boyfriend, and I began to get the impression that she still loved him. I began to realise that she'd felt guilty about what was about to happen.

As I listened to her sob story and saw her upset and hurt, I realised I had two possible options. Take the bull by the horns and fight for her love and attention. Or, concede that she was still in love and let her try a reconciliation. At this stage, I didn't want to play dirty games. I didn't want to be second best. I didn't need all the hassle. Yes, I liked her a lot, but I'd liked lots of other ladies in the past. I decided to take the latter option and almost acted as a counsellor, as I advised her to try again with her long-term lover. Within the space of an hour, I'd gone from the excitement of a potential new girlfriend to feeling low again. But I'd made the right decision. When she left, I gave her a cuddle and vowed to remain friends. Deep down, though, I knew it'd be the end.

As I'd met Olga the Polish prozzy, in a dodgy bar, I reasoned that the only way to meet someone special was online again. I tried yet again to develop more conversations with several ladies and agreed to meet up with a woman called Melissa. She was a bubbly character, with a mop of blonde hair and a pretty face. When we met, though, Melissa was a lot shorter than I anticipated and a little bit dumpy. I'm not saying that she lied about her height – maybe I just overlooked it.

I was past the point of studying every detail in their profile about every woman I met. So many of them blatantly lied anyway, that I reckoned it didn't matter. Meeting up was the only way to discover the truth. By this point, after all the pizzas I'd devoured I'd put some pounds on myself and tried to be more understanding – especially after the episode with Wendy in Tenby. I'd reflected on that and realised I needed to be more appreciative, considerate and savvy.

I met Melissa for a drink one night and we had a few interesting chats about our respective interests. I didn't feel that much spark to be honest but agreed to meet her again and have a night out together, in another town. It was possible that things may improve, after all. When I saw Melissa again, she did look nicer actually. Although, it appeared that she'd applied her make-up with the lights off and used a trowel in the process. She was still quite small though, despite her 6-inch heels. Nevertheless, her personality was bubbly – though at times she could be loud and laughed like a hyena.

Our night out was mainly fun, as we got merry and the laughs were frequent. In the taxi, on the way back, Melissa asked if I wanted to stay at her house that night. We'd not been particularly romantic throughout the night but had held hands and cuddled a couple of times. Of course, I wouldn't turn this opportunity down. We'd had a pleasant night, so why not? We made our way to her bedroom and I began to get amorous. Then, she turned the lamp off so I couldn't see anything at all. I asked her to put it back on so I could see what I was getting, but she was insistent that we were in the dark. Now, of course, being a man, I wanted to see the goods on full display. It was like buying a piece of fresh fruit from the supermarket. Before making a purchase, I liked to examine carefully, touch and squeeze.

Melissa didn't seem to understand that men were very visual creatures indeed. That's why men loved ladies wearing sexy underwear or erotic uniforms. That's why ladies usually spent half a day getting ready for a night out and spent all day choosing the perfect dress. That's why you witnessed distraught men nearly fainting after being dragged around the shops for six hours, whilst their partner chose an outfit to wear. Time and again I'd been asked to go shopping with a lady and give my opinion on every fucking outfit known to man. 'What's this one like?' she'd ask. 'It's nice yeah,' I replied. But that wasn't enough, of course. 'Just nice? I'm not getting that then. I want to look beautiful. Does it make my bum look big?'

Let's be honest, during sex it also turned men on to see our tool sliding in and out from various angles. It made us feel like real men. Doing it in the dark was the equivalent of taking part in a treasure hunt whilst blindfolded. Melissa didn't see it that way. Whereas I just couldn't see anything at all. I was fumbling about down there and was fingering the mattress most of the time. I couldn't normally find a clitoris with the big light on, never mind in the fucking dark.

First, I tried to find her pussy with my mouth, but started licking the covers. Who knew what her lady-bits looked like? Maybe they were all spotty or full of warts. Maybe that's why she didn't want me to see anything. It would've helped if she'd had glow in the dark pubes or a neon sign above her clit. It occurred to me that a luminous clitoris would've helped men tremendously. Then, I realised that if we were meant to have sex in the dark – women would've been designed that way. Their clit would glow bright yellow like a cat's eye on the motorway. It just wasn't meant to be though – so I had more chance of finding a rogue paper clip on a factory floor.

After fumbling about for ages and feeling lumps all over the place, I tried my best to make it happen. The truth was, however, that being in the dark just didn't do it for me. I may as well have had a blow-up doll and pretended she was real. It made me think about those life-like dolls I'd seen in Amsterdam on my European travels. Only, they seemed just as real as Melissa at this point.

Melissa laid there like a corpse and I felt a bit like a necrophiliac in a mortuary. I pumped and pumped the mattress and then eventually managed to find the right hole. The problem was, it didn't feel much different. Melissa was pleasant enough, but she wasn't my type in bed. I wanted someone who was confident in themselves. I wanted someone who'd let me look at them naked. I wanted someone who enjoyed sex, not someone who wanted to hide it away.

Melissa wanted it in the dark – and now I was in a dark place again. Why the hell couldn't I meet my soulmate? I began to realise that my dreams of meeting someone special were negligible. I had more chance of winning the bloody lottery – and I'd given up playing that. I nearly gave up dating sites too, but just like the lottery, I realised you've got to be in it, to win it.

Rob Morgan

CHAPTER 34: PEA AND PIES

Once again, I decided to venture to Manchester for my next date. I'd been talking to another lady online who appeared to have a zest for life and a great sense of humour. She'd posted some silly photographs on her profile, which I liked the look of. She also looked attractive, with a big smile and a nice set of teeth. In the pictures she also had long blonde hair and a shapely body. She was also about 7 years younger than me. She stated in her profile that she was known as Pea and that her main interest was travelling and visiting places of interest. Her main message, put simply, was that, 'If you want to be with me, you must be prepared to travel and visit new places.' I must admit, this kind of attitude appealed to me. I wanted to travel more too and be more adventurous.

As a child, my parents had never taken us abroad on holiday – although I once went on a football trip to Germany with school. My parents had a caravan and we usually went camping in the West Country – Somerset and Devon were fantastic counties that we explored. As I became a father, we took our children on caravan holidays down south as well. I remember going to places such as Cheddar, Weymouth, Minehead and Cornwall. We also went on caravan holidays to the Lakes, Wales and Scotland. The holidays were always fun, and we tried to visit places like stately homes and gardens, parks, farms, zoos and other places that you took kids – such as the beach. We couldn't afford foreign holidays or expensive treats, but it never occurred to us that we were missing out. There were so many great places around England and in Wales and Scotland that we just felt lucky to go away.

I'd had a taste of foreign travel, however, when I visited my university friend Nick in Cyprus. Afterwards, when I'd gone back-packing around

Europe as a student I'd managed to visit six countries in the process. But now though, my circumstances had changed, and my children were older. I reckoned it was time to see more of the world if I could. I just needed the perfect companion to travel and enjoy life with. It sounded great in theory – but I'd not met anyone to do these things with. It wasn't for lack of trying, that's for sure. Pea obviously wanted the same thing – so it seemed she was in a similar situation to me. Therefore, I was hopeful once again, as I sat on the train to Victoria Station.

When I arrived at the train station, I saw a tall attractive blonde stood in a corner who looked similar to Pea. However, in all the pictures online Pea's hair had been long. This lady had short hair. I wasn't convinced it was her – so walked to the taxi rank outside and sent her a text to say I'd arrived.

As I waited, a pug-faced woman with long blonde hair walked towards me. I thought I was down on my luck again. It'd happened a few times before. Women had lied about their age and took photos from strange angles – so I was prepared to expect the worse. As she approached and got nearer, I gulped and got ready to introduce myself. Thankfully, she walked straight past me. It wasn't to be pug-face this time. Then, as I looked up, I realised I was in luck. It was the lady I'd seen earlier waiting. As I saw her pretty face walking towards me, I thought to myself, 'She'll do.'

We exchanged pleasantries and began walking to Oyster Bar in the city centre. It was a lovely sunny day so we hoped we could sit outside and enjoy some sun. We chatted as we walked, and I asked about her hair. She told me that she'd only had it cut the week before. I was going to tell her that I normally preferred longer hair and then refrained, as I looked into her big wide eyes.

Oyster Bar, as always, was jam-packed when the sun was out. I said I'd go to the bar and she agreed to look for a seat outside. Pea surprised me when her drink of choice was a pint of lager – but she went up in my estimation straight away. There was no point ordering a half anyway, when it was so busy. She said she was saving my shoe leather on having to go back for another.

When I ventured outside, I saw her on a table with a few blokes and she was chatting to them. Maybe I hadn't made a good impression after all. This was not what I had in mind, but thankfully they soon left. However, they were soon replaced by an old couple from Wigan. They were really friendly and started talking to us, almost immediately. Wigan was famous mainly for its Rugby League team and its love of pies. So, for some strange reason to make conversation I asked if they liked rugby - and then pies. Of course, this led to a long chat about the best pies you could buy and moved on to pasties too. So, I was out with a girl called Pea and we were chatting about pies. Thankfully, she loved pies and pasties – this was a northern lass who loved a pie and a pint, what could be better so far?

The conversation with the couple from Wigan was rather bizarre, to say the least. Pea and I seemed to hit it off so well that they assumed we were a couple already. They asked how long we'd been together – unaware that this was our very first date and we'd only just met. There did seem to be a real connection between us and a chemistry that I'd seldom experienced. I mean with Pea, not with the couple from Wigan.

Not only did I fancy her, which was obviously important, but she appeared to have a super personality with a great sense of fun. Her zest for life would complement my sheer pessimism and grumpiness. I tried to have a laugh most of the time but was a natural worrier about life generally. For example, I'd be concerned about the fact that mass deforestation was ruining the Amazon rainforest and killing Jaguars. In short, I tended to worry about things I simply had no control over. Pea appeared to be a far more optimistic character – the sort of person who'd plant a few trees and be very positive about the future.

After a few cheap drinks in Oyster Bar, we moved down to Deansgate and continued our conversations. I was surprised that she hadn't had many boyfriends in the past, but she'd told me that she'd been working a lot of the time and had been a travel rep for a number of years too. This job had allowed her to visit a few places and probably explained her optimism. Being able to sort out numerous room problems and dealing with complaining Brits on holiday with a big smile on your face, must prepare you for anything in life.

She told me that she'd worked seasons in Austria, Spain and Turkey and at a skiing camp in the USA. She'd also travelled around Australia for three months, been on holiday to the Maldives and had visited many

190

European cities too. She could ski, scuba-dive and had even flown a small plane. I'd pissed out of a window in Whitby, burnt my feet in Rhodes and smashed a valuable Chinese vase in Cyprus. We were just so well-matched.

At one of the bars in Deansgate, she bumped into another man who she knew. I must admit, I became a bit jealous for a minute or two as she chatted to him. I just assumed, wrongly, that he was an ex-boyfriend. In fact, she told me she knew him from a previous job at the gas board. Being rather silly, I made the joke that I hoped he wasn't an old flame and there was no longer any spark between them. Pea's face said it all. My jokes had to be a bit better than that to impress her.

The date was going fantastically well so we decided to go for a Spanish Tapas somewhere on Deansgate. Or rather, Pea wanted to go for a Spanish. After drinking all afternoon, I'd have chosen a burger meal at *Wetherspoons*, or maybe a big steak pudding with chips and gravy. However, she insisted on paying about £5 for two king prawns. I'll be honest – at this point in my life I'd never had a Tapas before. It was all new to me. The idea was to choose lots of little dishes and taste the exquisite flavours of each, savouring each morsel.

I discovered that Tapas was all about taking your time and being elegant. It was about the indulgent sophisticated experience of eating, whilst drinking wine or sangria. After about six pints of lager, however, I was just ready to gobble the whole fucking lot in one go. I had the beer munches so bollocks to all this pretentious bullshit, I thought. At this point, I simply wanted to be stuffing a whole KFC family bucket down my throat, with the coleslaw and gravy poured on top.

Despite my cravings to actually eat some proper food, I tried my best to reign in my bursting appetite. I wanted to show Pea that I was not a pisshead, nor a lager lout. I wanted to show her my sophisticated side. So, I sipped the sangria, nibbled on my solitary prawn and devoured each mushroom as though I'd been stranded at sea on my own for two months in a small life raft. In simple terms, I tried to impress her. I was even going to pay for the lovely meal which took three hours to eat, until I realised that I was short. I'd come out with a wad of cash, but it still wasn't enough for this culinary experience. Luckily, Pea was a modern woman who believed in equal rights. That, of course, also meant paying half towards the bill which she duly did.

I must have been making some impression, because after the expense of the tapas, we made our way for a cheap drink at *Wetherspoons*. We found a nice quiet spot in a corner and sat close to each other. The day had been so fantastic that I didn't want it to end – but I didn't want to spoil it either. I gingerly put my arm around her, and we cuddled up a bit, but I didn't know whether to go for a kiss. But, after all those drinks including sangria, I was now merry, and it just felt right. I slowly moved my lips towards her and thankfully she responded in kind. So, after our posh meal I'd made my move on more familiar territory. The kiss was part romantic and part sloppy – I'm sure I got my tongue in there at least once, but it seemed to go well.

After meeting up in the early afternoon, we'd made it through the whole day and until the last train home. Before she departed at her stop, I remember kissing her neck and asking her last name. My plan was to invite her to a forthcoming cricket presentation evening, which included a three-course dinner. Wow, I must have liked her. I was even thinking ahead to another date – if she was agreeable. It'd been an incredible date, although I still had to buy a big bag of chips to eat on my way home, having arrived at my stop. As I dribbled tomato sauce all down my shirt, I was somewhat elated. I couldn't wait to see her again.

CHAPTER 35: MADEIRA MAGIC

Of course, I was anxious whether Pea would feel the same way as me and want to meet up again. We'd had a great date, but the pessimist in me doubted anything would progress further. I asked whether she'd like to attend a cricket presentation evening dinner in a couple of weeks, and she agreed to go. I must have liked her as I even paid £25 for her ticket too. Before that, however, we arranged to go for a walk in the local countryside. This was an opportunity to have another long chat, when we were both sober. It allowed us to develop a greater bond and share our views of the world. By this point, Pea already knew I had three children and didn't want anymore. She also knew I'd had the snip and seemed comfortable about the situation. I was honest right from the outset and hoped she'd accept my situation.

That particular date also ended well when I cooked her baked sea bass, courtesy of Marks & Spencer. She was really impressed, but I'd only banged the fish in the oven. In all honesty, I also wanted to bang her - but I knew I'd have to be patient with such a classy lady. The meal I cooked was certainly a step up from frozen pizza and fish fingers though, which showed how much I was trying to impress.

The cricket dinner that followed was also a major success. She related well to all my cricket mates and their partners and we had some cracking banter at our table. She was also impressed that I'd remembered her surname from our first date, as we had place names where to sit. On the whole, the night was superb, and I was really proud to have her as my date. She looked stunning in her dress and made me happy.

As time progressed, we continued to see each other most weekends. We even started making the effort to see each other during the week, if we could. We simply enjoyed being together and the distance between our respective towns didn't dampen our enthusiasm. Everything seemed to be progressing very nicely. After a couple of months, we agreed to have a few nights away in the lovely city of Chester. By now, of course, nature had taken its course and it'd been everything I was hoping for. We were not only compatible in everyday life - but importantly to me - also in the bedroom. We seemed so relaxed with each other very quickly and being intimate was very natural and loving.

It's hard to explain how I felt about Pea, but everything seemed different this time. She understood my sense of humour; she got my shit jokes. She understood my views and listened to me. We didn't agree about everything but could have a mature debate about current affairs and politics. She was intelligent, trustworthy and on the same wavelength as me. We fancied each other, but basically just clicked as people. The first date in Manchester had been simply amazing and things had continued in the same vein.

As part of our break, we decided to spend one day at Chester Zoo. This was a place I'd visited a few times as a kid, and again when my children were young. It was a fantastic day out for the whole family. It was quite a cold day at this time of year and Pea wore her hat and gloves. I'd made a picnic for us and we decided to eat it outside for some reason, on a picnic table. The thing I remember most was that Pea ate her sandwich wearing her bloody gloves. I'd never seen that before - or since. I thought it was a bit daft to say the least but told her so. In some ways it was quite endearing, although she did struggle to eat her crisps.

We went inside the bird and reptile house and watched all the exciting geckos and lizards stood there motionless. Why would anyone keep those boring fuckers as pets? We then tried to find the snakes in their tanks and all the camouflaged insects, examining the glass containers with eagle eyes. As we looked at the crocodile, a bird shat on Pea's shoes. It was a massive shit in all honesty. I was going to impress her like a true gent by licking it off but thought I'd offer her a tissue instead. We took some photos inside the reptile house and tried to avoid the same bird who obviously had the shits that day. It seemed to be flying around, trying to shit-bomb the visitors. There was bird poo everywhere, but hey, it was all part of the fun. As long as the crocodile didn't escape, we'd be fine.

A little later we played a game, whilst sat on a bench outside. It was called 'spot the red panda' and, funnily enough, involved trying to spot a red panda. We sat there for ages staring into the trees, trying to spot a red panda. At first, we couldn't spot a red panda. Then, I reckoned I'd spotted a red panda, but it was just a funny looking branch. Then Pea exclaimed at the top of her voice, 'I've spotted a red panda!' and I said, 'Have you really spotted a red panda?' in defeat. Unfortunately, she'd spotted a red panda and won the game of 'spot the red panda'. Without doubt, though, the highlight of our day at the zoo was watching the chimpanzees. Wow, they were so much like human beings. The way they moved and acted and looked was similar to some people I'd fucked.

Our break to Chester went so well that we decided to book a summer holiday together. We considered the options and plumped for the island of Madeira - which was known as the 'Jewel in the Atlantic' by all accounts. I'd not really been to such an exotic sounding place before. I mean Madeira just sounded fucking amazing before I'd even got there. It turned out to be a fantastic place, with lots of friendly people - although there was a distinct lack of beaches. If you liked sand between your toes and in your bum crack, then it wouldn't be the place for you.

During the first couple of days we sunbathed beside our lovely little pool. I remember reading Graeme Swann's autobiography, *The Breaks Are Off,* and Pea asking me lots of questions about cricket. I'm sure she loved me telling her all about the game in great detail - but I vowed to take her to Old Trafford to watch a game when we got back. I could tell by her face that she was very excited by the prospect.

After two days of sunbathing, I'd made a tit of myself once again. This time, it was my fucking knees. Yes, you've guessed it - I'd severely burnt the bastards. I'd applied sun cream but had fallen for a trap. My shorts were covering my knees whilst in a standing position and applying the lotion, so I figured I'd be okay. What I hadn't anticipated was that they'd ride up when I lay down on a sun lounger. It was a schoolboy error - but when it came to holidays in the hot sun, I was out of my depth. My knees were red raw and painful. Pea tried her best to apply after-sun without making me scream and did her best to placate me. Although, for the rest of the holiday every time I sat down, I exposed my shiny red knees.

It was Pea's birthday whilst we were in Madeira, so we decided to have a special meal out. It was basically steak on a stone. We'd never encountered this before – it sounded fantastic in theory – because the hot stone cooks the steak as you wish, right under your nose. To be fair, when the steak was sizzling there and then in front of us, it sounded great. Then, it dawned on us that we were cooking our own fucking meal. We had to keep an eye on it and concentrate just in case the steak burnt. It was certainly different – but I'd draw the line at a steak. I wouldn't want to be cooking my own stir fry, chopping my own salad or frying my own fish and then leave a bloody tip for the service. They may as well get you to do the washing-up as well.

As it turned out, the meal, the company and whole evening was amazing. One day we walked into Funchal, the lovely capital, and saw these alien-like creatures in the fish market. They were the ugliest fish you've ever seen. They were called Scabbard and were apparently a popular dish on the island. I always liked to try the local produce so ordered a Scabbard that night, which tasted lovely with bananas. Pea thought they were disgusting; I mean the Scabbard – not the bananas, so gracefully declined.

The next day I was persuaded to go up the mountains in a cable-car. Now, I was scared of heights and suffered from vertigo. But I was trying to impress Pea and from where I was stood, it didn't look too bad. The cable-car height was hidden from view by some buildings in front of us. So, we jumped into the glass bowl, along with another couple. As it started moving, I was fine at first – and then it went over and above the buildings. The true scale of the mountain then became apparent and my hands and feet began to sweat.

I squeezed Pea's hand so tight, she said I was hurting her. My heart began to pump faster, and I was nearly having palpitations, as I looked at the drop below. For fuck's sake, why had I agreed to do this? The other lady could see I was in a bad way and tried to reassure me by asking questions about my life. At the time, though, I thought my life was about to end imminently and didn't give a shit. I was having a panic attack as the glass bowl swirled around in the wind.

Pea tried to calm me down as we got higher and higher. She told me they were built by top engineers and to her knowledge none had ever fallen from the cable. This wasn't doing anything for my vertigo, however, and by now I was almost shitting myself. The other lady chipped in again and started asking about our hotel and where we'd been. I felt like telling her to shut the fuck up, in my useless and hopeless state. Then, with one final shudder, the cable-car reached the top of the mountain. I literally ran to the nearest toilet block and emptied my bowels. The journey to the top had literally made me shit myself. Afterwards, it dawned on me that I'd have to get back down. There was no way I was going on a cable-car, so I vowed to walk it – even if it took ten hours. Pea then persuaded me to go back down on the famous Madeira Wicker Toboggan Sled. Now, this was basically a ride down the mountain in a basket on wheels. Fortunately, we didn't have to steer it as well, as an expert wearing clogs was behind us to steer round those tight bends. What could possibly go wrong?

I was nervous too as I sat in the wicker sled at the top of the mountain, but I was now close to the ground and felt much better. As I sat down, my shorts rode up once more and my bright red knees were on display. I was worried that we didn't have knee pads or crash helmets to wear, whereas Pea was just giggling in excitement. I wanted this nightmare to end, but as we set off down the mountain, I began to enjoy the thrill. This, in contrast to the cable-car, was fantastic. The man behind us, who was steering the sled with his special boots, even stopped for us at one point and took a photograph. It was a great experience and I wasn't even sick. Pea must have been so impressed by my manliness. I was a macho man and had now proved to her that I could make it in the SAS. Ant Middleton would have been so proud of me. I'm quite sure he would've praised my bravery and courage in the sight of so much adversity.

That night we'd booked a dinner at a posh hotel, with a big band playing. We were sat next to a young Swedish couple who were on their honeymoon. They were a likeable couple who told us about what they'd been up to on their honeymoon. Well, not everything obviously. I even refrained asking them if they shopped at IKEA or drove a Volvo, just like in Torquay many years earlier when I'd questioned Ami in the street. We got talking to them and it transpired there was a casino in the hotel on another floor. We'd never been into gambling or seen a proper casino so decided to have a look. There was a Blackjack table there and a young lady was the croupier.

I fancied I could win some money as I'd played pontoon many times against my kids and usually won, so decided to show Pea how it was done. Of course, I lost all three games in a matter of minutes and was down about £15. Pea then lost too, and it was all over so quickly. It was the equivalent of enticing a beautiful lady into a hotel room ready for a night of passion and then coming in your pants at the sight of her bra. It made me realise just how easy it was to lose lots of money, in no time at all. People think they'll win the next game and play with hope. In reality, it's a dangerous addiction that'll chew you up and spit you out in bits. I was just relieved to get on the dance floor and strut my stuff. However, having seen my silly dances once more, I think Pea wanted to go back to the casino and lose more money.

Pea also liked swimming and sailing and booked us onto a boat trip in a catamaran, in order to go dolphin spotting. I was very sceptical that we'd actually see any dolphins and wasn't too keen to be on a boat, as I'd once taken the kids seal spotting in Wales and had to lie down after being dizzy for hours. Mind you, on that trip to Cardigan Bay, half the boat had puked up in choppy waters, including my son. I'd always had a problem with boats but was trying to make a good impression.

This time in Madeira, the sea appeared to be calmer – although we made a big mistake by arriving early and sitting on the boat for about 30 minutes before we set off. The boat was simply bobbing up and down as we waited to set off. I was sat next to a German bloke who was swigging a can of lager and looked at him with jealously – because by this time my stomach was already feeling tender and my head was starting to spin.

After an hour or so into the journey, my guts could take no more. The sea had become choppier and Pea's chirpiness was getting on my bloody nerves. She didn't understand how bad seasickness was. She could do spins in an aeroplane and feel fine. Nothing seemed to phase her at all. I tried to tell her I felt sick, but she wanted an alcoholic beverage from the bar. Then, I ran down the steps to the bog and puked my guts up good and proper. I remember feeling embarrassed by the whole episode – but surely, I'd not been the only passenger who'd suffered in this way.

After a while, I heard a knock on the toilet door. Pea shouted and said that dolphins had been spotted nearby and that I should come back up. I gingerly made my way up the steps and looked out to sea. There, in front of my very eyes, I saw three dolphins jumping out of the water. They were magnificent creatures and seemed so close to us.

Was I hallucinating? I didn't know what reality was as my fucking head was spinning round like a top. I felt like I'd just ridden the waltzer about fifty times. But people were muttering how beautiful they were and taking pictures of them. It was all very real - the dolphins were real, and my fucking seasickness was all too real. As we turned back to shore, I knew I couldn't last without being sick again - so went back to the boy's room below deck.

Sometime later, there was another knock on the door. It was bubbly Pea once again, asking how I was and if I could take some photographs. I staggered back up to the deck once more and she handed me the camera. This time, she was going for a swim and wanted a picture or two of her in the sea. I looked in the digital camera and tried my best to focus. The problem was my eyes couldn't focus at all and my head was spinning, as we bobbed up and down on the Atlantic Ocean. She shouted me from afar, but I couldn't see her. I pointed the camera at her, but the big German man told me that was his wife. I thought he was going to push me in, but he asked if I was okay and stopped me from falling over. I was fucking delirious by now and salivating at the mouth like a rabid dog. As this was unfolding, Pea shouted, 'Yoo-hoo,' from the sea and tried to smile for the camera shot. I think I took twenty snaps of my fucking trainers.

Walking back to our apartment from the boat was a chore I had to endure. I staggered most of the way and Pea did her best to hold me up and help me. As we walked up a big hill, I looked at the restaurants above and smelt a curry. Unfortunately, this turned my guts again and I puked up right outside an Indian restaurant with people watching me, as they tucked into a chicken bhuna. However, as I looked down at the pool of sick on the pavement it looked more like a vegetable biryani.

I was in a bad way but managed to make it back and had a lengthy lie down. I'd seen some dolphins, but realised I was nothing like Pea when it came to a sense of adventure. She wasn't frightened of heights; she didn't get seasickness and she didn't get burnt. I was a lightweight in comparison, but at least I'd given things a go. Either I'd carry on trying and make a go of it or give up and find someone more boring like myself. I'd loved most of our time together, though, and vowed it would be the former. I was determined to try and live life to the full – I wanted Pea's sense of adventure to make me a new man. I wanted to try new things and hoped that she'd try them with me.

CHAPTER 36: TRAVELLER'S TALES

As time progressed, my relationship with Pea grew stronger and more stable. She was a reliable person who never let me down - something I believed was an endearing quality. If she said she'd do something, she did it. If she said she'd meet me somewhere, she was always there - usually early. After being pissed about by women in the past, this was something I admired and had craved. Someone who genuinely cared about me and wanted to be with me. The feeling was mutual too, as I not only fancied her, but enjoyed her company in abundance. She often made me laugh and giggle and, put simply, made me happy again.

I'd not introduced any woman to my children by this stage, despite having several brief relationships. It was a massive step for me, but now it just felt right. After months together and Pea staying at mine quite often, it just seemed the next step in our relationship. I'd already met Pea's dad and siblings by this point and had bonded well with them. Sadly, I couldn't meet Pea's mum as she had died a few years previously. Understandably, she was still raw at times about that, but said that I'd have got on well with her mum. It was great, though, that I'd been out for several meals with her family and things had gone well. They made me very welcome and feel part of the family, very quickly.

After much deliberation, we arranged a walk in a local park and Pea met my children for the first time. It was certainly a stepping-stone to developing a relationship with them. Of course, I was a little anxious at first, but Pea tended to get on with most people and had a very friendly and likeable persona. Thankfully, my kids gave me very positive feedback from the off and I felt a hurdle had been bridged. The more and more we saw each other together, the more of a family unit we appeared to become. Of course, Pea wasn't there to be another mum – but it was important that they bonded with her for the sake of our future.

After a while, we decided to book a short break with the youngest two of my children and had a few nights away in a caravan in Somerset. It took about six hours to get there, mainly because of the M6 again. In hindsight, maybe we should've gone somewhere a little closer, but after plenty of moaning on the journey we finally made it. The moaning was mainly by me, though, as I was the one who had to drive on our shitty roads.

Having arrived at our caravan and unpacked our luggage, we decided to go for a walk on the local beach. We were tired from the journey but wanted to look for crabs and explore. However, after about half an hour, the heavens opened, and we got absolutely drenched. All of us were soaking wet and water dripped from us like a shaggy dog that'd just run through a river. But then, as we got back to the caravan, we all started laughing loudly. We were dripping wet, but happy.

In the caravan we played board games and watched television in our little cosy lounge. There was also a pool on site and some great waterslides, which we used. The campsite itself was pleasant enough, but the evening entertainment was shockingly bad. It was full of third-rate singers, silly party games for all the family and a few plain weirdos.

I tried to put a positive spin on things, but even after a few pints it was hard to. I felt like grabbing the microphone myself and telling a few knob gags to all the hyperactive kids, just to make things a bit better. My children just wanted to go back to our caravan and play *Trivial Pursuit*. After hearing several songs murdered by the so-called entertainer, I couldn't have agreed more.

We visited Dunster Castle and had a great day there, which included a fantastic bird display with several birds of prey. On another day we visited a local zoo and also made a stop at Weston-Super-Mare beach, which was like going back in time. Until, that is, you needed to use the toilet and had to fucking pay. I never agreed with having to pay to fulfil a bodily function. Imagine being desperate for a shit, only you didn't have the twenty pence to gain entry. It's no wonder kids always brought a bucket and spade to the beach. They could bury Grandad's turd, if need be. If you genuinely had the trots it'd cost about a fiver – unless you stayed there all day to get your money's worth. Anyway, it was a memorable holiday because we continued to bond, and all had fun.

Over the next couple of years, our relationship went from strength to strength. Pea certainly encouraged me to travel more widely and we visited some great European cities. For example, we visited Barcelona, Rome, Salzburg and Munich. In Barcelona we visited the Nou Camp football stadium, which was huge and impressive, the old Olympic village from the 1992 Olympic Games and a couple of fantastic parks – including Gaudi's park which contained much of his celebrated sculpture work. We ate genuine Spanish Tapas with a bottle of wine and had a romantic drink of sangria on the famous La Rambla – until I saw the fucking price. To be fair, I did moan a little about prices in Barcelona – but Pea tried to make me see sense on more than one occasion. Of course, she was correct. It really was worth £9 for a glass of sangria.

We went to Rome in December to celebrate New Year. I'd never been away at this time of the year before but thought it would be something different. It certainly was. Trying to look around the Vatican at new year was similar to a fly infestation around a fresh piece of dung. It seemed as though there were thousands of people all trying to gain entry at the same time. We were shoved through the place like cattle and got told to look out for pickpockets. There was so much bumping and barging, nobody would know if a pickpocket was around. I'm just glad that I had bad wind after some dodgy prawns the previous evening. It meant most people kept their distance from me – about two inches, but it's all relative.

This expedition, of course, was all to see Michelangelo's great Renaissance art, the Sistine Chapel – which took him from 1508 until 1512. Now, don't get me wrong, it was pretty amazing. I did wonder, though, that it may have taken him less time if he'd have done the painting on a wall instead. It may have been a bit easier than dangling upside down for four years. In the Sistine Chapel, we were told to be silent and couldn't take photographs. I was dying to break wind but couldn't risk my fart echoing around the sacred structure. Thankfully, I held it in until we got to St Peter's Basilica, which was an incredible piece of architecture. It was even good enough for a Pope.

The best attraction in Rome, in my view, was the magnificent Colosseum. It was the largest amphitheatre ever built and historically the fights there usually involved slaves, criminals or prisoners. Most of the modern-day fights involved pushy salesman trying to use various techniques to attract the tourists. Our guide, however, was knowledgeable and courteous throughout and made our trip thoroughly enjoyable.

On New Year's Eve we made our way to one of the city's main squares and soaked up the atmosphere. Well, I say atmosphere. It was more like trying to avoid being fire-bombed by a firecracker, thrown by a silly teenager from afar. The firecrackers were going off all over the bloody place and it could've been dangerous. Thankfully, Pea was there to shield me and keep me safe once again. What would I do without her? She was becoming my rock.

On New Year's Day, we stood on the famous Spanish Steps whilst listening to a full-blown orchestra playing a concert. It was great – if you didn't have a hangover that is. Rome certainly had fabulous architecture everywhere you looked, for sure. The only downside was the boring food – pizza and pasta that was overpriced and tasted better from a supermarket back home. I liked an Italian meal for sure, but I was disappointed with the pizzas. I'd had that many in the past, I reckoned I was a bit of an expert. To me, a pizza should have an actual topping on it and a sauce that covers all the base rather than being dry and bare.

The most romantic part of our break, though, was when we went to the gorgeous Trevi Fountain at night. It was all lit up and looked amazing from our angle, not looking at the tacky shops nearby. I gave Pea a lengthy kiss and thought I was being so romantic for once. I was a new man and was changing for the better. I was becoming more cultural, more sophisticated and more loving. I was even beginning to show my emotions more in public. I even held her hand a few times.

Our trip to Salzburg and Munich was definitely one of my favourites. Salzburg was the birthplace of Mozart and had views over the Eastern Alps. The town itself was lovely and we had a great time exploring its cobbled streets and sampling some hearty food. A goulash soup I tasted there was simply the best soup I've ever had. One of our best days was when we visited a small German town on the border with Austria. It was called Berchtesgaden and was in the Bavarian Alps.

Just south of the town was Hitler's *Eagle's Nest* retreat. We went for a boat ride on Königssee Lake, which was surely one of the most beautiful Alpine lakes in Europe. The cliffs beside us rose up into the sky as we sailed through the impressive ravine. As we reached a patch of land to stop and look at a magnificent church named St Bartholomew's, it began to snow. I looked up at the mesmeric snowflakes and then looked at Pea. At that moment, I knew I didn't want to be with anyone else but her. It was magical.

Having had a few days in and around Salzburg, we caught the train to Munich. On arriving at our very modern hotel, we discovered that the space age room had a sort of capsule in the room that was, quite frankly, housing the toilet. The problem was that this capsule was almost transparent and was not separated from the room itself. In other words, we could probably watch each other have a dump.

I'd have thought that in a modern room the toilet would be part of the bathroom, but this was just plain weird. It was certainly a new level to our relationship. Every couple, I guess, has to go through this 'shitting in front of each other stage' at some point. Luckily, there was a large television too so we could turn up the volume and watch that, when one of us had to drop the kids off. It was another box ticked in terms of our relationship. At this rate we'd be moving on to threesomes and swinging parties soon. I much preferred the transparent shower glass, though, to be honest. I could watch Pea take a shower and bash a quick one out before she'd finished.

Going away on these city breaks, and other holidays certainly made us grow closer as a couple. Being confined to a hotel room in a foreign country could make or break a relationship. Luckily for us, we had a mutual understanding whilst we were away. Basically, Pea told me what we would do that day and I agreed to along for the ride. She liked to be organised, well planned and fit everything into our busy schedule. To be fair, she was a leader and I was happy to concede to her suggestions. She planned everything with military precision, and everything usually ran smoothly. I appreciated her approach and occasionally she even consulted me. Occasionally, she even let me choose what pub we could go in or let me watch some cricket in a sports bar, if we were in England.

The one thing we argued about at times, was where we would eat our main meal. I tended to look at the price on the menu before making a choice, based solely on value for money. Pea just looked at the place itself, if it looked busy and nice and clean inside. I must admit, I was a tight git at times and didn't want to be ripped off like many tourists. I'd walk an extra mile to get a good deal and consider all options carefully. Pea was the sort of person who'd enjoy the experience, if possible, and not be too worried about price whilst on holiday. She also couldn't be bothered traipsing around every restaurant in the resort before deciding where to eat. In the end, we seemed to find a compromise on our trips away. She chose the restaurant - and then I paid.

CHAPTER 37: LIVING THE DREAM

By this point in time, it was becoming apparent that Pea was the one for me. We'd been staying over at each other's houses for part of the week and loved being together most of the time. We'd also travelled to several European cities by now and been on a couple of beach holidays too. In addition, she'd bonded well with my kids and they'd developed a relationship with her too. In these circumstances, it seemed a natural step to move in together on a permanent basis. I was ready to take the plunge and give up some of my independence.

Nevertheless, the problem that existed was that we both had our own houses and so we agreed that Pea would put her house up for sale and move in with me. Clearly, this was another big step as I'd been used to my own independence for so long. I could watch sport whenever I wanted, I could eat whenever I wanted, and I could bash the bishop whenever I wanted.

All this would change, however, when Pea moved in. I'd have to watch programmes about animals, fashion and cooking. I'd have to eat when she was hungry. I'd have to wank in secret when she popped out to the shops. But these were small sacrifices to make to have her with me. No longer was I a sad lonely bastard who thought the highlight of the night was eating a Bombay Bad Boy Pot Noodle, whilst watching cricket highlights. Although, that was still rather good at times actually.

We also agreed that I'd have to put the heating on at times, especially in the depths of winter. Pea was fed up of covering herself with a blanket and wearing her bobble hat inside. She even made sure that we had hot water so the dishes could be washed properly, and my plates would be totally clean. I didn't mind the cold or a bit of dirt, but she was definitely having a positive influence. She insisted that I changed my bed covers on a more regular basis and washed my clothes more than once a month.

In addition, she made me get rid my cricket porn which had built up in the bathroom, in particular. Basically, she insisted that hundreds of cricket magazines scattered everywhere around the house had to go. She also bought girlie things herself like candles, ornaments and cushions and vegetables. We also agreed that seeing our own friends was also important. We didn't want to restrict each other's independence too much and become suffocating. Being together 24 hours a day seven days a week was never a good option.

One thing we had in common was our love of food and drink. At university I was never a foodie and my diet had been, quite frankly, shit. I rarely ate vegetables and I certainly didn't buy fruit. I also couldn't cook, and food was just a fuel to get me through the day. As I got older, however, my love of food grew like a solitary apple tree developing into a fine orchard. Unfortunately, my waistline also grew as well. I'd been skinny at university and had a decent body most of my life. But now, I'd put on some timber and my body-shape was changing.

Pea was certainly a bad influence on me, in this respect. She enjoyed dining out and I'd become accustomed to eating out more often than ever before. We both enjoyed trying different restaurants and different cuisines. On holiday too, we always wished to try the local dishes and different types of food. It was becoming one of life's pleasures. The more I ate out, the more my culinary skills improved too. I went from shitty microwave meals for one whilst living on my own, to cooking lots of dishes from scratch.

I could cook a superb chilli-con-carne, spicy curry, prawn foo yung, spaghetti carbonara and paella. I also did lots of different roasts, grilled steak and pan-fried fish. I was inspired by some of the thousands of cooking programmes on television. It seemed that every time the TV was on, there was another bloody cooking show. My favourite presenters, though, were the Hairy Bikers because they cooked hearty food with a smile on their face and brought humour to the show. I even tried some of their recipes.

I'm sure Pea appreciated my efforts in the kitchen too, as I tried to be a new man and satisfy her through her stomach. I also knew that making a simple cup of tea would do me a favour, as she loved a brew and drank about ten cups a day. I discovered that if I cooked Pea a lovely meal and made her a nice cup of tea after, I was almost on a promise. She'd call it romance, I guess, but I called it being savvy. We also both enjoyed a few drinks including wine, beer, cider, prosecco, vodka, rum, gin, Irish cream and cocktails. In fact, we'd try most drinks other than whisky and brandy – though not usually on the same night. This mutual love of food and drink certainly allowed us to bond more closely. It'd be shit if she was teetotal.

We tended to go on pub crawls in different places, often with a country walk or a meal thrown in. We tried to refrain from drinking alcohol during the working week, but at weekends we'd let ourselves go. It was a kind of release after working hard all week and we would usually have at least one night out on the razzle somewhere. If Pea's brother, Ian, was there then the sessions could get messy. He could drink far more than me, but I did my best to keep up - like a silly teenager trying to impress their mates. These days or nights out, however, allowed me to get to know Pea's family much more and integrate as part of the family.

Though Pea had put her terraced house on the market, she was struggling to sell it. The area in which she lived had deteriorated somewhat and the housing market was in decline. It caused her some worry and stress and was certainly difficult at times. On one occasion she thought she'd sold it – only for the buyer to renege late in the day. It was a real blow to us, as we wanted to progress with our plans and move on. Eventually, after quite a while of disappointment Pea had to drop the price of her house once more, in order to make a sale. This ploy worked in the end – but she sold at a loss. At this point, I still had to sell my house too, so the process started all over again.

This period of living together, however, allowed us to get used to each other's foibles and idiosyncrasies. For example, I didn't particularly like it when she forgot flush the toilet. She didn't like it when I farted whilst her head was resting on my lap. I didn't like it when she looked at her mobile phone all the time. She didn't like it when I displayed my lack of knowledge about social media, modern technology, DIY, cars, clothes, handbags and anything else that she knew about, that I didn't. She certainly had more practical skills than me and was much better with her hands.

I was crap at DIY and fixing anything that broke. Pea put me to shame at times. At least I put the bin out, though, and cut the grass. Before we put my house on the market, I pulled down my manky shed and decided to buy another to help the sale. Ian came around to help us put it up. He was an engineer and could do anything with his hands. Basically, I made brews and a bacon butty whist Ian and Pea spent all day doing the job. I felt a little inadequate, but at least I made a good cup of tea.

When I put my house on the market, I had some immediate interest. I soon had an offer, but it was much lower than what I really wanted to accept. Nevertheless, as it was a buyer's market and we wanted to buy our dream home together, I had to accept in the end. We'd been looking at some new estates about ten miles or so from where I lived, in a nice relatively rural area.

One estate in particular was a favourite to us and Pea felt there was a positive signal too. She'd discovered that her mum had grown up in a house down the road from this estate. She felt it was a sign and was keen to identify the best plots. Having looked around the show homes about 3000 times, we found a good plot and put a deposit down. Now, it was a matter of waiting for our brand-new home to be completed. We knew it'd be a few months but had no alternative but to move out of mine as the buyer wanted to occupy, which was understandable, I guess.

Due to the wait for our new home, we had to spend some time living out of a suitcase in a hotel and other weeks staying at my sister's house and Pea's sister too. Of course, we were very grateful for their help and though this was a waiting game for us, we tried to make the best of it. Whilst living in a hotel room, we had to eat meals whilst sat on our bed on quite a few occasions and even had to borrow a fork as we'd packed our cutlery away in a storage unit.

It seemed strange eating a Chinese with a fork, whilst sat on our bed. On one occasion, we bought a mixed kebab for two from a takeaway nearby. On arriving to our room, we opened the boxes of meat given to us and scattered them on the bed. It was huge pile of meat and looked like we'd cut up a massive animal in the room. There was enough food to feed us for a couple of days.

This period of moving about was difficult, as we lacked any real stability at this point in time. Pea enjoyed looking after her sister's dog though when we stayed there. It was a little Shih Tzu called Winston. He was a lovely dog and we tried to take him out every evening. I'm sure she loved him more than me. I was the one who always picked up his shit though. I began finding poo bags in all my pockets, every time I went out. One time, I even took my sandwich to work in one. A clean one, I hasten to add. Winston was loveable and I could tell Pea wanted a dog in the future. I was happy, however, if we just had him as a house guest every now and then, as long as he didn't crap all over the carpet.

Eventually, after what seemed like years, we had a date for the keys. It was all very exciting to move into our dream home with help from our families. We'd arranged to move all our things the next day over the weekend so on the day we got the keys it was just us two, a takeaway and a bottle of champagne to share. As the day drew to a close, we sat in our new family room on cheap wooden chairs and toasted our new home with the fizz. We'd certainly come a long way since that first meeting at Victoria Station. It was amazing to think that we'd met each other through a dating site and now we were celebrating moving into our new home together. It felt strange being in our new house, a strange but delightful feeling. It was a new start for both us and one that we were determined to make the best of.

CHAPTER 38: SANTORINI SURPRISE

Buying our new home together was, at times, a stressful experience as you can imagine. Not only did we have to spend some time living in different hotels and with our families, but it also meant endless weekends shopping at stores, for buying essentials such as carpets, curtains, blinds, sofas, a table and chairs, new kitchen utensils and light fittings. Of course, whereas Pea thought carefully about colour schemes and patterns, I was fine as long as we bought a big new television. Once she'd agreed we could buy a new TV, she knew she'd have the final say on everything else. To be fair, she was well planned and had ideas swirling around in her head about different colour combinations for each room – whereas I just wanted to watch sport.

The one item we had disagreements over was a new fireplace. We visited a local showroom and saw one on offer, which was lovely, but I wasn't quite sure it was what we were after for our lounge. On the other hand, Pea was insistent that it was perfect for us. In the following weeks, we ventured to every conceivable showroom in the North West looking at bloody fireplaces.

In the end, after many miles on the road and many afternoons staring at fireplaces – we bought the first one we'd seen. It was a pattern that could reflect our relationship in all reality. We'd discuss things in depth and listen to each other's opinions – and then I'd decide Pea was right all along. In all honesty, at times I struggled deciding even what I wanted for tea. Once, she asked me if I was indecisive and I replied, 'I don't know.'

Obviously, it took some time to make our new house a home, as it was brand new and needed our stamp on it. We didn't even have a proper garden at the rear upon purchase – but simply a plot of land full of topsoil. The next job was turning this soil into our own garden design. Again, Pea had visions about what it should look like and studied garden design books in depth. To be fair, we discussed this part in detail and disagreed about the size of the patio we wanted. Pea had seen a garden table and chairs set that she'd liked and reckoned we needed plenty of room to sit outside. I was more inclined to have a smaller patio and a larger lawn.

When our massive patio was completed, it looked like Pea was correct yet again. Our table and chairs looked rather nice and there was plenty of room for a barbeque and a five a side football pitch. Well, not quite, but you get the idea. We were certainly happy with Pea's design. The next stage was buying some trees and plants for the border. We trailed around the area to lots of garden centres which was lots of fun, trying to find some bargains. Eventually, we found one that sold lovely trees and shrubs at very reasonable prices and had them delivered by some old wrinkly bloke who looked like he'd keel over at any moment. He insisted on helping to carry some of the trees into the back and nearly collapsed on our new patio. We nearly had to dig a hole for him too – at least we'd already got a spade.

One Sunday morning, we got up early with the children and spent the day planting everything around the edge of the lawn. When the job was done, it was actually very rewarding looking at our new completed garden. I'd never been interested in gardening, but now I thought I'd enjoy looking after our new special place. The problem always turned out to be those fucking weeds though. Within weeks, these little bastards were springing up all over the place. Maybe Pea would enjoy gardening more than me after all – she'd never had a garden and was excited about watching all our trees and bushes grow. It would always be my job to cut the grass, though she had more experience of trimming down bushes.

Doing all these jobs around the house and garden may have been a chore at times, but it also meant that we were always busy, and time seemed to fly by. We also had a house-warming party a few months after moving in and family and friends visited us in our new home to wish us luck. Everything seemed to be coming together at last. We were settling into our new place and certainly enjoying life together. We booked our next summer holiday to the beautiful Greek island of Santorini. I felt there was something magical about the Greek islands and the people were so welcoming and friendly. We'd already been to Kefalonia on one summer holiday and had also taken the kids to Corfu. These holidays were both fabulous and we encountered some amazing beaches and delicious Greek food, which we both loved.

We stayed at a fairly quiet spot in Santorini but had a lovely pool and a picturesque beach not far away. We couldn't really afford to stay in the exclusive resort of Oia, which was famous for its white-washed buildings and was pictured a thousand times in glossy travel magazines. Many of the buildings were even carved into the cliffs and overlooked the majestic Aegean Sea. It was the place where many celebrities stayed – but we went one day to visit and experience it for ourselves.

The buildings were certainly beautiful, the narrow-cobbled streets were pretty on the eye and the ambience of the place was magical. When we looked out to the sea too, it was obvious why this place was sought after as a village to visit. We noticed that there were some restaurants near the bay and made our way down the steep slopes and the numerous steps that took us down. We thought that we may take a ride on a donkey on the way back to the top, but when we saw their sad faces at the bottom of the slopes, we decided it may be best to walk it back. We saw some people swimming in a natural lagoon at the base of the cliffs and decided to join them. Swimming in that lagoon whilst the hot sun beamed down, was a memory I'll always cherish.

On one evening, we'd booked a table in a well-known winery quite near to where we were staying, called Santos Winery. Apparently, it was well regarded for having fabulous sunset views, from the terrace where our table was located. It was, quite simply, one of the most romantic settings I'd seen. As we sat down at our lovely table and ordered our huge cheese board and a selection of ten tasting wines each, I felt something inside. Obviously, I was a little concerned about the price, but this feeling was something else.

I just knew this was right time to take our relationship forward. I honestly thought I'd never get married in my lifetime, but now I'd met Pea, my views on marriage had changed. I was going to ask her to marry me! I didn't have a ring with me, but I wouldn't be able to choose the right size anyway. I'd have chosen the wrong design too and fucked everything up. So, it was best to pose the question and choose the ring later, in my view.

The problem was, I began to get nervous like never before. What if she rejected my proposal? What if I made myself look like a knob? Everything was swirling around my mind, as I thought about the possible outcomes. I thought she loved me and wanted to get married, but maybe now was not the right time for her. So, I vowed to wait a little longer – until she'd drunk some more wine. The sunset views were magnificent, and we took about a hundred photographs, just like everyone else. But I was also keeping an eye on the amount of wine that was being supped, as we tasted our local cheese selection.

At one point, I was going to do it, but there were too many people in the vicinity. I didn't want it to be a public show, but rather a private moment between us. I waited and waited, until we reached glass number nine. It dawned on me that time was running out and I had to make my move. So, I looked at Pea and held her hand tight. Then, still slightly nervous despite the wine, I asked her to marry me. She seemed surprised by the proposition, but in a positive way. She smiled and kissed me and said 'Yes'. My life was about to change forever.

As I woke up in the morning with a sore head, it felt great. I really didn't think I'd ever get married at all. I honestly didn't think I'd meet the right person. But now, after meeting my fiancée on a dating site, it was full steam ahead to plan the wedding. Well, from my point of view it was a gentle approach, but Pea approached this challenge like a military operation once again.

Within weeks, we were looking at venues and setting a date. We'd get married the following summer in July, almost a year to the day from the proposal. We looked at wedding packages and venues, including a farm, but decided on a local venue which was just about perfect for what we wanted. It seemed that we'd agreed to book it in no time at all, and preparations were well under way in respect of every other detail.

I was even dragged to a wedding show and realised what I'd let myself in for. There were fancy cars parked outside that could be hired and inside was an array of wedding stuff that I'd not even considered. For example, there were violinists, pianists and jazz bands that could be hired. Though, when a harpist played some amazing music in a show on stage, we fell in love with it and put a harpist on the list. There were also models strutting their stuff, modelling suits and wedding dresses on a catwalk. One good looking lad seemed to be getting excited by all the women staring at him, but I was focusing on the fit women modelling the dresses. The women, I mean dresses, looked stunning. Pea would have plenty to choose from, that's for sure. As each dress was being displayed, she kept asking my opinion. To be honest, I'd have shagged any of them. Looking back, maybe she was asking about the dresses.

I'd never really thought about everything that was required to make the day so special. There were florists, cake stalls, jewellery stalls, hair and make-up products, wedding stationary, sweet stalls, photographers, travel firms for honeymoons and even chocolate fountains. It was fucking mind-blowing what was needed just to get married.

Luckily, we'd agreed a budget between us and tried to stick to that. It wouldn't be a cheap registry office wedding, but it wouldn't be ridiculously priced either. It would've been so easy to go overboard and book every conceivable item. I mean, who wants a chocolate fountain making a mess everywhere? If it was up to me, I'd give everyone pie and peas and have the reception in a tent in our back garden and utilise our massive patio. Thankfully, it wasn't up to me. I barely did anything to help at all. I had no fucking choice.

CHAPTER 39: YORK YARNS

Pea chose Marbella for four nights, with nine friends for her hen do. I managed to get nine blokes to sunny York for my stag do for two nights, including Big Col, Mart, Ash, Dainty Dan and my brother-in-law to be, Ian. I'd once taken my kids to York on my own for a short holiday break and thought it was a fantastic place. The city was steeped in history and had lots of great attractions including the magnificent York Minster which is the second largest Gothic cathedral in Northern Europe and took over 250 years to be built from 1220 to 1472. It also had the York City Walls, some great museums and The Shambles – an historic street dating back to the 14th century.

My only hope was that my stag party wouldn't turn into a shambles. Of course, we wouldn't be visiting all the museums and the educational Jorvik Viking Centre, like I'd done years before with my kids. We'd be visiting all the disparate public houses scattered around the city. Famously, it was said that there were once 365 pubs in York – one for every day of the year. However, it was estimated that there were still over 200 within the city walls, which should've been enough for us lads over a couple of days. My best man leading this bunch of reprobates was Mart. He knew the city of York, or so he said, because he'd been to university there and lived in the city.

The plan was that a few of us would catch the train to York one Friday morning, and that some would drive or catch a later train after work and meet us for the evening. As I sat on the train, Big Col opened his bag and out popped some cans. We'd be starting on the booze early it seemed. Mart was due to get on the train at a later stop. As it pulled into the station, I tried to spot him amongst the other passengers. I saw his face, then realised he was holding something but couldn't make out what it was, before he boarded. Then, as he walked down the aisle of the train, I sunk into my seat with embarrassment. He was carrying a bloody blow-up doll. Not only that, but this doll was wearing a black dress and a big photograph of Pea's face was attached to its head. This was a complete surprise and I laughed as Mart placed the doll beside me on a seat.

At the next stop, more passengers boarded the train. Each and every one who walked past sniggered as they saw the doll and one or two jokers said 'Hello.' When the conductor came to check tickets, I asked jokingly if she needed one. Thankfully, he was in good spirits and said it was free for her as long as she didn't cause any trouble.

The lads took some photographs of me and the doll and I began to relax a little more, after supping a couple of drinks. Eventually, the train became full and I had to move my blow-up doll and sit her on my knee. But even though there was a vacant seat next to me, nobody dared sit down next to me and the doll. I felt a bit bad that an old lady was stood up nearby, but she could've sat next to me and blow-up Pea if she'd wanted. I would've been nice to her and introduced them.

As part of the journey, we'd have to change trains at Leeds station. Obviously, this was a much bigger station and brought the potential for far more embarrassment. The lads refused to carry the doll, so I had to trudge through the crowds with everyone staring at me. I probably wouldn't have been as embarrassed if I'd had a shit stain on my jeans. Talk about conspicuous, the train manager may as well have introduced me over the loudspeaker with the phrase, 'Your daily dickhead today can be seen on platform 2 carrying a blow-up doll right now.'

When we arrived in York at our Premier Inn, we checked in and headed straight out into the centre by the lovely River Ouse. This river had burst its banks several times over the years due to heavy rainfall and subsequent flooding. A pub we went to beside the river had recorded marks on the wall to identify the water levels the flood had reached. As it was a sunny afternoon, though, we could sit outside beside the river and got chatting to a group of ladies who were out on the piss. They were from the Durham area, I seem to remember, and had fairly strong accents. I had to listen carefully to understand what they were saying. We had a couple of drinks with them and the atmosphere was great, as the sun shone, and everyone was getting merrier.

After drinking all afternoon, we headed back to our hotel and got changed for the evening session so to speak. The others would be arriving soon, and it was agreed that we'd all wear Hawaiian shirts – the crazier the better. However, as such an effort was made to the blow-up doll, I'd have to carry her around with me all bloody night. Obviously, the doll attracted some attention and people got talking to us quite easily. In one pub, me and Ian got talking to a lady with melon like boobs who was wearing a tight white top, which left nothing to the imagination.

She said, 'I'm a medium you know,' in a serious voice. 'Well you look like a large to me,' said Ian as we chuckled. 'No, seriously I'm a medium. I've got psychic abilities,' she proclaimed. Me and Ian looked at each other and smiled. He said to her, 'Would you like a drink?' and without much hesitation she said, 'Gin and tonic please. Thanks so much.' But Ian had other ideas and stated quite forcefully, 'If you were really a psychic, you'd have known that I wasn't actually going to buy you a drink.'

At some point in the night, Pea got popped. I don't know how, but she started deflating. When we went for some food, Mart was sat in the pub trying to inflate her. It just looked so wrong at that time of night. Most of us ordered a giant burger for our meal and after drinking most of the day, it was one of the best I'd ever had. Around this time, I realised I hadn't actually been in contact with the real Pea. Maybe having a blow-up Pea to play with had got me distracted. But now she was deflating, I texted the real one and described how Mart was trying to blow her back up. She was just happy that I was still alive.

The following morning, we all met up in a local pub and ordered a big full English breakfast, to set us up for the day. Even by this stage in the morning, there were some groups of lads on the booze and there was a feeling that this could be a top day. We'd all put on our crazy Hawaiian shirts and Big Col had brought some bright garlands for us to wear too. Mart had booked the York Dungeons for us to visit, before we hit the booze again. The Dungeons depicted itself as a scare fest of live performances by actors in different rooms, with different scary themes. It tried to replicate some of York's dark history by using special-effects and props. Some of the characters included *The Torturer, The Plague Doctor, The Highwayman* and *The Executioner.*

As you can imagine, there was some unease in our party, and I could sense that a couple of the lads were trying to pretend they weren't scared at all. Some of the actors were outstandingly frightening in their depictions of death and destruction. During a walk down a dark passageway between rooms, I hid behind a wall. As Ian walked in front of me, I pounced on him from behind and shit him up good and proper.

The only problem was, I knew he'd try and get his own back as we went into more dark rooms. This just made me on edge even more. Thankfully, when it came to the torture room, it was Big Col who got selected for the demonstrations. Firstly, he had to bend over whilst a red-hot poker was shoved up his anus. Then, he had his cock chopped off with some shears. We were all in stitches as this ghastly torture took place, although my dick shrivelled up just a tad.

The Dungeons were brilliant entertainment and the day continued to be a ball. We had some drinks by the River Ouse, but actually got refused entry to a couple of pubs on the basis that they didn't serve stag parties. Then, we wandered into another pub and saw a big group of lads wearing similar Hawaiian shirts, clearly celebrating a stag do. As we walked in, they all gave us a high five and the atmosphere was electric.

We made our way to the sizeable beer garden and as the sun came out, the drinks started flowing. We were planning on a pub-crawl, but the party atmosphere was so fantastic that we decided to stay most of the afternoon. As we got merrier, it seemed that lots of hen parties and other stag dos arrived at the pub. By this stage, I was pretty mellow and telling all my mates that I loved them dearly.

Some of the lads bought me shots too and as I couldn't drink any more pints, I'd started on the rum. A group of girls from the Durham area came over and began talking to us. It was suggested by one of these ladies that she could give me a make-over. The lads encouraged her to do so and by this point I really didn't give a shit. So, she took off my glasses and proceeded to put foundation and eyeliner on me. Then, she got out her bright red lipstick and did my sexy lips. All the lads were taking photos and showed me what the rather amusing result was. I looked like a fucking lady-boy.

Shortly after the laughter had died down, I had to have a piss and so made my way to the toilet. As I went to the bogs, people were simply staring at me. I was wearing an orange Hawaiian shirt, a yellow garland and had lots of make-up on, including red lipstick. Jeez, I felt bloody great dolled up like a woman. After I'd syphoned the python, I looked in the mirror. I began to purse my lips and pull contorted faces. I was pissed by now, but thought I'd even shag myself if I'd been a bloke. I was simply stunning as a lady and I'm pretty sure lots of guys were giving me the eye.

After a while, however, we had to leave the pub as Mart had booked a Thai restaurant for our evening meal. We were all inebriated by now and somehow managed to stumble our way to the quiet and quaint place. Obviously, being a Saturday night, it was full of couples enjoying a nice romantic meal together. Suddenly, I walked into the restaurant made up like a lady-boy followed by nine others, all pissed up and wearing their silly shirts. Everyone looked at us in sheer horror, as they tucked into their Thai banquets. Their faces reminded me of Big Col's when he was made to bend over ready for a poker to be shoved up his soggy arsehole.

We ordered the most expensive Thai banquet on the menu and some beers too. Unfortunately, a couple of lads wanted to play drinking games at the table, but soon after arrival we were warned by the management about our behaviour. Being drunk, some of the lads didn't realise how loud they were, and the language was as colourful as our bloody shirts. Dainty Dan had a loud enough voice when he was sober, but now he was deafening. He even said a few words which turned out not to be expletives.

I looked at a young lady in the corner of the restaurant, on a table for two. She looked disgusted and a tear tried to roll down her cheek. I tried to maintain order by banning drinking games at the table and telling everyone to 'shut the fuck up,' though I was on a losing battle with some of them. Another round of beers was ordered, as we tucked into our hot and spicy soup.

The banquet itself was fantastic and though we cleared the place quite quickly, we spent a fucking fortune in there. Shortly after, we found yet another pub and some women approached us, somehow guessing we were on a stag do for some reason. After talking a while and showing me a photograph of a tit ring through her nipple, one lady bought me a shot.

I rather suspected she was after a shot of semen at the end of the night – but it wouldn't be from me. In every pub we went the atmosphere was buzzing.

We made our way to the *Bier Keller* and found ourselves a great dancefloor. One of the lads just dived across it and then began dancing with a sexy girl, who appeared to be high on drugs. At one point, she went on the stage and threw herself off, to be caught by him. Unfortunately, he mistimed the catch and she banged her head on the wooden floor. It was hilarious when she slapped him and then chased him around the place. Following that, it was still too early to call it a day so some of us decided to go to *Popworld* and continued to drink and dance.

After a while, however, I was flagging and realised the night was coming to an end. I'd managed at least fifteen drinks, plus shots, and hadn't been sick. I looked like a lady-boy but was very proud of myself indeed. I'd thoroughly enjoyed the weekend away and was just happy that it'd all worked out well. I'd not been stripped naked, thrown in the river or arrested and everyone seemed content.

In a little over a month, I was to lose my single status. As I sat on the train back with a stinking hangover, I contemplated how Pea had changed my life for the better. I looked at Big Col and thought about the night he came around to my house to help me set up a dating profile. I realised that without being online, without using dating sites, without my perseverance and without good fortune, I may not have been on this journey. Then I thought, jeez, I've forgotten to text her!

CHAPTER 40: AND FINALLY, ...

Having survived my stag do with flying colours, it was time to see if I could survive all the wedding preparation shit. The closer we got to the big day, the more that needed to be done apparently. We visited the venue a couple of times to discuss things like table decorations and the drinks package that we wanted. Then it was suggested that we add a post-box, so that guests could post cards.

Next, of course, there was a wedding ring to choose. It seemed that every time we ventured out of the house it was to sort something else out in respect of the wedding. To be fair to Pea, she played an amazing role in organising everything. I was basically clueless and relied on her big time. To make her think I was actually interested, I even agreed to watch every bloody episode ever broadcast of the TV programme *Don't Tell the Bride.* We ended up discussing dresses, suits, flowers, photography and any other crap associated with weddings.

Although Pea had taken her sister and friend to choose a wedding dress, it still had to be determined what suit the men would wear. I tried a few places but settled on the quality of Marks and Spencer. It had been agreed that five of us would wear the same suit – myself, the best man Mart, the father of the bride who, funnily enough was Pea's dad and two ushers - my son and Pea's brother Ian. We all met up one day to try on the suits I'd selected and for Pea to give her final approval.

The selection of suits went rather smoothly in the main, although my lad's slim-fit pants had to be changed later on, after he put loads of weight on devouring pizzas and KFC at university. He'd also discovered women and had a new girlfriend who he'd met on a well-known dating app, after taking my advice. Even the young ones were now using and becoming hooked on these shag apps, I mean dating sites.

After trying on our suits, we ended up going for a drink in the city centre and stayed most of the afternoon. Any excuse for a few drinks. Mart had told us that he'd recently bought his partner Leanne a new designer bag for her birthday. He'd ordered it online and had it delivered and placed in his recycling bin, as he was out at the time. He vowed to move it the following day, without her knowing, so that it'd be a surprise.

However, the next day he simply forgot about it and started his journey to work. On the way there, he had a terrible sinking feeling. He'd remembered about the expensive designer bag, but that it was also bin collection day! He rushed back as quickly as he could, with his heart pounding and sweat down his brow. Luckily, he saw the bin lorry around the corner from his house and managed to save the precious bag in time.

As our wedding day approached, we checked the weather forecast about a thousand times. This was the summer of 2018, the hottest summer in 40 years but whilst they forecast it was going to be sunny, there was a chance of rain too. In other words, the weather forecasters didn't fucking know a thing. Anybody could guess the forecast they predicted half the time. By now, I'd been sucked into the enormity of what I was about to do.

I'd also written a reflective and humorous poem about Pea and our relationship that was to be read during our marriage service, by Big Col. Whilst writing it, it made me realise how she'd changed my life. I realised I was a lucky man to be marrying her. At the point of meeting Pea, I was beginning to lose hope that I'd meet a woman who'd be just right for me. I'd had so many knockbacks and rejections along the way that it would've been so easy to give up. I'd certainly had some low points, that's for sure. Now, I was in a stable relationship and we'd bought our dream home together.

As the big day arrived, I decided to book a room at the 18th century manor house hotel that we'd chosen as our venue. I shared a room with my son the night before we got married. The day before, we used the spa facilities and went for a swim in the pool, and in the steam room and jacuzzi to relax. After all, it'd clearly been a rather stressful time for me sorting everything out. It was also great that my mate from school, all those years before, had made the effort to attend all the way from Canada. Graham had been on those trips to Torquay, when we were in the Sixth Form, as well as the field trip to Whitby. He now lived in a place called West Kelowna in British Columbia. It was nice to catch up with him. I told him there was no fucking way I'd have travelled to Canada if he'd got married there! But I told him that we'd try and visit him one day, if we could.

Also staying the night before the wedding were Mart, Ian, Pea's dad and a few others. It was a steady night, nothing too heavy, but we had an enjoyable chat and I felt at ease. I was surrounded by good people. As we had a civil evening in our posh surroundings, Pea had invited all the girls over to our house for a few drinks and nibbles, including my daughters. She vowed not to get drunk, just like me, as we didn't want to spoil the big day. I can't deny that I wasn't a little nervous. All the people who meant anything to us would be in attendance the following day and I didn't want to fuck up my vows.

As I woke up in the morning, it was a funny feeling. This was the day that mattered, the day that'd change my status to a married man. One of the most important days in my life. I looked outside the hotel window and was optimistic about the weather for the day ahead. I wanted it to be nice, as we'd paid a fucking fortune for this. Luckily, after a brief light shower which frayed my nerves, the sun began to shine. As I tucked into my full English, my mind wandered all over the place. Should I have more toast? Where's the brown sauce? Am I actually getting married in a few hours?

I remembered to have a shower and made sure I was nice and clean, having sprayed half a can of deodorant all over my body. Then, there was a knock at the door as I was drying my balls. It was the florist who'd come to deliver the Buttonholes. Having slipped some pants on, I let her in, and she pinned the Buttonholes on my suit and my son's too. Soon after, I was ready to rumble and get to the bar.

I needed a quick drink to settle my nerves, as some guests began to arrive. But then, I was called into meet the registrar who seemed rather formal and refused to let me have my pint, as we discussed the programme of service and signing of the marriage certificate. I guess she had a job to do, whereas I just wanted a quick drink to relax. She also told me that she'd met Pea and I was most definitely a lucky man and punching well above my weight. Cheeky sod!

Then, as the harpist was setting up in the corner and the photographer spoke to me, I knew the ceremony was approaching fast. The photographer had already been to our house and taken photos of Pea and the Bridal party getting ready. I checked with Mart about the ring. Luckily, he had possession of it but had forgotten his fucking belt. He'd have to spend most of the day holding his pants up, as they were a bit too big for him. But at least he had that precious ring and had prepared a speech for later.

As guests started to arrive and sit down, I stood at the front nervously. My parents were sat at the front and Mart was there beltless, but not ringless. My mum stared at me and smiled and told me to relax. Some of my mates gave me the thumbs up, as they arrived. As the harpist started to play our selection of songs, I was ready. I was finally prepared for Pea walking down the aisle with her father and composed myself so that I wouldn't cry like a baby.

Firstly, the bridesmaids walked down the aisle. My daughters looked beautiful in their dresses as they made their way to the front and I was a very proud dad, for sure. Then, as I heard John Legend's romantic song *All of Me* playing, I knew it was time for Pea to enter. I hadn't a clue what her dress was like, but when I saw her for the first time I was bowled over. She looked stunning – not just nice, or lovely, or alright – but stunning. All those hours of choosing a dress and getting ready had paid off. Once Pea was in front of me, I relaxed and felt at ease. Her dad looked as proud as punch too and had a big smile on his face. The ceremony itself flew by. None of us mucked up our lines and Mart's pants didn't even fall down. Big Col also did a fantastic job reading my poem, which got a few giggles in all the right places. In fact, just to prove that I wrote one for the big day – here it is:

> You're the one who makes me smile
> You're the one who goes the extra mile
> You're the one who's the filling in my pie
> Because of you, I can hold my head up high

You're the one who makes me laugh
You're the one who puts up with me bein' daft
You're the one who prevents my sigh
Because of you, I feel like an eagle in the sky

You're the one who makes me tingle
You're the one who makes me jingle
You're the one who completes my soul
Because of you, I feel whole

You're the one who makes my heart flutter
You're the one who made me get rid of the clutter
You're the one who fills me with glee
Because of you, I feel like me

You're the one who encouraged me to travel
You're the one who made my feelings unravel
You're the one who stole my heart
Because of you, life at 40 did start

You're the one who makes me complete
You're the one who even plays with my feet
You're the one I call my rock
Because of you, I'm getting married, I'm in shock!

You're the one who I admire so much
You're the one with the magic touch
You're my world and my life
And from today, you'll be my wife

Thank you for being you and being mine.

When I kissed Pea at the end of the ceremony, I felt like the whole room was watching us. Next, the photographer took more pictures and we left to a magical round of applause. We were officially married, and it was time to get drunk and party. We managed to mingle and had lots of snaps taken in the sunshine, which had decided to appear by now.

The vibe was great as the harpist continued to play some more music. Afterwards, it was time for the wedding breakfast, and we got a rousing reception as we made our way into the reception room. It was a special feeling that everyone had come to support our big day. As well as Graham, who'd travelled from Canada, some others had travelled from London and the south-west.

After our delicious three-course wedding breakfast, it was time for the speeches. Pea's dad was a lovely man who'd I'd always got on well with. By now, he was in his late seventies. He was very proud to give Pea away and managed to say all the right things in his speech. Of course, I paid tribute to him and my parents too in my speech as well as a mention for Pea's mum and best friend, who she'd also lost a couple of years before. My parents had been really supportive all my life and were always there if I needed them for anything. In my darkest days, after separating, they kept me going and looked out for my mental wellbeing.

My dad had always been there to give me plenty of advice about life itself. When I was a young immature man, I always thought he talked a load of bollocks. But as I matured and got older, I realised it really was a load of bollocks. My parents had been together nearly fifty years since meeting as childhood sweethearts. It was an amazing achievement, of course, and once I asked my dad the secret of longevity in marriage. He thought for a second or two and then stated, 'tolerance!'

My speech seemed to go down well, as I reminisced about meeting Pea online and our journey together. Next, Mart gave a funny speech about some of my dating mishaps and travails. He created a mock sleeve for a book cover, and it was entitled something like, 'Tales of an Internet Dater,' believe it or not. Yes, that's right. The idea of my book had been swirling around in my head for quite a while, but on this very day, my wedding day, I had a feeling that I should actually write it.

As the afternoon merged into the evening, more party guests arrived. After the speeches, me and Mart could relax more, and the drinks began to flow. We were asked to cut the splendid cake, which was kindly and expertly made by Leanne, in the reception room and entered to emphatic cheers. After that, it was an embarrassing first dance. Well, it was embarrassing for Pea as I did a few spins and nearly fell on her. I didn't care what anyone thought by now. I was up for a great night and intended to get merry. Towards the end of the night, everyone was dancing on the dancefloor and a pissed-up Pea even danced on a table. I started ripping my shirt off at one point, only to hear people groaning and Mart shouting at me to get it back on.

Thankfully, I refrained from a full striptease and Mart managed to keep his pants up too. Then, the DJ played the song *Can't Take My Eyes Off of You* by Frankie Valli. The whole room sang the lyrics in unison...*I Love you baby.* It was magical as we sang it again and again. Although my drunken dancing left a lot to be desired, it was all fantastic fun and singing that song will live long in the memory.

Our honeymoon was in Crete, a few days after our wedding. We stayed at a quiet resort and had a lovely relaxing break, after the stresses leading up to our marriage. We had a delightful pool and met some affable and friendly people at our complex. We dined out in some charming restaurants and ate some fabulous Greek food. All in all, it was just what we needed. One day, as I lay on the beguiling beach, I looked at Pea who was now my wife. Wow, she was my WIFE. I reflected about my life and how things had turned out so far. We'd been on an extraordinary journey together. In my view, everything in life happened for a reason.

Joining a dating site was almost a last throw of the dice to meet someone, for me. All the dates I went on moulded me as a person. All the experiences I had, whether they were good, bad or indifferent, were meant to be. Everything I learned about the opposite sex and the personalities I met, influenced my views. It transpired that fuck buddies were very common and certainly served a purpose for many individuals. However, what I discovered was that, at the end of the day, most people wanted something similar out of life. Although rampant sex could be great and friendship was therapeutic, a loving relationship was altogether more powerful.

An equal partnership of companionship, mutual trust and love was what people craved – men and women alike. I'd been a lad at times and played the field, and I'd done some stupid things. But women had also used me in equal measure for their intimate needs. It was usually a reciprocal understanding, at times when people simply wanted physical fulfilment.

Now, however, I was a married man and I was happy. You could say I'd been lucky to find Pea. Or, you could say that the sheer number of women I dated through various sites would eventually lead to success. Whatever you believe, the statistics show that over 17% of couples who get married met online. So, the world of dating apps and dating sites clearly work and lead to love. The answers to my questions that I posed in the Prologue, as I began internet dating, were finally reached at the end of my journey – I did find love by tapping away at a keyboard; I did find my perfect match and no it's not just about bonking!

On my journey, I discovered that a loving relationship can't be sustained by lust alone. It's much deeper than that, but in my view, it's basically how you relate to each other. Being able to accept your partner's faults; being able to compromise; being able to discuss issues after an argument; being able to understand your partner's point of view; always being there for one another no matter what; being able to trust each other implicitly. See, once I was rather crude, insensitive, undiplomatic and as subtle as a brick. Now, I'm all lovey-dovey and I've actually developed some romantic feelings. Well, I've got *feelings* anyway. It's amazing what true love can do to you.

Printed in Poland
by Amazon Fulfillment
Poland Sp. z o.o., Wrocław

50731282R00141